PASTORAL CARE IN
LATE ANGLO-SAXON ENGLAND

The tenth and eleventh centuries saw a number of very significant developments in the history of the English Church, perhaps the most significant being the proliferation of local churches, which were to be the basis of the modern parochial system. Using evidence from homilies, canon law, saints' lives, and liturgical and penitential sources, the articles collected in this volume focus on the ways in which such developments were reflected in pastoral care, considering what it consisted of at this time, how it was provided and by whom. Starting with an investigation of the secular clergy, their recruitment and patronage, the papers move on to examine a variety of aspects of late Anglo-Saxon pastoral care, including church due payments, preaching, baptism, penance, confession, visitation of the sick and archaeological evidence of burial practice. Special attention is paid to the few surviving manuscripts which are likely to have been used in the field and the evidence they provide for the context, the actions and the verbal exchanges which characterised pastoral provisions.

Dr FRANCESCA TINTI has worked as Research Associate for the Prosopography of Anglo-Saxon England at the University of Cambridge. She is a Fellow of Wolfson College, Cambridge and currently lectures in medieval history at the University of Bologna.

Anglo-Saxon Studies

ISSN 1475–2468

General Editors
John Hines
Catherine Cubitt

'Anglo-Saxon Studies' aims to provide a forum for the best scholarship on the Anglo-Saxon peoples in the period from the end of Roman Britain to the Norman Conquest, including comparative studies involving adjacent populations and periods; both new research and major re-assessments of central topics are welcomed.

Originally founded by Professor David Dumville as 'Studies in Anglo-Saxon History', the series has now broadened in scope under new editorship to take in any one of the principal disciplines of archaeology, art history, history, language and literature, and inter- or multi-disciplinary studies are encouraged.

Proposals or enquiries may be sent directly to the editors or the publisher at the addresses given below; all submissions will receive prompt and informed consideration.

Professor John Hines, Cardiff School of History and Archaeology, Cardiff University, Colum Drive, Cardiff, Wales, UK CF10 3EU

Dr Catherine Cubitt, Centre for Medieval Studies, University of York, The King's Manor, York, England, UK YO1 7EP

Boydell & Brewer, PO Box 9, Woodbridge, Suffolk, England, UK IP12 3DF

PASTORAL CARE IN
LATE ANGLO-SAXON ENGLAND

Edited by
Francesca Tinti

THE BOYDELL PRESS

First published 2005
The Boydell Press, Woodbridge

ISBN 1 84383 156 2

The Boydell Press is an imprint of Boydell & Brewer Ltd
PO Box 9, Woodbridge, Suffolk IP12 3DF, UK
and of Boydell & Brewer Inc.
668 Mt Hope Avenue, Rochester, NY 14620, USA
website: www.boydellandbrewer.com

A CIP catalogue record for this book is available
from the British Library

Library of Congress Cataloging-in-Publication Data
Pastoral care in late Anglo-Saxon England / edited by Francesca Tinti.
   p. cm. – (Anglo-Saxon studies, ISSN 1475–2468 ; 6)
   Summary: "The role of pastoral care reconsidered in the context of major
changes within the Anglo-Saxon church" – Provided by publisher.
   Includes bibliographical references and index.
   ISBN 1–84383–156–2 (hardcover : alk. paper)
   1. Pastoral theology – England – History.   2. Pastoral care – England –
History.   3. England – Church history.   I. Tinti, Francesca,
1971– II. Title.   III. Series.
   BV4011.P3453 2005
   253'.0942'09021–dc22   2005005792

This publication is printed on acid-free paper

Typeset by Pru Harrison, Hacheston, Suffolk
Printed in Great Britain by
Athenaeum Press Ltd., Gateshead, Tyne & Wear

Contents

Illustrations

Contributors

Julia Barrow, University of Nottingham

Jo Buckberry, University of Bradford

Helen Gittos, University of Southampton

Dawn M. Hadley, University of Sheffield

Sarah Hamilton, University of Exeter

Francesca Tinti, University of Cambridge

Victoria Thompson, New York University in London and Birkbeck College, London

Jonathan Wilcox, University of Iowa

Abbreviations

ASE	*Anglo-Saxon England*
B	W. De G. Birch, ed., *Cartularium Saxonicum* (London 1885–99), 3 vols
BAR	British Archaeological Reports
CBA	Council for British Archaeology
CCSL	Corpus Christianorum Series Latina
Councils and Synods	D. Whitelock, M. Brett and C.N.L. Brooke, ed., *Councils and Synods with other Documents Relating to the English Church I: AD 871–1204*, 2 vols (Oxford, 1981)
EEMF	Early English Manuscripts in Facsimile
EETS	Early English Text Society
EME	*Early Medieval Europe*
K	J.M. Kemble, *Codex Diplomaticus Aevi Saxonici*, 6 vols (London, 1839–48)
MGH	*Monumenta Germaniae Historica*
os	original series
PL	*Patrologiae cursus completus, series latina*, ed. J.-P. Migne (Paris, 1844–64)
S	P. Sawyer, *Anglo-Saxon Charters: an Annotated List and Bibliography* (London, 1968)
ss	supplementary series

Introduction

Francesca Tinti

'Pastoral care' is not easy to define. The phrase can be stretched to accommodate different definitions, which obviously depend on the historical period for which it is used. In general terms it can be employed to refer to all the activities carried out by the clergy to assist and support the spiritual life of the laity.[1] The adjective 'pastoral' derives from the image of the shepherd used in both the Old and the New Testaments as a metaphor for God's continuous love and care of His people. Sacraments have always had a special place among the activities and the liturgical celebrations which constitute pastoral care, although in the early Middle Ages the doctrine regulating them was still rather fluid. As will emerge from the articles contained in this volume, late Anglo-Saxon sources give special attention to baptism, penance and visitation of the sick. Pastoral care, however, also comprised other more common tasks and activities, such as preaching. It had a crucial role in so many important facets of people's lives that a study of this topic necessarily leads to a more general appreciation of the role of the Church in society as a whole.

The publication of this volume stems from one fundamental premise: late Anglo-Saxon pastoral care deserves to be studied for its own sake. For a long time, in fact, the evidence for tenth- and eleventh-century Church organisation and delivery of pastoral care has been treated as a useful tool to be employed regressively, that is, to try to reconstruct the situation in the earlier period, for which the evidence is noticeably scarcer. This seems to have been particularly the case with those publications which, about ten years ago, led to the development of the so-called 'minster debate'.[2] The debate arose following the emergence – during the late 1980s and the early 1990s – of a specific hypothesis about the

---

[1] Giles Constable has defined pastoral care as 'the performance of those ceremonies that were considered central to the salvation of the individual Christian and that were the primary responsibility of ordained priests working in parish churches under the supervision of the diocesan bishop or his representative': G. Constable, 'Monasteries, rural churches and the *cura animarum* in the early Middle Ages', in *Cristianizzazione ed organizzazione ecclesiastica delle campagne nell'alto medioevo: espansione e resistenze*, Settimane di studio del centro italiano di studi sull'alto medioevo 28 (Spoleto, 1982), pp. 349–89, at p. 353.

[2] E. Cambridge and D. Rollason, 'Debate: the pastoral organization of the Anglo-Saxon Church: a review of the *Minster Hypothesis*', *EME* 4.1 (1995), pp. 87–104; J. Blair, 'Debate: ecclesiastical organization and pastoral care in Anglo-Saxon England', *EME* 4.2 (1995), pp. 193–212.

origins and early development of an English system of ecclesiastical organisation.[3] According to this hypothesis the seventh and eighth centuries saw the spread of a network of religious houses (called *monasteria* in the Latin sources of the time, and 'minsters' by modern historians) served by communities of clergy responsible for pastoral supervision in the districts attached to those minsters. Later on, in the post-Viking period, local private churches began to proliferate and acquire the parochial rights which had previously been reserved for minsters. This would have led to the fragmentation of the minsters' large *parochiae* and, eventually, to the emergence of the modern parochial system. In the debate which followed the initially favourable reception of this hypothesis, many of its aspects were criticised: in particular the terminological choices adopted by its exponents, the lack of attention to the major role played by bishops in the delivery of pastoral care, and the assumption that all seventh- and eighth-century religious houses would have been more or less equally involved in pastoral activities. These problematic areas have now been reconsidered in order to revise any previous attempts to establish a 'minster model'.[4] It is important to stress here, however, that most of the criticism arising at the time of the debate was directed at those aspects of the hypothesis that concerned the earliest phases of English ecclesiastical organisation. As can be noted by a careful examination of relevant studies published in the mid 1990s, exponents and opponents of the 'minster hypothesis' mostly disagreed on the situation in the seventh and eighth centuries, without really engaging in a proper discussion of the late Anglo-Saxon system of parochial organisation.[5] The aim of this book is to start that discussion without trying to revive the minster debate. Although some of the contributions in this volume do refer occasionally to pre-tenth-century aspects of Church organisation, none of the contributors has tried to reopen the debate on the seventh and eighth centuries. This is mainly for one incontrovertible reason: we do not have enough sources to be able to establish with any degree of certainty whether anything like a minster system was then in place.

By contrast, evidence for the study of pastoral care in the later Anglo-Saxon period is much fuller, and its very existence is the main reason behind the publication of this volume. Considering the quantity of homilies, canon law material, saints' lives, liturgical and penitential sources available for the tenth and eleventh

---

[3] The main publications which led to the emergence of the minster hypothesis are those contained in J. Blair, ed., *Minsters and Parish Churches. The Local Church in Transition 950–1200* (Oxford, 1988), and J. Blair and R. Sharpe, ed., *Pastoral Care before the Parish* (Leicester, London and New York, 1992). See also J. Blair, 'Secular minster churches in Domesday Book', in *Domesday Book: a Reassessment*, ed. P.H. Sawyer (London, 1985), pp. 104–42; J. Blair, 'Local churches in Domesday Book and before', in *Domesday Studies*, ed. J.C. Holt (Woodbridge, 1987), pp. 265–78 and J. Blair, 'Minster churches in the landscape', in *Anglo-Saxon Settlements*, ed. D. Hooke (Oxford, 1988), pp. 35–58.

[4] See J. Blair's introduction to his monograph, *The Church in Anglo-Saxon Society* (Oxford, 2005). I am very grateful to Dr Blair for allowing me to consult some relevant sections of his volume before publication.

[5] Cf. Cambridge and Rollason, 'Debate: the pastoral organization' and Blair, 'Debate: ecclesiastical organization'. At the Leeds International Medieval Congress of 2002 John Blair and David Rollason were invited to readdress the debate, trying to move it on to the later Anglo-Saxon period. However, interestingly enough, the discussion which followed their two papers concentrated once again on the earlier situation.

centuries, it is rather surprising that this material should not yet have been used in any extensive way to provide a historical analysis of the pastoral context in which those texts were produced. Since a very large portion of this source material is in Old English, most of the research conducted on such texts has concentrated on their linguistic and literary aspects. Anglo-Saxon England represents a unique case in early medieval Europe because of the extensive employment of the vernacular in texts of this nature, and in particular in liturgical ones.[6] Historians, however, have rarely tried to approach that material in the same way they have done for the earlier texts, written mostly, if not exclusively, in Latin. But there seems to be no real justification for such a distinction. Relevant works by Ælfric and Archbishop Wulfstan deserve just as much attention as Bede's texts. Furthermore, they provide us with a much clearer sense of the way in which the Church was organised on the ground as well as a lot of information on the clergy's education and the material they could rely upon while carrying out their pastoral duties.[7] The fact that Old English was employed extensively in later homiletic and liturgical texts gives us a much better sense of what the laity would have been able to understand. However, no terminological investigation comparable to those conducted on Bede's choice of such words as *monasterium* or *ecclesia* has ever been carried out on the later material.[8]

There seems to be a general consensus that the tenth and eleventh centuries saw the origins of what became the modern parish system, as many local churches were founded at this time. England was not the only country in Europe to experience such developments. New churches were being built everywhere, as is testified in a much-quoted passage by Ralph Glaber, who, looking back over the early decades of the eleventh century, wrote: 'It was as if the whole world were shaking itself free, shrugging off the burdens of the past, and cladding itself everywhere in a white mantle of churches.'[9] The archaeological evidence and the diversified but still valuable records of churches in Domesday Book confirm that England was deeply affected by this process.[10] Several archaeological studies have identified some crucial developments which took place in the late Anglo-Saxon period. Parish church excavations in the east of England and the Midlands have shown the remains of timber or rubble-walled churches, which mostly date back to the

---

6 See Helen Gittos' article in this volume.

7 On Bede's reluctance to say more about church organisation on the ground, see A. Thacker, 'Monks, preaching and pastoral care in early Anglo-Saxon England', in *Pastoral Care before the Parish*, ed. Blair and Sharpe, pp. 137–70, at p. 137.

8 For an example of a terminological analysis of Bede's works conducted by a historian, see S. Foot, 'Anglo-Saxon minsters: a review of terminology', *ibid.*, pp. 212–25.

9 J. France, ed., *Rodulfus Glaber: The Five Books of the Histories*, Oxford Medieval Texts (Oxford, 1989), iii.13, pp. 116–17.

10 For the Domesday Book evidence see Blair, 'Local churches' and R. Morris, 'Churches, settlement and the beginnings of the parochial system', in *The Church in British Archaeology*, ed. *idem*, CBA Research Report 47 (London, 1983), pp. 63–76, at pp. 68–71. For a more recent review of developments in excavations of minor churches see J. Blair and C. Pyrah, ed., *Church Archaeology. Research Directions for the Future*, CBA Research Report 104 (York, 1996). For a full report on one specific church see A. Boddington, *Raunds Furnells. The Anglo-Saxon Church and Churchyard*, English Heritage Archaeological Report 7 (London, 1996).

tenth and eleventh centuries. Furthermore, it would seem that in England small churches started to be built with more durable materials from the mid eleventh century. From that time until about 1150 new churches were built on an unprecedented scale.[11] Although many more excavations are needed to establish regional variations, the sheer number of new buildings which appeared in the late Anglo-Saxon and early Anglo-Norman period must have had an enormous impact on both ecclesiastical organisation and pastoral care provisions.[12] It seems natural that people's lives would have been affected by the increased number of churches in which religious services could be attended. It is with the pastoral care provided at this crucial period of English Church history that this book is mostly concerned.

The proliferation of small churches, which characterised the period from the tenth to the twelfth century, seems to have been determined by some other important developments which took place at the same time. Crucial among such developments was the emergence of a new class of small landowners, interested in building their own private local churches. It was in the context of developing local lordship and changes to the settlement pattern that the new churches were founded, thus providing the basis of the later medieval parochial structure.[13] Some features of this process of progressive localisation have already received a certain degree of attention, especially with regard to the impact of the foundation of minor churches on territorial ecclesiastical organisation. The evidence provided by some tenth- and eleventh-century law-codes has played a crucial role in the development of studies concentrating on such aspects. From the time of King Edgar legal codes repeatedly refer to various types of churches, with different rights and different pastoral responsibilities. In II Edgar senior churches are called 'old minsters' in order to distinguish them from the new local churches which were being built in that period.[14] By the time of King Æthelred four classes of churches may be distinguished. In a passage of one of his laws, known as VIII Æthelred and issued in 1014, violation of sanctuary is described as a crime that has to be compensated for according to the type of church in which it has been committed. The highest fine has to be paid if sanctuary is breached in a chief minster. Fines then decrease progressively with reference to medium minsters, smaller ones and field-churches.[15] A similar but definitely more relevant picture is provided by legal codes dealing with church tributes. From the second half of the tenth century up to the time of Cnut, these become increasingly specific in

[11] J. Blair, 'Churches in the early English landscape: social and cultural contexts', in *Church Archaeology*, ed. Blair and Pyrah, pp. 6–18.

[12] As far as regional variation is concerned, John Blair has noted that the contrasts emerging from Domesday Book are probably genuine. It would seem that the higher incidence of minor churches recorded in the eastern counties reflects a higher presence of such small foundations in that area, whereas superior churches were probably more numerous in southern counties. By comparison, these would appear to be less important than those recorded in the south-western region, which, however, were probably less numerous: Blair, 'Secular minster churches', pp. 112–13.

[13] Richard Morris has noted that the change in ecclesiastical geography probably reflects a society in transition: R. Morris, *Churches in the Landscape* (London, 1989), p. 167.

[14] 'Man agife ælce teoðunge to þam ealdan mynstre': II Edgar, c. 1.1, in *Councils and Synods*, i, pp. 97–8.

[15] VIII Æthelred, c. 5.1, *ibid.*, i, p. 390.

restricting such payments to older superior churches, whose parochial rights were being threatened by the rival claims of new minor foundations.[16]

In spite of the interesting picture provided by legal sources, it should not be forgotten that they can be rather problematic, in that they may represent theory rather than practice and may also give the impression that the situation was the same all over the country. It would seem that it was by trying to make local studies fit into the picture described in legal texts that the minster hypothesis originated in the first place. This is a danger which is very hard to avoid when conducting research on institutional features of Church organisation, and it is probably for this reason that in recent decades such aspects seem to have ceased to attract the attention of historians. The inevitable tension between the general picture and the specificity of local studies has led to a moving away from research on the institutions in favour of a more specific interest in the people who manned them. In many ways this book reflects such a trend: the articles here do not focus on relations between mother churches and dependent ones, or on the territorial origins of the parish system, though they do not ignore institutional matters altogether. In fact, a great deal of attention is given to the context in which late Anglo-Saxon pastoral care was provided.

The first essay, by Julia Barrow, discusses the provenance, recruitment and patronage of those who were mostly involved in pastoral activities: the clergy. It also takes into account the relations between priests and the bishops in charge of the dioceses within which the former carried out their pastoral tasks.[17] My essay focuses on the development of a system of church dues and the more or less explicit connections that sources draw between the delivery of pastoral care and the need to sustain the clergy responsible for *cura animarum*. Jonathan Wilcox's contribution also deals with institutional matters by placing preaching in context, trying to identify the types of churches in which Ælfric's homilies could have been delivered, and bearing in mind the ecclesiastical organisation of the diocese in which the homilies were composed. It is in these first three essays particularly that the book examines an institutional framework for the delivery of pastoral care in late Anglo-Saxon England. Meanwhile, Hadley and Buckberry's contribution on the archaeological evidence for late Anglo-Saxon burials also takes into account institutional factors, by discussing changes in size of cemeteries, which could reflect a change in function of the churches to which they were attached. The reduction of a church's burial grounds might be due to a parallel reduction of the size of the district for which it provided pastoral care: a few cases are discussed as possible examples of former minsters whose function shifted to that of a parish church. Therefore, although the focus of the volume is not on institutional issues, the latter are duly borne in mind.

---

[16] In Edgar's time minor private foundations with a graveyard were allowed to receive the third part of a landlord's tithe. II Edgar, c. 2, *ibid.*, i, p. 98.

[17] On the relationship between bishops and their clergy and in particular on the evidence provided in Archbishop Wulfstan's manuscripts on possible periodic examinations of his diocesan clergy, see C.A. Jones, 'Wulfstan's liturgical interests', in *Wulfstan, Archbishop of York*, ed. M. Townend (Turnhout, 2004), pp. 325–52, at pp. 333–4.

There are further aspects that need to be pointed out in this introduction in order to illustrate the rationale behind this volume and to provide a proper context for the contributions that follow. Several essays are more concerned with the pastoral care available at minor centres. In our attempt to move from the institutional framework to the practice of delivery and reception of *cura animarum*, our main aim has been to investigate pastoral provisions at local level; hence the efforts directed at identifying the tools that could have been used by local priests for their daily work.[18] Furthermore, most contributions focus on rural areas rather than urban settlements. As Wilcox points out, the fact that Ælfric's unprecedented systematic collection of vernacular homilies was produced in a relatively remote centre such as Cerne Abbas probably reflects the impact that the late Anglo-Saxon reorganisation of pastoral care had in the countryside.[19] However, it should not be forgotten that urban settlements were also going through some very significant changes. English towns developed extensively in the tenth and eleventh centuries, as their populations increased and their economies grew through the flourishing of urban manufacturing and the circulation of silver coin. Urban churches were very directly affected by such developments: many of them were founded at this time, and others were re-founded or rebuilt.[20] This volume also considers pastoral activities in towns. Wilcox discusses Sherborne cathedral as a very likely place in which Ælfric's *Catholic Homilies* could have been preached by Bishop Wulfsige to a mixed audience of clergy and laity. He also examinies the preaching and pastoral context provided by several other minor Dorset towns with minster communities. The relationship between major town churches and smaller local ones is a topic which features in other contributions as well. In her presentation of the possible provenance and history of the Red Book of Darley, Helen Gittos suggests that the manuscript might have been compiled at Sherborne for someone who was studying there and was about to become the priest of a local church. In her discussion of penitential practice in late Anglo-Saxon England, Sarah Hamilton refers to the efforts made by bishops to promote such practice amongst the rural clergy, pointing out that we probably do not know much about penance at the local level because very few relevant manuscripts have survived. This confirms the importance of contacts between major ecclesiastical centres and minor ones: local provisions for pastoral care cannot be properly understood without taking into account their relations with major religious houses, which had a crucial role in providing the tools that local priests would have needed to carry out their duties.

For a proper understanding of the role played by the major late Anglo-Saxon religious houses within the pastoral care system it is necessary to introduce another element into this discussion, the so-called 'Benedictine reform', which would seem to have had a dramatic impact on English ecclesiastical organisation in the second half of the tenth century. The reform has been described as the

---

[18] See especially Helen Gittos, Sarah Hamilton and Victoria Thompson's articles in this volume.
[19] See Wilcox, below.
[20] Morris, *Churches in the Landscape*, p. 169.

phenomenon which 'drew a firm line between "true" monasteries and the mass of "secular" minsters'.[21] It is when dealing with tenth- and eleventh-century religious houses that historians find it easier to choose between the terms 'monastery', normally used to refer to a primarily contemplative community living by a rule, and the less specific 'minster'. Whereas the earlier period is perceived as highly problematic, because it does not allow for a proper distinction between secular and monastic communities, the reform is seen as the crucial event which permits such a distinction. However, this appears to be too simplistic, as the evidence at our disposal shows that the situation after the monastic reform was not so clear-cut. For instance, it would seem that not enough attention has been paid to the pastoral implications of the fact that the three main leaders of the Benedictine reform, Dunstan, Æthelwold and Oswald, had episcopal responsibilities, and that monastic cathedral communities – led by monastic bishops – were a very distinctive characteristic of the English Church for a long time after the reform. Such cathedrals were to be found in towns where contacts with the local population were probably very frequent.[22]

Although the *Regularis Concordia*, the main source for the study of the reformers' intentions and aspirations for their communities, does not provide specific directions in this respect, it would seem that contacts between monks and the laity were not at all exceptional. The *Regularis Concordia* assumes a regular presence of lay people at mass, and the sizes of the churches built or rebuilt as a result of the reform confirm that they were intended for large congregations and not just for the use of monastic communities.[23] Moreover, it would appear that the construction of new churches might not necessarily have been linked to the monks' need to retreat from the world. At Worcester, for instance, Bishop Oswald preached to the people outside the old cathedral church of St Peter in the second half of the tenth century, before the new church of St Mary was completed.[24] The old cathedral was too small for Oswald's popularity, and the construction of the new church of St Mary can be better understood if placed within the general context of a growing town.[25] William of Malmesbury reports that in the following century St Wulfstan started his pastoral mission as a monk in the same church of St Mary. When he was still a prior, he preached there on Sundays and feast-days. On one occasion he attracted the criticism of a foreign monk, who did not think it appropriate for Wulfstan to be involved in such pastoral activities: in his

---

21 Blair, 'Introduction: from minster to parish church', in *Minsters and Parish Churches*, ed. *idem*, pp. 1–19, at p. 1.

22 Mary Clayton has discussed monastic bishops and monastic churches with reference to Ælfric's homilies, which often seem to assume a mixed audience of both monks and lay people. In Clayton's words: 'such a situation must have been relatively common after the Benedictine Reform': M. Clayton, 'Homiliaries and preaching in Anglo-Saxon England', *Peritia* 4 (1985), pp. 207–42, at p. 239. On this topic see also Wilcox, below.

23 For the presence of lay people at mass see T. Symons and S. Spath, ed., *Regularis Concordia*, in *Consuetudinum Sæculi X/XI/XII Monumenta non-Cluniacensia*, ed. K. Hallinger, Corpus Consuetudinum Monasticarum, vii.3 (Siegburg, 1984), pp. 61–147, at ch. 28, p. 88.

24 The story is reported in Hemming's Cartulary: T.H. Hearne, ed., *Hemingi chartularium ecclesiae Wigorniensis* (London, 1723), ii, p. 342.

25 Cf. N. Baker and R. Holt, 'The city of Worcester in the tenth century', in *St Oswald of Worcester: Life and Influence*, ed. N. Brooks and C. Cubitt (London and New York, 1996), pp. 129–46, at p. 143.

experience preaching was a bishop's task, not a monk's.[26] This story seems to confirm the fact that in late Anglo-Saxon England monastic houses, especially those attached to cathedrals and located in towns, were still very much involved with the laity. In some cases that could also lead to less pious incidents or situations, as the same source shows with regard to St Wulfstan himself. When the latter was still prior of St Mary's, a wealthy female citizen of Worcester was very assiduous at attending the church, but as William of Malmesbury reveals, her main aim was to court Wulfstan with words of flattery.[27] One day, while he happened to be standing next to her in the church, she took hold of his garment and prayed him to listen to what she had to say: she suggested that he give up his ecclesiastical position, rule her household and share her bed. In order to justify Wulfstan's pausing to listen to her, the text says that he thought she wanted to confess her sins, thus providing yet another instance of the ways in which the prior of an eleventh-century monastic cathedral community could be involved in delivering direct pastoral care to the laity living in town and attending the cathedral church. At Winchester the reform probably had a greater impact than at Worcester, considering the way in which it affected the layout of the town: by the end of the tenth century Winchester had the largest complex of monastic buildings in the whole country, and the drainage system created by Æthelwold went on to serve the town for many centuries afterwards.[28] When secular canons were expelled from the Old and New Minsters in 964 and replaced by monks, new domestic buildings were constructed for both communities. Furthermore, in the 960s-70s the construction of a boundary to enclose the Old Minster, the New Minster and Nunnaminster was only made possible through the demolition of some secular buildings.[29]

The monastic reform was not the only factor which affected the ecclesiastical geography of towns in the late Anglo-Saxon period. In fact, it would seem that the majority of urban minsters were secular rather than monastic at this time. As has been pointed out by several scholars, the monastic propaganda, which characterised the time of the reform, has probably obscured the activities which were still taking place at non-reformed houses.[30] Most cathedral communities remained

---

[26] *Vita Wulfstani*, i.8, in *William of Malmesbury: Saints' Lives*, ed. M. Winterbottom and R.M. Thomson, Oxford Medieval Texts (Oxford, 2002), pp. 36–7.

[27] *Ibid.*, i.6, pp. 30–3.

[28] J. Crook, 'Winchester', in *The Blackwell Encyclopaedia of Anglo-Saxon England*, ed. M. Lapidge, J. Blair, S. Keynes and D. Scragg (Oxford, 1999), pp. 480–2, at p. 481; M. Biddle and D.J. Keene, 'Winchester in the eleventh and twelfth centuries', in *Winchester in the Early Middle Ages*, ed. M. Biddle, Winchester Studies 1 (Oxford, 1976), pp. 241–448, esp. pp. 306–23. Groups of churches standing within the same architectural complex were not unusual in late Anglo-Saxon towns; for a discussion of their possible complementary functions see G. Rosser, 'The cure of souls in English towns before 1000', in *Pastoral Care before the Parish*, ed. Blair and Sharpe, pp. 267–84, at pp. 272–4.

[29] For a detailed discussion of Winchester in the tenth century see M. Biddle, *'Felix urbs Winthonia*: Winchester in the age of monastic reform', in *Tenth-Century Studies. Essays in Commemoration of the Millennium of the Council of Winchester and 'Regularis Concordia'*, ed. D. Parsons (London and Chichester, 1975), pp. 123–40.

[30] Cf. Blair, 'Secular minster churches', p. 104, and J. Campbell, 'The church in Anglo-Saxon towns', in his *Essays in Anglo-Saxon History* (London and Ronceverte, 1986), pp. 139–54, at p. 143.

secular, and some of these also adopted rules regulating their *uita communis*.[31] Other non-episcopal secular communities left even fewer traces of their activities. James Campbell has examined the examples of Saint Frideswide's, Oxford and Cirencester. The pre-Conquest evidence for the former is relatively richer, comprising both written sources and archaeological findings. By contrast, for the latter example there is no mention of an ecclesiastical foundation in any Anglo-Saxon source, although archaeological excavations have proved the existence of an earlier church under the remains of the Norman one.[32] Such secular churches would have had much more contact with the local population than monastic ones, although they have left no comparable evidence of their activities.

The phenomenon which by and large had the biggest impact on the ecclesiastical geography of late Anglo-Saxon towns was the above mentioned proliferation of minor churches. Towns with many churches were very common at this time. Such places as Ipswich (with at least 11 churches in 1086) or Norwich (with at least 46) are examples of a group of large towns in which at least three quarters of their later parish churches had already been founded by the end of the eleventh century.[33] In such towns – just as in rural areas – laymen were mostly responsible for ecclesiastical foundations which could be the result of both private and corporate initiatives.[34] It is not easy, however, to establish the extent to which such foundations would have affected the late Anglo-Saxon pastoral system. Small urban churches began to acquire some sort of parochial status from the eleventh century, sometimes usurping the rights of major older churches. But new churches, both in towns and in rural areas, could also be founded with the agreement of old minsters.[35] Any attempt to describe the process which led to the foundation of the parochial system must bear in mind that the new local churches were not yet parish churches and that the tenth and especially the eleventh centuries were a period of negotiations and adjustments between major and minor foundations.[36]

As Gervase Rosser has pointed out, in many respects major churches continued to exercise a crucial role because of the more attractive features they possessed. Among such features the ownership of saints' relics was probably

---

[31] On secular cathedral chapters in late Anglo-Saxon England, see N. Brooks, *The Early History of the Church of Canterbury* (London and New York, 1984), pp. 255–6 and J. Barrow, 'English cathedral communities and reform in the late tenth and eleventh centuries', in *Anglo-Norman Durham 1093–1193*, ed. D. Rollason, M. Harvey and M. Prestwich (Woodbridge, 1994), pp. 25–39. The main examples of secular cathedral communities which adopted a form of *uita communis* include Exeter, York, Wells and London.

[32] Campbell, 'The church in Anglo-Saxon towns', pp. 143–4. For further examples of both urban and rural late Anglo-Saxon secular minsters, see Blair, 'Secular minster churches'.

[33] Morris, *Churches in the Landscape*, p. 169.

[34] Rosser, 'The cure of souls', p. 274. Some corporate foundations were associated with the activities of guilds, as seems to have been the case at Cambridge, Exeter and Winchester; cf. Morris, *Churches in the Landscape*, p. 213.

[35] Some interesting examples of such cases are provided in Blair, 'Secular minster churches', pp. 127–31.

[36] Whereas some eleventh-century minor churches had their own priests, others were still served by priests sent from the local minster, but, as John Blair has noted, 'the further we go beyond the year 1000, the more likely we are to find local churches with their own lands – and pretensions to their own parochial rights': Blair, 'Local churches', p. 270.

unbeatable: experiencing or witnessing a miracle could often lead to profound pastoral consequences.[37] The relation between pastoral care and the cult of saints is a topic which deserves much more space than can be allocated in this introduction. However, it is important to bear in mind that though more exceptional and less frequent than other aspects of *cura animarum*, the rituals and celebrations which were connected with later Anglo-Saxon saints' cults must have had a remarkable impact on the laity. In a way this topic takes us back to the pastoral potential of monastic centres, as in late Anglo-Saxon England such communities were the major promoters of saints' cults. Tenth-century reformers were extremely keen to assemble relics in their monasteries, as is attested by the number of translations which involved reformed centres between the 970s and the 1020s.[38] The first example which comes to the mind is the cult of St Swithun, which originated in late tenth-century Winchester and spread during the following centuries. The translation of Swithun's remains in 971 and the writing – within the following 30 years – of four accounts of that event and the post-mortem miracles performed by the saint testify to the great publicity promoted by the Winchester community in the last decades of the tenth century.[39] The healing miracles and visions reported in Lantfred's *Translatio* and the other slightly later texts dealing with Swithun's cult depict a very high number of lay people coming to the Old Minster at Winchester from far and wide. Lantfred says that he personally saw more than two hundred sick people cured in ten days.[40] Those who were healed at St Swithun's shrine, as well as those who accompanied them, would necessarily meet the monks of that community. The latter were expected to gather in the church whenever a miracle took place. Those who decided to disobey the rule because they were so frequently awakened from their night-time sleep were seriously rebuked by Bishop Æthelwold.[41] Lantfred also tells of people who were healed by St Swithun before reaching his shrine and who would subsequently go to Winchester to report the miracles to the monks.[42] Pilgrimages and visits to such places as the Old Minster at Winchester would obviously help to gather lay people in the churches and thus provide a perfect occasion for the delivery of pastoral care, especially in the form of preaching. Lay people would also participate in some of the liturgical celebrations which took place at saints' shrines. Such exceptional events as the translation of St Swithun were characterised by large gatherings, but the same can be said for feast-days and peak periods of pilgrimage. Portable relics were used in public celebrations such as church

---

[37] Rosser, 'The cure of souls', p. 276

[38] Cf. D. Rollason, 'The shrines of saints in later Anglo-Saxon England: distribution and significance', in *The Anglo-Saxon Church*, ed. L.A.S. Butler and R.K. Morris, CBA Research Report 60 (London, 1986), pp. 32–50.

[39] The four texts in question are Lantfred's *Translatio et miracula Sancti Swithuni*, Wulfstan of Winchester's *Narratio metrica de S. Swithuno*, the *Epitome translationis et miraculorum S. Swithuni* and Ælfric's 'Life of St Swithun'. For editions, translations and detailed discussion see M. Lapidge, *The Cult of St Swithun*, Winchester Studies 4.ii (Oxford, 2003).

[40] Lantfred, *Translatio*, ch. 4, in Lapidge, *The Cult of St Swithun*, pp. 286–7.

[41] *Ibid.*, ch. 10, at pp. 292–6.

[42] *Ibid.*, chs 27, 29 and 35, at pp. 314–17, 316–19 and 324–9.

consecrations or penitential processions, a practice which seems to have become particularly popular in later Anglo-Saxon times.[43] Saints and relics, therefore, would have acted as a powerful tool through which ecclesiastical institutions, and especially monastic reformed houses, would have attracted the laity in the late tenth and eleventh centuries. As has been pointed out by several scholars, the cult of saints was often promoted with due consideration for the political and financial advantages that the possession of saints' relics would normally generate.[44] However, such matters should not be over-emphasised at the expense of those eminently religious components that characterised saints' cults. The growing popularity of saints and relics among the laity of both higher and lower social status probably contributed to creating successful pastoral situations, in which the miraculous mediation of the saints would act as a powerful link between the communities which kept their relics and the faithful who went to their shrines.

Although saints' cults affected the liturgical life of every single church, the small local foundations which transformed the ecclesiastical geography of late Anglo-Saxon England would not have been able to match the grandeur of the liturgical celebrations taking place at major shrines. However, as has been pointed out above, it is mostly with the pastoral care and the liturgy of such minor churches that this book is concerned. In order to provide a proper context for the issues discussed in the following contributions, it is necessary to deal with some aspects of minor churches' architecture. First of all, it is worth repeating what has been previously hinted at: the eleventh century was a turning point in terms of church construction, as it was from this time that minor churches started to be built or rebuilt with more durable materials. It is also necessary to emphasise that when dealing with small churches it does not seem possible to draw a definite line between buildings erected before or after 1066.[45] The post-Conquest developments in minor church construction cannot be compared to the massive programme of rebuilding which characterised the architectural history of English cathedrals in the decades after the Conquest. Eric Fernie has written of 'a school of minor churches, inhabiting the hundred years from the second quarter of the eleventh century to the second quarter of the twelfth, which is neither simply "Saxon" nor simply "Norman" '.[46] John Blair has noted that 'English technology . . . could have co-existed for some generations with methods derived from the great Anglo-Norman building projects' and that many of the churches of this period show a 'fusion of traditions: either Romanesque architectural ornament with English technology, or traditional English forms realized in the new Norman masonry'.[47]

Bearing in mind that many of the buildings which appear to be relevant for our period might in fact be later than 1066, we may still look at this group of minor ecclesiastical foundations in order to study possible architectural settings for the

[43] D. Rollason, *Saints and Relics in Anglo-Saxon England* (Oxford, 1989), p. 194.

[44] *Ibid.*, p. 180.

[45] Blair, 'Churches in the early English landscape', p. 13.

[46] E. Fernie, *The Architecture of the Anglo-Saxons* (London, 1983), p. 171.

[47] Blair, 'Local churches', pp. 272–3.

liturgy performed in late Anglo-Saxon local churches. Several excavations and analyses of standing buildings have shown that such churches would have had a simple two-cell plan, with a square chancel and a rectangular nave. The identification of the position of the altar has been the subject of several publications, given that the celebration of the Eucharist would have probably been the main ceremony among those performed at minor foundations. It would seem that in some earlier Anglo-Saxon churches, like that at Raunds Furnells, Northamptonshire, the altar was not positioned inside the chancel but at the east end of the nave, so that the priest would have celebrated facing west, towards the congregation.[48] But further archaeological excavations have proved that by the eleventh century the altar had been moved inside the chancel, although it is not entirely clear whether at this point the priest would have still celebrated facing the congregation.[49] The altar probably did not occupy the only space used for liturgy in small churches. Architectural evidence has shown that west doors were rarely used at this time. Doors were instead placed along the nave, so that one could turn either left or right when entering the building. This suggests that the west end of the nave could have also been used as a liturgical space. There are various hypotheses about possible uses, which go from the presence of another altar – since major Anglo-Saxon churches did have western altars – to the presence of a baptismal font at this end of the nave. Unfortunately there is not enough archaeological or documentary evidence to establish when minor churches began to celebrate baptism. On the Continent baptism was the crucial factor which would distinguish a mother church from a dependent chapel.[50] Written evidence available for late Anglo-Saxon England does not allow for such a specific distinction; it would actually appear that burial had a more important role in defining parochial status, as is attested by King Edgar's second code, according to which the only churches which were entitled to receive tithe payments were those with graveyards.[51] The basic two-cell plan was maintained until well after the Conquest, but at some point between the late eleventh and the twelfth centuries several buildings, especially in East Anglia, acquired some additional space at the west end in the form of a tower.[52] The exact original function of such towers is still matter of debate, although various suggestions have been made, including the

---

[48] For the results of excavations at Raunds, see Boddington, *Raunds Furnells*, pp. 63–4.

[49] Further examples include churches at Norwich, Lincoln and Barton-upon-Humber. On these issues see H.M. Taylor, 'The position of the altar in early Anglo-Saxon churches', *Journal of the Society of Antiquaries* 53 (1973), pp. 52–8; W. Rodwell and K. Rodwell, 'St Peter's church, Barton-upon-Humber: excavation and structural studies, 1978–81', *Journal of the Society of Antiquaries* 62 (1982), pp. 283–315; D. Parsons, 'Sacrarium: ablution drains in early medieval churches', in *The Anglo-Saxon Church*, ed. Butler and Morris, pp. 105–20; M. Biddle, 'Archaeology, architecture, and the cult of saints in Anglo-Saxon England', *ibid.*, pp. 1–31, at p. 20, and R. Gem, 'Church buildings: cultural location and meaning', in *Church Archaeology*, ed. Blair and Pyrah, pp. 1–6, at p. 3.

[50] For an overview of the Italian system of ecclesiastical organisation see C. Violante, 'Le strutture organizzative della cura d'anime nelle campagne dell'Italia centro-settentrionale (secoli V–X)', in *Cristianizzazione*, pp. 963–1158.

[51] On this point see Hadley and Buckberry, below.

[52] Cf. S. Heywood, 'The round towers of East Anglia', in *Minsters and Parish Churches*, ed. Blair, pp. 169–77.

possibility of their being employed as liturgical space for baptism.[53] Whatever the original function of such towers, it is probably safe to assume that the architecture of small churches began to develop as the latter started to acquire new functions and rights. The situation throughout late Anglo-Saxon England would have probably been rather varied, with small churches' architectural features beginning to reflect different stages of a steady development towards parochial status.

The main aim of the first part of this introduction has been to provide a context in which readers could place the following essays. It is now time to concentrate on the characteristics of the volume itself, starting with the terminology used to refer to the institutions on which the pastoral system was centred. Contributors were not given specific guidelines in this respect: all the ink which was spilled at the time of the minster debate on terminological issues has probably proved that no matter how hard one tries to define one's labels (or even how hard one tries to instruct other scholars on which words they should use – as has sometimes been the case), terminology remains one of the most sensitive issues in historical writing.[54] The principal issue here concerns the term 'minster', which has been the subject of several progressively more detailed definitions in the past few decades.[55] Not surprisingly in this volume the word occurs frequently in the essays which have been above identified as being most engaged in providing an institutional framework for pastoral care. Here, as in many other publications dealing with tenth- and eleventh-century England, the term is used to refer to major secular churches and 'monastery' to refer to the communities which were affected by the tenth-century monastic reform. As has been specified above, such a distinction seems to be more justified with reference to the later Anglo-Saxon period, although it should be borne in mind that the clergy of the time probably would not have used different terms to distinguish between such institutions. A more detailed terminological investigation is necessary to compare usage in both Latin and vernacular texts. What can be pointed out, however, is that terminology confirms the importance of the later Anglo-Saxon period in English Church history and the need for it to be studied for its own sake. After all, the use of the term 'minster' (derived from Old English *mynster*) to refer to the communities of the seventh and eighth centuries is not really justified on the basis of written evidence. Relevant written sources from that period are in Latin and generally employ the term *monasterium* to refer to religious communities. We can assume that in oral communication Old English *mynster* would have probably been used at that time as well, but it is only in the later period that vernacular texts give us a proper sense of the contexts in which the term would have appeared.[56]

---

[53] This section is based on the paper presented by Carol Davidson-Cragoe at the Leeds International Medieval Congress of 2002. For different hypotheses on the original function of these towers see C. Platt, *The Parish Churches of Medieval England* (London, 1981), p. 15.

[54] Cf. Foot, 'Anglo-Saxon minsters'.

[55] The climax of such attempts has been reached by John Blair in his monograph entitled *The Church in Anglo-Saxon Society*: his definition of 'minster' (p. 3) is more than eighty words long and is thus unlikely to be beaten by any future attempt.

[56] This is not the place for a detailed evaluation of the usage of the term 'minster' in modern historical

As has been pointed out, the main interest of this volume lies in what pastoral care really consisted of in late Anglo-Saxon England, how it was provided and by whom; hence the focus in Barrow's opening contribution on secular clergy, their recruitment, patronage and means of subsistence. The many examples and documents cited in this essay allow us to think of real people, with proper names, who were responsible for the ministry of specific churches. Such real people would have had to deal with the aspects of pastoral care discussed in the contributions that follow: payment of church dues, preaching, baptism, penance, confession, visitation of the sick, burial and so on. Most of the essays rely heavily on sources produced at the turn of the millennium, when such writers as Ælfric and Archbishop Wulfstan composed or compiled the texts which appear to be most useful for a discussion of the role, tasks and conduct of the late Anglo-Saxon clergy.[57] As a matter of fact, it would seem that whereas the late tenth-century material focuses on the characteristics of monastic life and liturgy, thanks to the vast amount of material produced at the time of the Benedictine reform, by contrast eleventh-century sources provide a much better understanding of the specificity of the secular clergy's life, education and pastoral responsibilities.[58] Hence the attention that several contributions pay to sources explicitly written to instruct the clergy on dogmatic, pastoral and liturgical matters. The production of this material appears to have been directly linked to the proliferation of smaller churches and the breaking up of a more centralised system. Bishops had to find new ways to reach their priests, as many of them had ceased living in large communities and had been put in charge of a local church.

A special place is also given to the texts which convey a sense of some direct interaction between the clergy and the laity: from such public occasions as the delivery of homilies on Sundays and feast-days to very private events like visitation of the sick or confession. Sarah Hamilton's contribution highlights the efforts made by the late Anglo-Saxon higher clergy to encourage confession among the laity, both at specific times of the liturgical year – as in Lent – and when approaching death. By comparing the instructions given in such prescriptive texts as Archbishop Wulfstan's *Canons of Edgar* with the contents of some vernacular

writing to refer to early religious houses, but it should be pointed out that the issue probably needs to be addressed, bearing in mind that the Old English term from which 'minster' derives is mostly attested in later Anglo-Saxon sources. It is probably worth investigating whether a regressive use of terminology is justified in this case or whether one should stick to Latin *monasterium* when discussing earlier communities.

57 Chief among such texts are Ælfric's Pastoral Letters and Wulfstan's so-called *Canons of Edgar*, which are repeatedly referred to in this volume.

58 Joyce Hill has suggested that both Ælfric and Wulfstan's activities can 'be seen as part of a second-generation extension of the reform to the secular church': J. Hill, 'Archbishop Wulfstan: reformer?', in *Wulfstan*, ed. Townend, p. 316. On the same point see also her earlier article: 'Monastic reform and the secular church: Ælfric's pastoral letters in context', in *England in the Eleventh Century*, ed. C. Hicks (Stamford, 1992), pp. 103–17, esp. pp. 103–8. For a slightly different view on Wulfstan's relations with the monastic world, with reference to liturgical material, see Jones, 'Wulfstan's liturgical interests'. Malcolm Godden has also noted that Wulfstan and Ælfric did not share the same views on matters concerning clerical discipline; the former, for instance, seems to have been less strict regarding priests' chastity: M. Godden, 'The relations of Wulfstan and Ælfric: a reassessment', in *Wulfstan*, ed. Townend, pp. 353–74, at p. 373.

penitentials and confessionals, this essay allows one to move from theory to practice, from what the clergy were expected to do to the tools they were given to carry out their pastoral duties. Victoria Thompson's contribution provides a detailed analysis of one of the very few surviving late Anglo-Saxon manuscripts (Oxford, Bodleian Library, Laud Misc. 482) which, given their dimensions and contents, were probably made for the practical use of the clergy in their ministry to the sick and dying. The analysis focuses on the relationship which came to be established between the priest and the parishioner in such a special context. Thompson draws attention to the contents of the exceptionally long and detailed vernacular rubrics commenting on the *ordines* for the sick and the dying in the Laud manuscript, pointing out the remarkable amount of direct speech they contain. This material takes us to the core of late Anglo-Saxon pastoral care, as it provides some very interesting evidence for the context, the actions and the verbal exchanges which characterised its delivery. Obviously linked to these matters are the enormous implications of the late Anglo-Saxon Church's reliance on the vernacular in pastoral situations. The issue is analysed in detail by Gittos with special attention to the presence of the vernacular in texts containing formal liturgy. In all such manuscripts Old English is used extensively for rubrics, often providing directions for the clergy on what to do during the celebration of mass, baptism, blessings and so on. Occasionally, however, the vernacular is used in the liturgy itself, in contexts requiring a direct address by a priest to an individual (as in confession or visitation of the sick) for which comprehension was crucial. Gittos suggests, therefore, that the vernacular was not considered as just a poor substitute of Latin in liturgy, or at least not any longer. Pastoral aims might have had a part in such a development.

In many ways this volume is 'about' texts, but not texts alone. The survival of a small group of manuscripts which might have been used in the field by the priests of the late Anglo-Saxon Church, and which is duly discussed in this book, is tangible evidence of the actual tools used in pastoral care provision. Archaeology allows us to go further. The survey by Hadley and Buckberry, which closes the volume, focuses on one specific aspect of pastoral provisions, namely the care of the dead. Through a detailed discussion of the burial evidence available for the tenth and eleventh centuries, the authors take us into a world in which the Church was exercising a growing control. Location of burials was obviously a crucial matter, as is testified by a number of late Anglo-Saxon law-codes dealing with churchyards. However, the form of burial appears to have been very significant as well, given the interesting variations that the archaeological evidence reveals, often even within the same churchyard. In spite of the efforts made by the higher clergy to control certain aspects of burial through normative texts and law-codes, choices of grave materials and artefacts were necessarily made at the local level, within a single community. Once again, it is the emergence of local churches with their own churchyards which seems to have played a major role. We are thus taken back to one of the very first points made in this introduction: the late Anglo-Saxon evidence testifies to a period of major changes in the pastoral system, a period of contrasting – but also complementary – developments: it was the spread of new, minor churches which called for the production of normative texts dealing with several aspects of ecclesiastical organisation and pastoral care. But the proliferation of local churches was not just a threat to older institutions: the higher clergy were also aware of the potential of such foundations. Hence the provisions made to assist priests in all their pastoral activities (from preaching to a wide variety of liturgical celebrations) and to ensure that church dues were paid by the faithful for whose souls care was provided.[59]

[59] Most of the essays contained in this book are longer versions of papers delivered at the International Medieval Congress held in Leeds in July 2002, in the course of four sessions dedicated to pastoral care in late Anglo-Saxon England. I am grateful to all participants and all contributors to this volume for the fruitful discussion which followed and led to the publication of this book. I am also grateful to John Blair for his comments on an earlier draft of this chapter.

1

The Clergy in English Dioceses c. 900–c. 1066

Julia Barrow

Now at that time there were in the Old Minster, where the bishop's throne is situated, cathedral canons involved in wicked and scandalous behaviour, victims of pride, insolence and riotous living to such a degree that some of them did not think fit to celebrate mass in due order. They married wives illicitly, divorced them, and took others; they were constantly given to gourmandizing and drunkenness. The holy man Æthelwold would not tolerate it.[1]

The clergy of late Anglo-Saxon England have not received the most favourable of presses, as the quotation above shows. Too often they are defined for us by the much more literate monks of the Benedictine reform movement, who, although they formed only a small part of the late Anglo-Saxon ecclesiastical establishment, set the tone and the agenda for the rest from the reign of Edgar onwards.[2] More problematic for the historian of the clergy is that they have not been recorded for us in sufficient detail. For the historian of the later Middle Ages, that is to say of the period from the Fourth Lateran Council of 1215 onwards, the standard approach to the clergy is a prosopographical one, made possible by the existence of enough pieces of information to supply biographical outlines for large numbers of individual clerics. Since the 1960s scholars have been steadily producing detailed lists of later medieval clergy in Britain – English cathedral canons between 1066 and 1540,[3] graduates of Oxford and Cambridge,[4] Yorkshire

---

[1] M. Lapidge and M. Winterbottom, ed., *Wulfstan of Winchester: Life of St Æthelwold*, Oxford Medieval Texts (Oxford, 1991), ch. 16, pp. 30–1.

[2] For the tensions between Benedictine monks and secular clergy in late Anglo-Saxon England, and for attempts by the former to prescribe patterns of behaviour for the latter, see J. Hill, 'Monastic reform and the secular church: Ælfric's pastoral letters in context', in *England in the Eleventh Century*, ed. C. Hicks (Stamford, 1992), pp. 103–17, and J. Barrow, 'English cathedral communities and reform in the late tenth and the eleventh centuries', in *Anglo-Norman Durham 1093–1193*, ed. D. Rollason, M. Harvey and M. Prestwich (Woodbridge, 1994), pp. 25–39; see also J. Barrow, 'Cathedral clergy', in *The Blackwell Encyclopaedia of Anglo-Saxon England*, ed. M. Lapidge, J. Blair, S. Keynes and D. Scragg (Oxford, 1999), pp. 84–7.

[3] John Le Neve, *Fasti Ecclesiae Anglicanae 1066–1300*, compiled by D.E. Greenway with J.S. Barrow and M. Pearson, 9 vols to date (London, 1968–, in progress); John Le Neve, *Fasti Ecclesiae Anglicanae 1300–1540*, compiled by J.M. Horn, B. Jones and H.P.F. King, 12 vols (London, 1962–7).

[4] A.B. Emden, *A Biographical Register of the University of Oxford to AD 1500*, 3 vols (Oxford, 1957–9); *idem*, *A Biographical Register of the University of Cambridge to 1500* (Cambridge, 1963); *idem*, 'Additions and corrections to *A Biographical Register of the University of Oxford to AD 1500*: supplemental list no. 2', *The Bodleian Record* 7 (1962–7), pp. 149–64.

parish clergy[5] and Scottish higher clergy and university graduates.[6] These schemes have numerous parallels across Europe, notably *Fasti Ecclesiae Gallicanae* for medieval French cathedral canons of the post-1200 period,[7] and more elaborate projects to list inmates of all ecclesiastical communities in Germany and Switzerland.[8] Even for the twelfth century, before the systematic survival of royal, papal and episcopal documents, attempting a very rudimentary prosopography of the English parish clergy would be feasible, and from naming practices and comments on advowson various hypotheses could be arrived at as to backgrounds and careers. But for the tenth and eleventh centuries evidence is quite exceptionally sparse.[9] Therefore this article can do no more than provide some hypotheses. It will survey the following topics: the source material, evidence for the recruitment of clergy, in particular the operation of family networks and patronage, and the institutional framework within which the clergy operated; finally it will compare and contrast tenth- and eleventh-century English clergy with their twelfth-century successors, for whom evidence is far more plentiful, in the hope that this might help to establish developing trends.

The sources which are most valuable for the study of the English clergy of the 150 years before the Norman Conquest are the *Liber Eliensis* and the *Chronicle of Ramsey*, both cartulary-chronicles of the twelfth century containing a large number of (usually summarised versions of) Anglo-Saxon charters, Anglo-Saxon wills (most of the ones relevant to this paper are connected with Bury St Edmunds), and Domesday Book, with some post-Conquest charter material.[10] Charters form a particularly valuable source for prosopographers because of the number of individuals for whom they provide evidence. There is a heavy imbalance towards East Anglia and the East Midlands in the sources cited, especially when one bears in mind that Domesday references to clergy are fuller for East Anglia than for most other parts of England. Even though the more plentiful Domesday material for East Anglian churches partly results from the fact that Little Domesday did not undergo the editorial slimming-down of the material in Great Domesday, the frequency of references to East Anglian clergy and

5　A.H. Thompson, C.T. Clay, N.A.H. Lawrence and N.K.M. Gurney, ed., *Fasti Parochiales*, 5 vols to date, Yorkshire Archaeological Society Record Series, 85 (1933), 107 (1943), 129 (1967), 130 (1971), 143 (1985).

6　D.E.R. Watt and A.L. Murray, ed., *Fasti Ecclesiae Scoticanae medii aevi ad annum 1638*, revised edition, Scottish Record Society, n.s. 25 (Edinburgh, 2003); D.E.R. Watt, *A Biographical Dictionary of Scottish Graduates to AD 1410* (Oxford, 1977).

7　*Fasti Ecclesiae Gallicanae*, gen. ed. H. Millet, 6 vols (Turnhout, 1996–, in progress); http://fasti.univ-paris1.fr/.

8　*Germania Sacra*, Max-Planck-Institut für Geschichte, Göttingen, original series 7 vols, new series 42 vols in 48 parts to date (Berlin, 1929–, in progress), with website at http://www.germania-sacra.mpg.de/; *Helvetia Sacra*, ed. A. Bruckner and others, 23 vols to date (Bern, Basel and Frankfurt am Main, 1972–, in progress).

9　The Prosopography of Anglo-Saxon England (PASE) project has tabulated evidence for all known Anglo-Saxons, including clerics, down to the mid eleventh century: see website at http://www.pase.ac.uk.

10　E.O. Blake, ed., *Liber Eliensis*, Camden third series 92 (London, 1962); W.D. Macray, ed., *Chronicon Abbatiae Rameseiensis*, Rolls Series (London, 1886); D. Whitelock, ed., *Anglo-Saxon Wills* (Cambridge, 1930); A. Farley and H. Ellis, ed., *Domesday Book*, 4 vols (London, 1783–1816); for the post-Conquest charter material see n. 43 below.

churches overall is largely a reflection of the denser population and the earlier increase in the number of churches in eastern England in the late Anglo-Saxon period.[11]

If we turn first to the recruitment of the clergy, we can discern three main routes of advancement: firstly family networking and inheritance, secondly purchase, and thirdly patronage. Priests made the most of family relationships in establishing themselves in their careers. All sorts of relationships could be exploited, but the most important ones were those between father and son and between brothers. It was valuable for families to enter kinsmen into the Church, since clerics might give prestige and assistance to those of their relatives who remained laymen. Andrew Wareham has shown how prominent, indeed dominant, the clerics were in the paternal family of Bishop Oswald of Worcester in the Fens in the tenth century – not only those of senior rank like Archbishops Oda and Oscytel but also those lower down the hierarchy such as Oda's brother Æthelstan and his kinsman Osweard.[12] Osweard and his own son, moreover, tried to preserve their family inheritance by claiming lands in which Ramsey Abbey had an interest.[13] At Horningsea Herulf the priest allowed his kinsman, another Æthelstan, to stand in for him and later, on Herulf's death, the latter succeeded him.[14] The obit book of Hereford cathedral records that when the Welsh sacked Hereford cathedral on 25 (or 24) October 1055, they killed Canon Eilmar and his four sons,[15] who were trying to defend the doors of the church,[16] presumably in an effort to protect their future inheritance. Links between brothers helped too: for example Æthelstan priest of Horningsea relied on assistance from his brother Bondi.[17]

Family networking was of assistance to clergy in all sorts of ways. Æthelstan of Horningsea was rescued from prosecution for criminal activities by the lobbying of a highly placed relative.[18] Land might be held in common between a priest and his kin, for example the unnamed priest and his sister holding at *Bricewolde* in Hertfordshire.[19] Above all there was the possibility of inheritance. The will of Siflæd, proprietress of Marlingford in Norfolk, says that Wulfmær

---

[11] H.C. Darby, *Domesday England* (Cambridge, 1977), pp. 92–4.

[12] A. Wareham, 'St Oswald's family and kin', in *St Oswald of Worcester: Life and Influence*, ed. N. Brooks and C. Cubitt (London and New York, 1996), pp. 46–63.

[13] Macray, ed., *Chronicon Abbatiae Rameseiensis*, p. 76.

[14] Blake, ed., *Liber Eliensis*, ii.32, p. 106.

[15] *Fasti Ecclesiae Anglicanae 1066–1300*, viii, *Hereford*, compiled by J.S. Barrow (London, 2002), p. 148. The year of the Welsh attack on the cathedral is not given in the obit book but is supplied by the Anglo-Saxon Chronicle: D. Whitelock, D.C. Douglas and S.I. Tucker, tr., *The Anglo-Saxon Chronicle: a Revised Translation* (London, 1961), pp. 130–1, and by John of Worcester: R.R. Darlington and P. McGurk with J. Bray, ed. and tr., *The Chronicle of John of Worcester*, ii, *The Annals from 450 to 1066* (Oxford, 1995), pp. 576–7; John of Worcester gives the day of the attack as 24 October.

[16] *Chronicle of John of Worcester, ibid.*, supplies the detail about the canons defending the doors of the church.

[17] Blake, ed., *Liber Eliensis*, ii.33, pp. 107–8.

[18] *Ibid.*, ii.32, p. 106. Æthelstan's successor Leofstan was later saved from prosecution for a different offence by pleading from the citizens of Cambridge: *ibid.*, p. 107.

[19] *Domesday Book*, i, fol. 142b (M. Newman and S. Wood, ed. and tr., *Domesday Book*, 12, *Hertfordshire* (Chichester, 1976), 42, 9).

and his children will sing at the church there as long as they are in holy orders.[20] Domesday contains several references to priests inheriting property: Stigand's brother inherited the church of SS Simon and Jude in Norwich *de patrimonio*,[21] and there are several examples of priests inheriting from their fathers,[22] while one Lincoln priest unsuccessfully claimed inheritance from a more distant kinsman.[23] The Domesday survey for Kent supplies the double list, *TRE* and 1086, of the clergy of St Martin's Dover, which shows that four of the canons in office in 1086 had succeeded their fathers.[24] Charter and other evidence shows that canons of both St Paul's and Hereford cathedrals often succeeded their fathers in prebends from the later eleventh well into the twelfth century.[25] These references are not numerous but they are casual and matter-of-fact, unlike the comment in the *Vita Æthelwoldi* cited at the opening of this paper, suggesting that hereditary succession to whole churches or to portions of churches or to lands associated with churches was normal and socially acceptable, however abhorrent it must have been to the Benedictine reformers.

Equally acceptable was the purchase of churches. Even the *Northumbrian Priests' Law* of the mid eleventh century seems to suggest that this was allowable when the previous incumbent had committed a capital offence.[26] The priests Burgred and Thorkell bought St Mary's church in Huntingdon, after it had passed through numerous other hands, in the mid eleventh century.[27] Nearly a hundred years earlier, St Oswald's kinsman, Thurcytel, after he had been ejected from his position as abbot of Bedford, had managed to persuade St Paul's cathedral in London to give him a place as a canon by offering to bequeath an estate which he would continue to hold in his lifetime for an annual rent of twenty shillings.[28]

However, as the careers of several of the clerks who have so far been mentioned suggest, family and wealth were not always sufficient to preserve priests in churches. The severe fluctuations in the land-market most noticeable in eastern England, influenced as they were by waves of political back-stabbing and carefully targeted prosecutions leading to outlawry and confiscation, affected

---

[20] Whitelock, ed., *Anglo-Saxon Wills*, pp. 92–3, no. 37.

[21] *Domesday Book*, ii, fol. 117b (P. Morgan, ed., *Domesday Book*, 33, *Norfolk*, 2 parts (Chichester, 1984), Part 1, section 1, 61); cf. F. Barlow, *The English Church 1000–1066*, second edn (London, 1979), p. 78 n.1 and M.F. Smith, 'Archbishop Stigand and the eye of the needle', *Anglo-Norman Studies* 16 (1994), pp. 199–219, at p. 210 n. 81.

[22] *Domesday Book*, i, fol. 211a (V. Sankaran and D. Sherlock, ed., *Domesday Book*, 20, *Bedfordshire* (Chichester, 1977), 14, 1); i, fol. 68c (C. and F. Thorn, ed., *Domesday Book*, 6, *Wiltshire* (Chichester, 1979), 19, 4); i, fol. 91c (C. and F. Thorn, ed., *Domesday Book*, 8, *Somerset* (Chichester, 1980), 16, 9).

[23] *Domesday Book*, i, fol. 336b (P. Morgan and C. Thorne, ed., *Domesday Book*, 31, *Lincolnshire*, 2 parts (Chichester, 1986), Part 1, C16).

[24] *Domesday Book*, i, fol. 1c–d, 2b (P. Morgan, ed., *Domesday Book*, 1, *Kent* (Chichester, 1983), M, P).

[25] *Fasti Ecclesiae Anglicanae 1066–1300*, i, *St Paul's*, compiled by D.E. Greenway (London, 1968), pp. 32, 34, 36, 45, 55, 59, 65, 67, 69, 71, 75, 77, 83; see also C.N.L. Brooke, 'The composition of the chapter of St Paul's, 1086–1163', *Cambridge Historical Journal* 10 (1950–2), pp. 111–32 at pp. 124–5; for Hereford, *Fasti Ecclesiae Anglicanae 1066–1300*, viii, *Hereford*, ed. Barrow, pp. 9, 44, 65, 75.

[26] *Northumbrian Priests' Law*, cc. 2, 2.1, 2.2: F. Liebermann, ed., *Die Gesetze der Angelsachsen*, 3 vols (Halle, 1903–16), i, p. 380; *Councils and Synods*, i, p. 452.

[27] *Domesday Book*, i, fols 203a, 206a, 208a (S. Harvey, ed., *Domesday Book*, 19, *Huntingdonshire* (Chichester, 1975), B12; 19, 9; D1).

[28] Blake, ed., *Liber Eliensis*, ii.31, p. 105.

priests just as much as laymen, both as owners of land and as owners of churches.[29] It was thus useful to have the protection of some figure in authority. The range of authority figures was very wide: from thegns of quite modest status up to kings. We may begin with the kings and then proceed to the rest.

Royal patronage of clerks, which is particularly well evidenced in Domesday Book, appears to have operated at two levels. At the top level were the curial clerks, men such as Stigand, Giso, Spirites and Regenbald, who would be rewarded with churches in numerous counties.[30] Very often they would receive the leading position in a minster church, as for example Spirites at St Guthlac's Hereford and at Bromfield in Shropshire, or Regenbald at Cheltenham, to name only one part of Regenbald's ecclesiastical empire.[31] Probably the other clerics attached to these churches would have carried out the liturgical and pastoral duties on a day-to-day basis, while the curial clerks would have paid only fleeting visits. It is not necessary here to say much about the court clergy, since detailed studies exist of the careers of Stigand, Regenbald and Giso. In contrast, the lower tier of royal clergy has excited less interest. These are the clerks who occur in Domesday Book as king's almoners, king's clerks or clergy holding land from the king (perhaps a hide or so); sometimes they occur among the king's thegns at the end of a shire entry; they tend to hold modest amounts of land in one shire only, usually on only one manor; some of them clearly inherited their positions from their fathers, and even after the Norman Conquest many of them bore English names, suggesting that at this level of patronage William was happy to leave the status quo intact.[32] In the cases of Thorkell, the king's almoner at Wymington in

---

[29] P. Wormald, 'Giving God and King their due: conflict and its regulation in the early English state', in *Legal Culture in the Early Medieval West. Law as Text, Image and Experience*, ed. *idem* (London, 1999), pp. 332–54, at pp. 339–42, and *idem*, 'Charters, law and the settlement of disputes in Anglo-Saxon England', *ibid.*, pp. 289–311, at pp. 307–9.

[30] Smith, 'Archbishop Stigand'; S. Keynes, 'Regenbald the chancellor (*sic*)', *Anglo-Norman Studies* 10 (1988), pp. 185–222; S. Keynes, 'Giso, bishop of Wells', *Anglo-Norman Studies* 19 (1997), pp. 203–71; for Spirites, see Barlow, *The English Church 1000–1066*, pp. 131–2, 135, 156, 174–5, 239n.; in general on this group of curial clerks, see M.F. Smith, 'The preferment of royal clerks in the reign of Edward the Confessor', *The Haskins Society Journal* 9 (1997), pp. 159–73.

[31] On Spirites: *Domesday Book*, i, fol. 183a (St Guthlac's, Hereford) and 252d (Bromfield, Shropshire); also F. and C. Thorn, ed., *Domesday Book, 17, Herefordshire* (Chichester, 1983), 7, 4; 7, 6; 7, 8–9; F. and C. Thorn, ed., *Domesday Book, 25, Shropshire* (Chichester, 1986), 3d, 6–7; for Regenbald, see Keynes, 'Regenbald', p. 196.

[32] The following list is of instances of king's clerks occurring as individuals, including those king's almoners not identifiable as nuns, with prominent royal clerks such as Regenbald named in square brackets. For Spirites see n. 30 above; for the canons of St Martin's of Dover, see n. 24 above. Domesday Book, i, fols 14c (*Domesday Book, 1, Kent*, 13, 1), 38a, 39b, 44b, 49b, 49d (J. Munby, ed., *Domesday Book, 4, Hampshire* (Chichester, 1982), 1, 1; 1, 44; 17, 2–3; 63, 1 [Nigel]; 64, 1–2; 66, 1 [Ranulf Flambard], 69, 8), 68c, 73d, 74a (*Domesday Book, 5, Wilts*, 18, 1; 18, 2 [Reginbald]; 67, 22; 67, 52), 79a, 84a (C. and F. Thorn, ed., *Domesday Book, 7, Dorset* (Chichester, 1983), 24, 1–5; 56, 7–8), 91bc, 99b (*Domesday Book, 8, Somerset*, 15, 1 [Bishop Maurice]; 16, 1 [Reginbald]; 16, 2–5; 16, 9–11; 16, 14 [Bishop Peter]; 45, 14 [Reginbald]), 117a, 117d (C. and F. Thorn, ed., *Domesday Book, 9, Devon*, 2 parts (Chichester, 1985), Part 1, 45, 1–3 [Gerald the chaplain]; 51, 6), 142b (*Domesday Book, 12, Herts*, 42, 9–11), 146a (E. Teague and V. Sankaran, ed., *Domesday Book, 13, Buckinghamshire* (Chichester, 1978), 11, 1 [Reginbald]), 157a, 160b (C. Caldwell, ed., *Domesday Book, 14, Oxfordshire* (Chichester, 1978), 14, 3–4; 14, 5–6 [Flambard]; 49, 1 [Reginbald]), 162d, 163b, 166cd (J.S. Moore, ed., *Domesday Book, 15, Gloucestershire* (Chichester, 1982), 1, 1 [Reginbald]; 1, 18 [Bernard the priest], 26, 1–4 [Reginbald]), 211a, 218cd (*Domesday Book, 20, Beds*, 13, 1- 2; 14, 1; 57, 8; 57, 21), 222d (F. and C. Thorn, ed.,

Bedfordshire,[33] and Colebern, the priest in the church of St Nicholas at Humbleyard in Norfolk,[34] their precise relationship with the king is explained: they prayed for him, saying weekly masses, and in Colebern's case the Psalter also. Similar duties were performed by the three priests of the king in Archenfield (the Welsh-speaking part of Herefordshire), who had each to say two masses for the king every week, as well as carrying messages for him into Wales.[35] Domesday Book refers to some royal clerks being royal almoners in King Edward's time also.[36] Perhaps Edward the Confessor would have used the term *bedesman* to describe such a cleric in place of the word *elemosinarius*. The latter term seems to have been introduced into England after the Conquest by the Normans. It emerges in England at the same time as the phrase *in elemosinam*, which indicates the concept that grants to priests or other objects of charity could be elemosinary, and which is found in some mid eleventh-century Norman charters and increasingly, from the late eleventh century, in English ones. While the idea of defining royal priests by their elemosinary status may have been new in post-Conquest England, the idea of prayer specifically for kings was of long standing: Anglo-Saxon kings from at least the ninth century onwards regarded prayers on their behalf as a necessary support for their rule, and included orders for such prayers in their legislation.[37] Saying prayers or a weekly or bi-weekly mass for the king would have been quite compatible with a parochial cure, and royal almoners were probably essentially village priests, though, thanks to their landholdings (often about a hide), of some status socially, rather like the clergy of better-off minsters.

The two levels of patronage can be also observed among clergy who were clients of noblemen and bishops, though many landowners could afford, and needed, only the lower tier. Several of the landowners whose wills survive refer to 'my priest' (sometimes to more than one of them).[38] These are in several instances

---

Domesday Book, 21, *Northamptonshire* (Chichester, 1979), 15, 1 [Ansger], 17, 1–5), 231b (P. Morgan, ed., *Domesday Book*; 22, *Leicestershire* (Chichester, 1979), 8, 1; 8, 4–5), 238b (J. Plaister, ed., *Domesday Book*, 23, *Warwickshire* (Chichester, 1976), 1, 8 [Albert]), 247d (A. Hawkins and A. Rumble, ed., *Domesday Book*, 24, *Staffordshire* (Chichester, 1976), 7, 13), 260d (F. and C. Thorn, ed., *Domesday Book*, 25, *Shropshire* (Chichester, 1986), 9, 1–2 [Nigel]), 294a (F. Thorn, ed., *Domesday Book*, 29, *Rutland* (Chichester, 1980), R21 [Albert]); ii, fol. 263b (P. Brown, ed., *Domesday Book*, 33, *Norfolk*, 2 parts (Chichester, 1984), Part 2, 44, 1; 45, 1).

[33] *Domesday Book*, i, 218d (*Domesday Book*, 20, *Beds*, 57, 21).

[34] *Domesday Book*, ii, fol. 263b (*Domesday Book*, 33, *Norfolk*, 45, 1).

[35] *Domesday Book*, i, fol. 179b (*Domesday Book*, 17, *Herefordshire*, A1). David Crouch points out that, with three priests each chanting two weekly masses, this would mean that ferial low mass would be sung for William I every weekday in Archenfield: D. Crouch, 'The origin of chantries: some further Anglo-Norman evidence', *Journal of Medieval History* 27 (2001), pp. 159–80.

[36] *Domesday Book*, i, fol. 142bc (*Domesday Book*, 12, *Hertfordshire*, 42, 10–11).

[37] On the term *elemosina* in Norman charters and in post-Conquest English charters, see F. Pollock and F.W. Maitland, *A History of English Law*, second edn, 2 vols (Cambridge, 1911), i, pp. 241–2, and B. Thompson, 'Free alms tenure in the twelfth century', *Anglo-Norman Studies* 16 (1994), pp. 221–43, at p. 225 and literature there cited. For Anglo-Saxon laws ordering prayer for the king, see V Athelstan, c. 3; VII Æthelred, c. 3.2 and VIIa Æthelred, c. 6.2 (Liebermann, ed., *Gesetze*, i, pp. 168, 261, 262); prayers for the Christian people, and prayers in danger, which evidently are also for the king, are stipulated in V Æthelred c. 4.1; VI Æthelred c. 2.2; VII Æthelred c. 2.2a; VIIa Æthelred, cc. 6.2–3 and I Cnut cc. 4.3 and 6a (Liebermann, ed., *Gesetze*, i, pp. 238, 246, 260, 262, 284, 288).

[38] Whitelock, ed., *Anglo-Saxon Wills*, nos 13, 14, 26, 34, 37.

identifiable as priests of village churches, or at least as priests associated with particular villages. One will, more specific, refers to 'my masspriest'[39] and Siflæd's will already quoted says the priest is to sing:[40] here again the priests seem to be village priests, but the stress on sacramental and liturgical duties perhaps suggests that the landowners wished the priests to say prayers particularly for their own souls. The Ramsey Chronicle refers to Ælfhild, widow of Earl Ælfwold, making arrangements for her 'chaplain'.[41]

However, noblemen and noblewomen could, if they desired more lavish liturgical arrangements, support communities of clergy. In two wills the testatrix and testator seem to be making arrangements for minster communities: Leofgifu for several priests at Colne, and Thurstan for a priest and two clerks termed *hirdprest*. Dorothy Whitelock translated this term as 'chaplain', but it might be possible to understand the *hired* element in the term *hirdprest* as a community of clergy rather than the landowner's household.[42] Alternatively, it might be possible to see the two meanings operating simultaneously – a priest might be both a member of a noble household and a member of a clerical community. Two post-Conquest charters from the West Midlands, Bishop Robert of Hereford's 1085 landgrant to Roger de Lacy and Earl Roger de Montgomery's 1086 foundation charter for Quatford, bear this out.[43] Between them they contain the names of clerics in three separate households, Bishop Robert's, Roger de Lacy's and Roger de Montgomery's, but these clerics were not only members of households (and presumably in attendance on their masters for much of the time) but also members of ecclesiastical communities. Bishop Robert's clergy formed about a third of his cathedral chapter,[44] Roger de Lacy's clerks might just possibly represent the clergy serving his father's foundation of St Peter's in Hereford,[45] and Earl Roger's household clerks (who of course included the father of Orderic Vitalis) were the beneficiaries of his new collegiate foundation at Quatford, which was later moved to Bridgnorth.[46]

So far, in looking at the roles of family and patronage in the recruitment of

---

[39] *Ibid.*, no. 20.

[40] *Ibid.*, no. 37.

[41] Macray, ed., *Chronicon Abbatiae Rameseiensis*, pp. 63–4 (S 1808, of the late tenth century).

[42] Whitelock, ed., *Anglo-Saxon Wills*, nos 29, 31.

[43] For Bishop Robert of Hereford's landgrant of 1085, see: V.H. Galbraith, 'An episcopal landgrant', *English Historical Review* 44 (1929), pp. 353–72; J. Barrow, ed., *English Episcopal Acta*, vii, *Hereford 1079–1234* (Oxford, 1993), no. 2; T.S. Purser, 'The origins of English feudalism? An episcopal land-grant revisited', *Historical Research* 73 (2000), pp. 80–92. For the foundation of Quatford in 1086, see W.G. Clark-Maxwell and A.H. Thompson, 'The college of St Mary Magdalene, Bridgnorth, with some account of its deans and prebendaries', *Archaeological Journal* 84 (1927), pp. 1–87, at pp. 1–4 and plate 1 facing p. 1; J.F.A. Mason and P. Barker, 'The Norman castle at Quatford', *Transactions of the Shropshire Archaeological Society* 57 (1961–4), pp. 37–62, at pp. 39–41.

[44] *Fasti Ecclesiae Anglicanae 1066–1300*, viii, *Hereford*, ed. Barrow, pp. 8, 23, 63, 64, 76, 88, 93.

[45] On the foundation of St Peter's Hereford, see W.H. Hart, ed., *Historia et Cartularium Monasterii S. Petri Gloucestriae*, 3 vols, Rolls Series, 33 (London, 1963–7), i, pp. 73, 84–7, 326; *Domesday Book*, i, fols 182d, 184a–185b and cf. also fol. 180a (*Domesday Book, 17, Herefordshire*, 10, 5; 10, 37; 10, 48; 10, 75 and cf. also 1, 10c).

[46] M. Chibnall, *The World of Orderic Vitalis* (Woodbridge, 1984), pp. 7–8; A.T. Graydon, ed., *Victoria County History of Shropshire*, II (London, 1973), pp. 123–4 on Quatford and the move of the collegiate community to Bridgnorth.

clergy, several aspects of the institutional framework of the Church have been touched on, and it is now necessary to look at this issue more generally. Although the word 'dioceses' occurs in the title of this article, bishops and diocesan institutions have barely made any appearance so far. Bishops in tenth- and eleventh-century England seem to have had very varying influence over the clergy in their bishoprics. Over their cathedral clergy, over the clergy in their proprietary minster churches (for example the bishop of Lichfield's church of St John's in Chester,[47] or the bishop of Hereford's church at Lydbury in Shropshire),[48] over household clerks rewarded with small manors,[49] and over the clergy serving small churches on their estates, their influence would have been considerable, but their powers over clergy in the service of kings or of thegns is less clear. Ordination would have brought them into contact with those clergy to whom they did not act as patrons, but only momentarily. The fact that Brihtheah ordained young Wulfstan is underlined in the *Vita Wulfstani*, but the two were kinsmen in any case.[50] Thurcytel of Bedford purchased his advancement to priest's orders in London, according to *Liber Eliensis*.[51] The jurisdictional framework in which bishops exercised discipline over clergy is not clear. The evidence of the *Northumbrian Priests' Law* suggests that in and around York the archbishops of York did exercise such discipline.[52] On the other hand, clerks prosecuted for crimes would appear in the shire court, where the bishop, though one of the presiding figures, might find his influence diluted by that of powerful ealdormen and thegns. It is true that the 'Laws of Edward and Guthrum'[53] say that criminous clerks should be reserved to the bishop for judgement, and possibly Wulfstan was aiming at restricting the role of secular members of the shire court in hearing such cases, though he may simply have been copying standard continental canon law here without thinking about its practical application in English courts. By contrast, *Liber Eliensis* shows clerics being prosecuted just like laymen.[54] The degree of authority which a bishop could exercise over his clergy would also have been affected by the rate at which new parishes were being established. Dioceses such as Worcester, with 150 or more churches in 1086, or Hereford, with between 60 and 70 in 1086, were in a quite different position from that of Thetford (the future diocese of Norwich, covering East Anglia), which had at least 700

---

[47] *Domesday Book*, i, fol. 263a (P. Morgan, ed., *Domesday Book*, 26, *Cheshire* (Chichester: Phillimore, 1978), B10–12).

[48] *Domesday Book*, i, 252b (*Domesday Book*, 25, *Shropshire*, 2, 1).

[49] The clerks on manors of the bishop of Hereford in Domesday are listed in J. Barrow, 'A Lotharingian in Hereford: Bishop Robert's reorganisation of the church of Hereford 1079–1095', in *Medieval Art, Architecture and Archaeology at Hereford*, ed. D. Whitehead, British Archaeological Association Conference Transactions 15 (Leeds, 1995), pp. 29–49, at p. 36.

[50] *Vita Wulfstani*, i.2, in *William of Malmesbury: Saints' Lives*, ed. M. Winterbottom and R.M. Thomson, Oxford Medieval Texts (Oxford, 2002), pp. 22–3.

[51] Blake, ed., *Liber Eliensis*, ii.31, p. 105.

[52] *Northumbrian Priests' Law*, cc. 1, 3, 4, 12, 24, 30, 45, 57.1: Liebermann, ed., *Gesetze*, i, pp. 380–2, 384; *Councils and Synods*, i, pp. 452–8, 461, 464.

[53] 'Laws of Edward and Guthrum', c. 4.2: Liebermann, ed., *Gesetze*, i, pp. 130–1; *Councils and Synods*, i, pp. 307–8.

[54] Blake, ed., *Liber Eliensis*, pp. 106–7, as n. 18 above.

churches in 1086.[55] It is difficult to see how bishops in Eastern England in the eleventh century coped before the introduction of archdeacons.

I would like to sum up by comparing the clergy in England in the tenth and eleventh centuries with their counterparts in the twelfth century. It is tempting to assume a wide gulf between the two, largely because of the huge difference in the quantity and type of source material, but also because of the steady disappearance of English clerics from the episcopate in the last three decades of the eleventh century.[56] However, at the level of parish clergy, English clerics survived in very large numbers. In cathedrals their numbers diminished as clergy of Norman and other French origins obtained preferment, but canons with Anglo-Saxon names are noticeable at St Paul's, Exeter and Hereford until well into the twelfth century, long after most indigenous English families had begun to give their children Continental Germanic names. Cathedrals founded on new sites, for example Salisbury and Lincoln, also had canons with English names, though far fewer.[57] Their eventual disappearance corresponds to the twelfth-century shift in the nomenclature of indigenous inhabitants from Anglo-Saxon to Continental German.[58]

Beyond the question of ethnic origin, some clerical characteristics remained remarkably similar. Family networking, though somewhat diluted by the Gregorian reform, persisted: father to son succession was still common in the twelfth century, and, although it was being very slowly brought to an end, it was to some extent being replaced by new family strategies in which uncles and older brothers in the Church assisted nephews and younger brothers.[59] Again, the influence of landowners over churches and clergy persisted, though now in the more formalised practice of advowson.[60] Other features changed enormously. Steadily, from the 1070s onwards, bishops created an administrative structure in their dioceses which permitted them to keep tabs more effectively on parishes, and thus also on

---

[55] J. Barrow, 'Wulfstan and Worcester: bishop and clergy in the early eleventh century', in *Wulfstan, Archbishop of York*, ed. M. Townend (Turnhout, 2004), p. 144, argues that the figure of churches which can be calculated for the diocese of Worcester from Domesday should be pushed upwards to allow for some urban churches; for Hereford, see J. Barrow, 'Clergy in the diocese of Hereford in the eleventh and twelfth centuries', *Anglo-Norman Studies* 26 (2003), at n. 46; for East Anglia, see J. Campbell, 'The East Anglian sees before the Conquest', in *Norwich Cathedral: Church, City and Diocese, 1096–1996*, ed. I. Atherton, E. Fernie, C. Harper-Bill and H. Smith (London 1996), pp. 3–21, at p. 20.

[56] F. Barlow, *The English Church 1066–1154* (London, 1979), p. 57; for comment on the situation see also E. Mason, *St Wulfstan of Worcester c. 1008–1095* (Oxford, 1990), pp. 120, 196–232.

[57] For general context, see A. Williams, *The English and the Norman Conquest* (Woodbridge, 1995), pp. 126–31; for St Paul's see *Fasti Ecclesiae Anglicanae 1066–1300*, i, *St Paul's*, ed. Greenway, pp. 4, 8, 23, 27, 29, 32, 36, 40, 47, 49, 57, 65, 71, 73, 77, 79, 85, 87, 89 and also Brooke, 'The composition of the chapter of St Paul's, 1086–1163', p. 122; for Hereford see *Fasti Ecclesiae Anglicanae 1066–1300*, viii, *Hereford*, ed. Barrow, pp. 8–9, 63, 65–6, 76, 79, 88, 97–8; for Lincoln and Salisbury see Le Neve, *Fasti Ecclesiae Anglicanae 1066–1300*, iii, *Lincoln*, compiled by D.E. Greenway (London, 1977), pp. 35, 121, 144–5 and iv, *Salisbury*, compiled by D.E. Greenway (London, 1991), pp. 13, 17, 112, 118, 121; for Exeter, see e.g. F. Barlow, ed., *English Episcopal Acta xi Exeter 1046–1184* (Oxford, 1996), nos 15, 33, 34 (Alfred) and 87 (Algar).

[58] C. Clark, 'Onomastics', in *The Cambridge History of the English Language*, II, *1066–1476*, ed. N. Blake (Cambridge, 1992), pp. 542–606, at pp. 552–3, 558–61.

[59] I intend to develop this theme at greater length elsewhere.

[60] A very valuable study of the ways in which advowson operated and its effects on clerical recruitment is provided by C. Harper-Bill, 'The struggle for benefices in twelfth-century East Anglia', *Anglo-Norman Studies* 11, ed. R.A. Brown (1989), pp. 113–32.

parish clergy;[61] from the 1120s, the quantity of documents issued by bishops began to increase noticeably, though for about a century the onus was on the recipients to keep these records and it was only in the thirteenth century that bishops found it necessary to register their charters.[62] Numbers of clergy soared as opportunities opened up for unbeneficed clergy who now could make a living performing private masses and anniversary services, paid for by people who found they had more ready money in their purses.[63] Finally, education pushed wealth aside as the main distinguishing factor between high-ranking clergy and those lower down the scale.[64]

---

[61] The starting point was the introduction of archdeacons in 1072, on which see C. Brooke, 'The arch-deacon and the Norman Conquest', in *Tradition and Change: Essays in Honour of Marjorie Chibnall*, ed. D. Greenway, C. Holdsworth and J. Sayers (Cambridge, 1985), pp. 1–19.

[62] D.M. Smith, C.R. Cheney and others, ed., *English Episcopal Acta*, British Academy, 26 vols to date (Oxford, 1980-, in progress); for a listing of, and introduction to, English and Welsh bishops' registers, see D.M. Smith, *Guide to Bishops' Registers of England and Wales* (London, 1981).

[63] J. Barrow, 'Vicars choral and chaplains in northern European cathedrals 1100–1250', in *The Ministry: Clerical and Lay*, ed. W.J. Sheils and D. Wood, Studies in Church History 26 (Oxford, 1989), pp. 87–97 at pp. 96–7; J. Barrow, 'The emergence of vicars choral to c.1250', in *Cantate Domino*, ed. R. Hall and D. Stocker, forthcoming.

[64] J. Barrow, 'Education and the recruitment of cathedral canons in England and Germany', *Viator* 20 (1989), pp. 117–37; J. Barrow, 'Origins and careers of cathedral clergy in twelfth-century England', *Medieval Prosopography* 21 (2000), pp. 23–40.

2

The 'Costs' of Pastoral Care: Church Dues in Late Anglo-Saxon England

Francesca Tinti

> Through the diligence of our legates, baptismal churches are ordered to be restored by those who are baptised or receive their sacraments [there], and it should be entrusted to the public administrators that through their insistence the children of the church be compelled to their restoration and obliged to give tithes to God there.[1]

This passage from Emperor Lothar's *Capitulare missorum* of 832 establishes a very specific and explicit relationship between the delivery of pastoral care and the obligation on the part of the recipients to pay tithes in return for it and to participate in the restoration of the church from which they receive their sacraments. The direct relation between the reception of *cura animarum* and the payment of church dues represents an important and recurrent aspect of Carolingian legislation on tithes.

Although in the Old Testament and in the early history of Christianity tithes were considered the special property of God, it soon became canonically accepted that they could be used for the support of the poor and the repair of churches.[2] Originally, the bishops and clergy who controlled such payments were not even entitled to a share, but with the development of a territorial ecclesiastical organisation, new elements began to appear. For instance, in 722 Pope Gregory II wrote a letter to Bishop Boniface in Thuringia (a region which was still missionary land), specifying that he had to divide the revenue of the church and the offerings of the faithful into four parts: one for Boniface himself (i.e. the bishop); one for the clergy; a third part for the poor; and the last part for the maintenance of ecclesiastical buildings. Regarding the share of the clergy, Gregory added that they should have their part *pro officiorum suorum sedulitate*, that is, for the assiduity of their offices: in other words, the diligence with which they performed their duties.[3]

---

[1] *MGH, Capitularia regum francorum*, ii, ed. A. Boretius (Hanover, 1897), no. 202, c. 9, p. 64: 'Ut baptismales eclesiae [. . .] diligentia missorum nostrorum ab his qui baptizantur uel sacra misteria percipiunt restaurari praecipiantur et ministris rei pubblicae committantur, ut filii eclesiae eorum instantia ad earum restaurationem compellantur, decimas quoque Deo dare ibidem cogantur.'

[2] See G. Constable, *Monastic Tithes. From their Origins to the Twelfth Century* (Cambridge, 1964), pp. 10, 51.

[3] M. Tangl, ed., *Die Briefe des heiligen Bonifatius und Lullus* (Berlin, 1916), no. 18, p. 32.

By the beginning of the tenth century the phrase *ecclesia mater* or *matrix*, which had previously been reserved for cathedrals, was frequently used to define baptismal churches. However, as the passage quoted above shows, the faithful, who could be identified as recipients of the pastoral care delivered by a specific baptismal church, had begun to be called *filii ecclesiae* much earlier.[4] It was this special relation between a church and its children which was at the basis of the obligation to pay tithes in the Frankish world. The decrees of the Council of Tribur of 895 state that every member of the faithful was to be buried at the church to which they had paid their tithes.[5] That would have normally been the church where they had also been baptised, thus creating a sense of continuous belonging from birth to death. By the end of the ninth century the Carolingian Church had developed an organic complex of ideas relating to what French historians often call *encadrement religieux*, a system that can be recognised in several normative sources of the period.[6]

The same cannot be said for Anglo-Saxon England. Specific evidence for the origins of church dues is very sparse here, and for the earlier period of English Christianity it is restricted to the information provided by just a handful of sources. The earliest relevant evidence does not concern tithes, but another tribute called *ciricsceat* (literally, 'tribute of the church') in Old English sources and usually translated as 'church-scot'. In King Ine's late seventh-century laws *ciricsceattas* are ordered to be paid at Martinmas.[7] But the evidence provided by this law cannot be compared with any other text earlier than the third quarter of the ninth century; and questions remain as to whether Ine's code as we have it dates from his time, given that it has only been preserved as an appendix to Alfred the Great's laws.[8] Ine's code does not specify the exact nature of the payment. On the basis of information provided by later sources we know that church-scot consisted of a fixed amount of wheat (a *mitta*) for each hide of land held by the payer. The origin of this tribute, which appears to have been paid only in early medieval England, is rather obscure. It has been suggested that it might date back to Anglo-Saxon pagan times or even to a very ancient Celtic custom taken over by the Church, but the evidence to substantiate either hypothesis does not seem to be conclusive.[9]

---

4 On this point see also C. Violante, 'Le strutture organizzative della cura d'anime nelle campagne dell'Italia centrosettentrionale', in *Cristianizzazione ed organizzazione ecclesiastica delle campagne nell'alto medioevo: espansione e resistenze*, Settimane di studio del centro italiano di studi sull'alto medioevo 28 (Spoleto, 1982) pp. 963–1158, esp. p. 1140.

5 *MGH, Capitularia regum francorum* ii, ed. Boretius, no. 252, c. 15, pp. 221–2.

6 Cf. J.F. Lemarignier, 'Encadrement religieux des campagnes et conjoncture politique dans les régions du royaume de France situées au nord de la Loire, de Charles le Chauve aux derniers Carolingiens (840–987)', in *Cristianizzazione*, pp. 765–800.

7 F.L. Attenborough, ed., *The Laws of the Earliest English Kings* (Cambridge, 1922), c. 4, p. 36: 'Ciricsceattas sín agifene be scē. Martines mæssan'.

8 See P. Wormald, *The Making of English Law: King Alfred to the Twelfth Century*, i: *Legislation and its Limits* (Oxford, 1999), pp. 103–5. Wormald believed that Alfred would have not tampered with Ine's code, although he admitted that some clauses might have been added to the original core in the course of the two centuries which separated Alfred from Ine.

9 See W.A. Chaney, 'Anglo-Saxon church dues: a study in historical continuity', *Church History* 32 (1963), pp. 268–77, esp. pp. 271–2, and N. Neilson, 'Customary rents', in *Oxford Studies in Social and Legal History*, ed. P. Vinogradoff (Oxford, 1910), pp. 188–201, esp. p. 196.

Another early but equally problematic source is the so-called 'Penitential of Archbishop Theodore' (669–690). It refers to an unspecified *tributum ecclesiae* as well as tithes in two clauses, which hardly suggest the existence of a well-established or coherent system of compulsory ecclesiastical taxation.[10] In fact, in the first clause Theodore allows for the possibility of different traditions coexisting in the country, according to the custom of each province. It is also interesting to note that the tone used in these two clauses seems to imply the possibility of abuses.

Even though they do not explicitly mention either tithes or church-scots, some of Bede's writings also refer to abuses concerning church dues. In his famous *Letter to Egbert* Bede writes of tributes claimed by bishops even in those cases in which they fail to provide their ministry.[11] For the present purpose it is interesting to note that the reproachful tone of the passage implies that those renders were supposed to be paid in exchange for episcopal pastoral care. A similar preoccupation can be recognised in some of Bede's exegetical writings, as has been recently pointed out by Scott DeGregorio. In a couple of passages from his *In Ezram* Bede writes in an even more critical tone of those who are supposed to teach and offer an example by their lives, but who, in spite of their failings to achieve that, are still eager to exact *immensum rerum saecularium pondus ac uectigal* ('an immense tax and weight of wordly goods') or *sumtpus . . . a populo* ('charges from the people').[12] DeGregorio has noted that the word *tributum* used in the *Letter to Egbert* might refer to church-scot, but it is not clear what Bede meant exactly by the use of such terms as *pondus*, *uectigal* or *sumptus*. In spite of the vague nature of Bede's vocabulary in this respect, it is important to underline the implied relationship between these tributes and the delivery of pastoral care. It remains uncertain whether Bede was simply criticising the negligence of some members of the clergy or whether he thought that such a system of taxation should not have existed at all.

[10] The first clause establishes that the 'tribute of the church (*tributum ecclesiae)* is to be according to the custom of the province, that is, so long as the poor suffer no oppression in [paying] tithes or anything': Constable, *Monastic Tithes*, p. 25, n. 1. The second clause is much more problematic and its interpretation has caused a number of problems. There are two slightly different readings of this clause: 'Decimas non est legitimum dare nisi pauperibus et peregrinis siue laici suas ad ecclesiam' (or 'ecclesias'). The reading 'ecclesiam' is given in P.W. Finsterwalder, *Die Canones Theodori Cantuariensis und ihre Überlieferungsformen*, Untersuchungen zu den Bussbüchern des 7., 8. und 9. Jahrhunderts, i (Weimar, 1929), c. 10, p. 333. The alternative reading ('ecclesias') is given in A.W. Haddan and W. Stubbs, ed., *Councils and Ecclesiastical Documents relating to Great Britain and Ireland*, iii (Oxford, 1878), p. 203, and is based on Cambridge, Corpus Christi College 320. Different interpretations have been provided for this tricky passage. McNeill and Gamer, who based their translation on the Corpus manuscript, suggested: 'It is not lawful to give tithes except to the poor and to pilgrims or for laymen [to give] to their own churches': J.T. McNeill and H.M. Gamer, *Medieval Handbooks of Penance* (New York, 1938), p. 213. However, this interpretation would imply the (unlikely) presence of *Eigenkirchen* in England at a very early stage. Giles Constable has used the reading given by Finsterwalder and has proposed a significantly different translation: 'It is not legitimate to give tithes except to the poor or to pilgrims or for laymen [to give] theirs [except] to the church' (*Monastic Tithes*, p. 25, n. 1). More work is probably needed on the manuscript transmission of the Penitential in order to identify the earliest reading. I would like to thank Rob Meens for useful discussion on this passage.

[11] C. Plummer, ed., *Venerabilis Bedae opera historica* (Oxford, 1896, repr. 1975), i, p. 410.

[12] D. Hurst, ed., *In Ezram et Neemiam*, CCSL 119A (Turnhout, 1969), pp. 236–392 at pp. 359–60, lines 825–33 and p. 386, lines 1863–74. I am grateful to Scott DeGregorio for this reference.

Some more explicit and direct references to tithe payments are contained in Bishop George of Ostia's report on the legatine councils of 786, although it does not provide any evidence for the actual enforcement of the practice in England. According to the report the councils had established that all people should give to God a tenth of all their possessions and live and pay alms out of the remaining nine parts. This text shows how influential the Carolingian example must have been in the introduction of a tithe system in England. As a matter of fact, this section of the legatine decrees was used extensively in the middle of the tenth century by Archbishop Oda for the composition of his so-called 'Constitutions', thus demonstrating that the later Anglo-Saxon Church was still relying upon their authority.[13]

The normative and exegetical nature of the earliest sources mentioning church dues does not allow us to establish whether and how regularly such tributes were being paid in England. Furthermore, these texts do not seem to hint at a compulsory system of ecclesiastical taxation and consequently do not show a direct connection between the delivery of pastoral care and the payment of church dues. It is not until the later Anglo-Saxon period that relevant sources become more numerous and it is only with reference to this period that it is possible to analyse the nature of such payments and their role within the system of pastoral care. However, before embarking on such an analysis, I should point out that the Anglo-Saxon system of church dues differed from the Carolingian system in one very important respect: whereas the latter system relied principally on tithe payments (proportional to the yearly produce of livestock and crops), the former – as already mentioned – relied from a very early date on church-scot (calculated on the amount of land held by the payer), with tithe payments being added only later. The close relationship between church-scot and land-holding deserves proper investigation. As we shall see, it seems to have affected significantly the later Anglo-Saxon development of church due payments.

By the end of the ninth century other church dues, such as soul-scot (i.e. mortuary), had made their appearance in documentary sources, without achieving, however, the level of importance which seems to have been reserved to church-scot and tithe.[14] The payment of some of these minor dues is also explicitly regulated in the legal codes of the tenth and eleventh centuries, but some other church dues seem to have been paid only on a very local scale. As a matter of fact, this is a factor which it is necessary to bear in mind, as it would seem that the system varied noticeably across the country. After all, notwithstanding all his activities aimed at introducing a proper ecclesiastical and diocesan organisation, Archbishop Theodore himself had established in his Penitential that the *tributum ecclesiae* had to be according to the custom of the

---

13 *MGH, Epistolae Karolini aevi*, ed. E. Dümmler (Berlin, 1895), no. 3, c. 17, pp. 25–6. On the synod and its report see C. Cubitt, *Anglo-Saxon Church Councils, c.650–c.850* (London, 1995), pp. 153–90. Regarding the use that Archbishop Oda made of the legatine decrees, it is worth underlining that only the canon concerning tithes was reproduced in the tenth-century 'Constitutions' in its entirety. See G.B. Schoebe, 'The chapters of Archbishop Oda (942/6) and the canons of the legatine councils of 786', in *Bulletin of the Institute of Historical Research* 35 (1962), pp. 75–83.
14 F. Stenton, *Anglo-Saxon England* (Oxford, 1971), third edn, p. 156.

province.[15] Local practices were kept up throughout the period under consideration, in spite of all the effort put into regularising the system through the production of a conspicuous and consistent body of legislation by the later Anglo-Saxon
kings.

Bearing in mind all the complications mentioned, in this article I shall try to do
two main things. First, I shall look at the role that church dues played within the
late Anglo-Saxon *cura animarum* system; in particular, attention will focus on
whether the available sources allow us to identify the connection between the
delivery of pastoral care and the obligation to pay ecclesiastical tributes that has
been observed in continental texts. Second, I shall examine the implications of the
contemporary presence of tithe and church-scot in tenth- and eleventh-century
England. As has been pointed out above, the existence of two main types of
church dues seems to be an English peculiarity and for this reason it deserves to be
properly investigated.

The first part of the article begins with an examination of the evidence of the
legal codes issued in later Anglo-Saxon times. This evidence is then compared
with some other tenth- and eleventh-century texts instructing the clergy on
various dogmatic, pastoral and liturgical issues. Such texts as the Pastoral Letters
written by Ælfric for Bishop Wulfsige III of Sherborne and Archbishop Wulfstan,
as well as other texts composed by Wulfstan himself for similar purposes, have
been described as the main products of the generation after the monastic reform,
whose interests had extended from the needs of monasticism to those of the
secular clergy.[16] I shall look at what these texts tell us about church dues, paying
specific attention to the way in which the clergy were instructed to demand such
payments from the laity. The focus will then shift from the means used to educate
the clergy to those employed to communicate directly with the faithful, that is, to
the Old English homiletic material produced in the tenth and eleventh centuries.
Homilies were probably the most direct means by which clerics could communicate with lay people, and the payment of church dues often featured among such
exhortations. This material will be examined in order to establish whether in
Anglo-Saxon England there was any sense of an explicit relationship between the
delivery of pastoral care and the lay people's obligation to pay church dues.

These specific topics have only recently begun to attract the attention of
Anglo-Saxonists. Up to the time when the minster debate reached its climax,
church dues had only made some occasional appearances, either in volumes
dealing with the general history of the Anglo-Saxon Church or in a couple of articles which seem to have gone largely unnoticed.[17] However, even the publications that appeared on the wave of the minster debate have considered only the

---

[15] See above, n. 10.

[16] J. Hill, 'Monastic reform and the secular church: Ælfric's pastoral letters in context', in *England in the Eleventh Century*, ed. C. Hicks (Stamford, 1992), pp. 103–17, esp. pp. 103–8.

[17] Church dues have been discussed briefly in various monographs, including Stenton, *Anglo-Saxon England*, pp. 152–7; M. Deanesly, *The Pre-Conquest Church in England* (London, 1961), pp. 212, 307–10; *eadem*, *Sidelights on the Anglo-Saxon Church* (London, 1962), pp. 114–18; J. Godfrey, *The Church in Anglo-Saxon England* (Cambridge, 1962), pp. 320–8; F. Barlow, *The English Church 1000–1066* (London and New York, 1979), second edn, pp. 145, 160, 179, 195–6, 199; H.

evidence coming from legislative codes and have rarely tried to compare their contents with any relevant documentary material.[18] This is what I intend to do in the second part of this article, as documentary sources can convey a better sense of the way in which the norms promulgated by the central government were or were not respected at a local level. By examining relevant charters and leases I shall follow the development of church due payments in the later Anglo-Saxon period, looking in particular at the relative distribution of church-scot and tithe both geographically and over time. In the course of such an examination, it should be borne in mind that documentary sources mostly reflect tenurial preoccupations and their main focus is not on matters related to pastoral care or ecclesiastical organisation. However, as several documents of this type, dealing primarily with church-scot, have been preserved, it is necessary to take them into account and compare their evidence with that provided by other sources.

CHURCH DUES IN LEGAL CODES

The laws of the tenth and eleventh centuries are the sources most often cited by scholars interested in Anglo-Saxon church dues. The supporters of the so-called 'minster hypothesis' have made use of these texts to prove the existence of a system of ecclesiastical organisation centred on a network of religious houses (called 'minsters'), which in many cases had been founded in the seventh and eighth centuries. These texts need to be analysed for their own sake and for what they tell us about the system in later Anglo-Saxon times.

As a result of Patrick Wormald's thorough and comprehensive analysis of the Anglo-Saxon legal system, the context in which these codes were issued is now much better known than it used to be. Furthermore, thanks to some of the more recent works of both Wormald and John Blair, it is now much easier to reconstruct the development of the legislation on church dues.[19] I shall not try to summarise that entire process again. What might be worth remembering here, however, is that tithe and church-scot are explicitly named together for the first time as two elements of the same system in Athelstan's first law-code, issued in the third decade of the tenth century.[20] This is a very significant text as it introduces tithe as a compulsory tribute in a long passage describing the way in which it should be paid from royal and episcopal estates. This clause also establishes

---

Mayr-Harting, *The Coming of Christianity to Anglo-Saxon England* (University Park, Pennsylvania, 1991), third edn, p. 135; H.R. Loyn, *The English Church 940–1154* (Harlow, 2000), pp. 29–31, 46. The two articles in question are Neilson, 'Church rents' and Chaney, 'Anglo-Saxon church dues'. For a discussion of the minster debate see my introduction to this volume.

[18] The obvious exception is represented by John Blair's work and in particular by his book, *The Church in Anglo-Saxon Society* (Oxford, 2005).

[19] Wormald, *Making of English Law*. Church dues were also to be dealt with in the second volume of this work, which Patrick Wormald was preparing before his death (*The Making of English Law: King Alfred to the Twelfth Century*, ii: *From God's Law to Common Law*). With his typical generosity he allowed me to consult relevant draft sections of his second volume. It is to be hoped that the book will be published posthumously.

[20] I Athelstan, in *Councils and Synods*, i, pp. 43–7.

that ealdormen and reeves should do the same on their own estates and that bishops and reeves should make the obligation known to all those who owe them obedience. The length of the passage is particularly striking when compared with the immediately following and much shorter clause dealing with church-scot. The difference in the amount of detail provided may be due to the fact that as far as church-scot was concerned, the legislator could rely on a much better established tradition of payment, at least in some areas of the country. This code represents, therefore, the formal fusion of two traditions, as it is here that for the first time both tributes are required together as compulsory payments. It should also be noted that according to Patrick Wormald's study of the manuscript transmission of Anglo-Saxon laws, originally tithes and church-scots were the only two church dues dealt with in this code. The references to soul-scots and plough-alms contained in some of the manuscripts in which the code has been preserved are likely to be the result of Archbishop Wulfstan's later intervention, aimed at increasing the range of church revenues.[21]

In spite of the length of the passage dealing with tithes, Athelstan's law-code does not allow us to see a direct connection between the delivery of pastoral care and the payment of church dues. Later laws are not much more explicit either. Edmund's code issued at London in the 940s states: 'tithes we enjoin on every Christian man by his Christianity' (*be his Cristendome*), thus simply pointing out that the payment of tithes was a specific Christian duty.[22] Edgar's Andover code of the early 960s is more interesting in that it specifies to whom church dues should be paid:

> And all tithe is to be given to the old minster[s] to which obedience is due (*þam ealdan mynstre [ealdum mynstrum] þe seo hyrnes to hyrð*); and it is to be paid both from the thegn's demesne and from his tenant-land (*ge of þegnes inlande ge of geneatlande*), as the plough go over it.[23]

The same code also refers to church-scot, saying that it had to be paid to the old minster, and follows Ine's law with regard to the date by which it was due and the penalties for default.[24]

For present purposes the most interesting aspect of this code lies in the phrase chosen to describe the recipient of tithe payments: *þam ealdan mynstre [ealdum mynstrum] þe seo hyrnes to hyrð*. As John Blair has pointed out, the term *hyrness* is the earliest known Old English word used to describe the parochial obligation due to an old minster.[25] Although it is not stated explicitly that tithes are due in

---

21 Wormald, *Making of English Law*, pp. 295, 314.

22 I Edmund, c. 2, in *Councils and Synods*, i, p. 62.

23 II Edgar, c. 1.1, in *Councils and Synods*, i, pp. 97–8. In this case I have preferred the translation given by Patrick Wormald in his draft second volume on *The Making of English Law* to the one provided by Whitelock in *Councils and Synods*.

24 Edgar's law also contains the first reference to the 'hearth-penny' (*heorðpæning*), known in later codes as *Romfeoh*, with detailed instructions for those who fail to pay it by the appointed day of St Peter. They would have to take it to Rome themselves, pay thirty pence in addition and bring back a document showing that it had been paid there. On top of that a fine of 120 shillings had to be paid to the king. II Edgar, cc. 4–4.3, *ibid.*, i, pp. 100–1.

25 Blair, *Church in Anglo-Saxon Society*, pp. 428–9. See also *idem*, 'Introduction: from minster to parish

return for pastoral care, as was the case in the Continental sources discussed at the beginning of this article, this code shows that by the early 960s a sense of obedience owed to a specific church was also well established in England.

Later texts show the employment of another word, equally interesting for present purposes: *scriftscir* or *rihtscriftscir* (from *scrifan*, 'to hear confession', and *scir*, 'district'). *Scriftscir* is the earlier one and is used by Ælfric in one of his homilies.[26] *Rihtscriftscir* appears in some of the laws that Archbishop Wulfstan wrote for Kings Æthelred and Cnut with reference to the payment of soul-scot:

> And it is best that *saulsceat* be always paid at the open grave. And if any body is buried elsewhere, outside the proper parish (*rihtscriftscire*), *saulsceat* is nevertheless to be paid at the minster to which it belonged (*þam mynstre þe hit to hyrde*).[27]

These laws allow us to recognise a direct relationship between church dues and the delivery of pastoral care. Soul-scot was paid in connection with a very important moment of any Christian person's life (its end), for which clerics had to provide specific forms of *cura animarum*. The use of the term *scriftscir* indicates the importance of confession as a means to define the extent of the territory on which a given church would have had jurisdiction. In this context the choice of such a term might be due to the fact that confession was one of the main elements of the pastoral care delivered to a person who was about to die.[28]

Wulfstan's codes are also revealing in other respects, as they allow us to recognise a much more coherent and systematic organisation of church due payments. The archbishop was eager to make the system as consistent and regular as possible. In the laws he wrote for both Æthelred and Cnut he incorporated all church renders into a coherent and detailed description of obligations. In VIII Æthelred (1014) we have a complete list of deadlines for tithes of livestock (Pentecost) and crops (Equinox, or All Saints' day at the latest), 'Rome-money' (St Peter's day), church-scot (Martinmas), plough-alms (fifteen days after Easter) and light-dues (Candlemas).[29] The same directions are reproduced in Cnut's laws. But however detailed these texts might appear, Wulfstan's lists of church dues do not allow us to perceive the specific relationship between the receipt of pastoral care and the payment of ecclesiastical tributes that we have identified in the Continental sources cited at the beginning of this article. Perhaps this is not surprising given the nature of these normative sources. The primary interest of such decrees was to make sure that everybody knew when, how and to whom

---

church', in *Minsters and Parish Churches. The Local Church in Transition 950–1200*, ed. *idem* (Oxford, 1988), pp. 1–19, at p. 1.

[26] Cf. Blair, *Church in Anglo-Saxon Society*, pp. 429–30.

[27] V Æthelred, cc. 12–12.1, in *Councils and Synods*, i, p. 352. In VI Æthelred the form which is used is *rihtscire*, rather than *rihtscriftscire*. However, the latter term also appears in Cnut's laws: I and II Cnut, cc. 13–13.1, *ibid.*, i, pp. 477–8. It should be noted that neither *scriftscir* nor *rihtscriftscir* is very well attested, probably also because they made a rather late appearance in the record. In the draft version of his second volume on *The Making of English Law* (ch. 8) Patrick Wormald suggests that *rihtscriftscir* might be Wulfstan's neologism.

[28] On this matter see the article by Victoria Thompson in this volume.

[29] VIII Æthelred, cc. 9–13, in *Councils and Synods*, i, pp. 392–3. This code also refers to the division of tithes into three parts. For a discussion of such a practice in England, see section below on 'Instructions for the clergy'.

ecclesiastical tributes should be paid. Anglo-Saxon legal codes as a genre do not allow much room for the type of information that we are looking for. It is thus necessary to take into account some other sources in order to investigate the way in which the late Anglo-Saxon Church considered such payments, how it ensured that they were going to be rendered and on what bases it justified such requests.

INSTRUCTIONS FOR THE CLERGY

Several late Anglo-Saxon texts written to instruct the clergy on various dogmatic and pastoral matters contain references to church due payments. Such tributes are mentioned, for instance, in the Old English letter that Ælfric wrote for Bishop Wulfsige III of Sherborne between 993 and 1002. This text, as well as the other Pastoral Letters that Ælfric produced in 1005–06 for Archbishop Wulfstan, was specifically composed for circulation amongst the clergy. The passage dealing with church dues follows some directions on the books that each *mæssepreost* should have, how he should keep his mass-vestments and his altar, and what topics he should preach about on Sundays and feast days. Regarding church dues, Ælfric wrote:

> The holy fathers appointed also that men shall pay their tithes into God's church. And the priest is to go there and divide them into three: one part for the repair of the church, and the second for the poor, the third to God's servants, who look after the church (*þam Godes þeowum þe þære cyrcan begymað*).[30]

This letter is one of the earliest English texts containing instructions on the division of tithes into three parts, which seems to have been the most common practice in Anglo-Saxon England.[31] This was probably due to Carolingian influence, as the practice is described in various Continental sources which were available in the tenth and eleventh centuries and which Ælfric appears to have used in the composition of his Pastoral Letters.[32] What is interesting about this passage is the

---

30 For an edition of this letter see B. Fehr, ed., *Die Hirtenbriefe Ælfrics in altenglischer und lateinischer Fassung* (Darmstadt, 1966), pp. 1–34, at c. 68, p. 16. An edition with accompanying translation can also be found in *Council and Synods*, i, pp. 191–226, at pp. 209–10.

31 Other Anglo-Saxon texts referring to the division of tithes into three parts include a homily by Ælfric ('First-fruits and tithes'), published in J.C. Pope, ed., *Homilies of Ælfric. A Supplementary Collection* (Oxford, 1968), i, pp. 806–8; the so-called *Canons of Edgar* composed by Archbishop Wulfstan (*Councils and Synods*, i, c. 56, p. 333); and the law-code known as VIII Æthelred, also written by Wulfstan (*Councils and Synods*, i, c. 6, pp. 390–1). I have been able to identify only one late Anglo-Saxon text in which a slightly different type of division is suggested. This is a largely derivative Latin homily entitled *De decimis dandis*. It is preserved in a manuscript containing material assembled at the order of Archbishop Wulfstan. The first three paragraphs are taken from a sermon of Caesarius of Arles, but the last section on the division of tithes into four parts seems to be original. According to this text, tithes had to be used for the repair of the church, for priests and clerics, for other varied uses of the church and for the poor and strangers. This type of division differs from the most common one in that it takes care of some unspecified *varii usus ecclesiæ*. For a facsimile see J.E. Cross and J. Morrish Tunberg, ed., *The Copenhagen Wulfstan Collection: Copenhagen Kongelige Bibliotek Gl. kgl. sam. 1595*, EEMF 25 (Copenhagen, 1993), fols 43r-45v. The homily is discussed in the 'Introduction', at p. 19. I would like to thank Tom Hall for bringing this text to my attention.

32 Among the Carolingian texts mentioning the division of tithes into three parts that Ælfric might have

fact that the process is described in detail, as if Ælfric was thinking in very concrete terms of the churches in which the division of tithes had to take place. The final part of the passage refers to a specific group of clerics: those who looked after the churches to which tithes had been paid. Other Continental and Anglo-Saxon texts refer to this division in very general terms, simply listing the legitimate recipients of tithes; by contrast, Ælfric is thinking of a very concrete situation in which the priest in charge (*sacerd*) had to go to the church and divide the tithes paid there into three, making sure that the third part went to the clerics responsible for that church.[33] Therefore, although the link with pastoral care is not explicit, it appears that the clerics entitled to the third part of tithe payments were those who looked after the church and who would have celebrated mass and other sacraments there: in other words, the clerics responsible for the pastoral care of the people who paid their tithes to that very church.

In the first Old English letter that Ælfric wrote for Archbishop Wulfstan c. 1006, the emphasis is on the abuses committed by those priests who tried to obtain church tributes to which they were not entitled. Although it is not spelled out, Ælfric must have been thinking of soul-scot when he wrote the following passage:

> Some priests are glad when men die and they flock to the corpse like greedy ravens where they see a carcass, in wood or in field; but it is fitting for him to attend the men who belong to his jurisdiction (*hyrnysse*), at his minster (*mynstre*); and he must never go into another's district to any corpse, unless he is invited.[34]

Once again there is an explicit interest in regularisation: priests were assigned to a specific minster responsible for the delivery of pastoral care (including burial) within a given district. Church dues had to be paid by the people who lived in that district to the clerics who duly administered the sacraments at their church. Given the tone used in this passage, it would seem that abuses were fairly frequent.

This preoccupation with possible abuses is confirmed by a chapter of

---

used for the composition of this letter it is worth mentioning the *Statuta* by Gerbald of Liège (previously known as the Capitulary of Aachen of 802) and the Enlarged Rule of Chrodegang. Both texts were well known in Anglo-Saxon England. The former was used extensively for the compilation of the collection known as *Excerptiones Pseudo-Ecgberhti* (see J.E. Cross and A. Hamer, ed., *Wulfstan's Canon Law Collection* (Cambridge, 1999), p. 35), whereas the latter was even translated into Old English. For a parallel edition and translation of both Latin and Old English versions, see B. Langefeld, ed., *The Old English Version of the Enlarged Rule of Chrodegang* (Frankfurth, 2003). Cross and Hamer have identified three modern editions of Gerbald's *Statuta*. The most recent one is in *MGH, Capitula episcoporum*, i, ed. P. Brommer (Hannover, 1984), pp. 16–21. On the possible sources for the composition of Ælfric's letter for Wulfsige see *Councils and Synods*, i, p. 195. On the influence of the Enlarged Rule of Chrodegang on Ælfric's Pastoral Letters, see M. McC. Gatch, *Preaching and Theology in Anglo-Saxon England: Ælfric and Wulfstan* (Toronto and Buffalo, 1977), pp. 41, 45 and Langefeld, *Enlarged Rule of Chrodegang*, p. 20. Ælfric's Pastoral Letters have not yet been investigated by the Fontes Anglo-Saxonici Project.

33 In VIII Æthelred, c.6, for instance, directions on this issue are much vaguer as the law does not specify which clerics were entitled to the payment. Cf. *Councils and Synods*, i, pp. 390–1.

34 'Sume preostas fægniað þonne men forðfarað, 7 gegaderiað hy to þam lice, swa swa grædige hremmas þær þær hy hold geseoð, on holte oþþe on felda; ac hym gebyrað to bestandenne þa men þe gehyrað to his hyrnysse into his mynstre; 7 he ne sceal na faran on oþres folgoðe to nanum lice, butan he gelaþod sy': *Councils and Synods*, i, cc. 182–4, pp. 295–6. This letter is also edited in Fehr, ed., *Hirtenbriefe*, pp. 68–145.

Wulfstan's *Institutes of Polity* which employs the same image of the greedy ravens used by Ælfric. The passage on church dues starts with a quotation from the prophet Hosea:

> 'Woe to those priests', he said, 'who devour and swallow up people's sins'. Those are they who will not or cannot, or dare not warn the people against sins and punish sins; but nevertheless want their monies for tithes and for all church dues; and neither lead them well with examples, nor teach them well with preaching, nor cure them well with penances, nor intercede for them with prayer, but seize whatever they can grasp of men's possessions, just as voracious ravens do from a carcass wherever they can get to it.[35]

The structure, the tone and the content of this passage are reminiscent of what Bede had written about three hundred years earlier on the same matter.[36] Once again the link between pastoral care and the payment of church dues is clearly implied in the negative terms used by the author to describe negligent clerics, who wanted a share of church dues without performing their pastoral tasks. Wulfstan's text provides a detailed description of their duties: priests were expected to lead the lay people by their example, to teach them through preaching, to cure them through penance and intercede for them through their prayers. The implication is that priests were entitled to receive church dues only if they were prepared to carry out their pastoral responsibilities.

In another text that Wulfstan wrote between 1005 and 1008 (the so-called *Canons of Edgar*) for circulation amongst the clergy, making extensive use – among various other sources – of Ælfric's Pastoral Letters, there are further references to church dues:

> And it is right that priests remind the people about what they must render to God as dues in tithes and in other things. And it is right that they be reminded of this at Easter, the second time three days before Ascension Day, a third time at midsummer, when most of the people is assembled.[37]

This passage is then followed by a complete list of tributes with respective deadlines, mirroring the norms that Wulfstan inserted in the laws he wrote for King Æthelred in the same period. The archbishop wanted to make sure that the clergy knew exactly what they had to do about church dues: not only did he list all the dates by which each type of render had to be paid, but he also instructed priests as to the exact days on which they had to remind the laity of their duties in this respect. Very interestingly, Wulfstan chose three specific days on which people were most likely to attend church. This text shows how English ecclesiastics were getting seriously organised about the payment of church dues, trying to make sure

---

35 ' "Wa þam sacerdum", he cwæð, "þe fretað and forswelgað folces synna". Þæt syndon þa, ðe nellað oððe ne cunnon oððon ne durron folc wið synna gewarnian and synna gestyran, ac gyrnað þeah heora sceatta on teoþungum and on eallum cyricgerihtum, and naðor ne hi mid bysnungum wel ne lædað, ne mid bodungum wel ne lærað, ne mid dædbotum wel ne lacniað, ne mid gebedrædenne fore ne þingiað, ac læccaþ of manna begeatum, loc hwæt hi gefon magan, eallswa gyfre hræmnas of holde doð, þær þær hi to magon': K. Jost, ed., *Die 'Institutes of Polity, Civil and Ecclesiastical': ein Werk Erzbischof Wulfstans von York*, Schweizer Anglistische Arbeiten 47 (Bern, 1959), pp. 98–101. The English translation is from M. Swanton, ed., *Anglo-Saxon Prose* (London, 1975), pp. 125–38, at p. 132.

36 See above at notes 11 and 12 and related text.

37 *Canons of Edgar*, c. 54, in *Councils and Synods*, i, pp. 331–2.

that as many people as possible were duly informed about what they were expected to pay and when. This attitude is confirmed by another eleventh-century text, probably later than the other sources mentioned in this section, known as the *Northumbrian Priests' Law*. It deals with offences committed both against and by priests. In one of the chapters dealing with the latter type of offence it is stated that those priests who did not demand yearly dues had to compensate personally for such negligence.[38]

This brief discussion of the texts which were composed between the tenth and the eleventh centuries for circulation amongst the clergy shows how important the payment of ecclesiastical tributes had become by that time. The late Anglo-Saxon Church could rely on a system which was regulated by the law-codes issued by kings with the assistance of such figures as Archbishop Wulfstan. At the same time, the Church was making sure that its members were correctly trained on the means by which the laity had to be informed about their duties in this respect. Possible abuses were also being taken care of, by reminding priests that they were entitled to church dues only if they duly performed their pastoral tasks. A specific link between delivery of pastoral care and receipt of ecclesiastical tributes is often implicit in the texts that have been analysed here. It is now necessary to take into account late Anglo-Saxon homilies to see whether the link is made any more explicit there.

CHURCH DUES IN LATE ANGLO-SAXON HOMILIES

There is a number of late Anglo-Saxon homilies dealing with the payment of church dues.[39] In most cases these texts contain generic admonitions reminding people of the Christian duty to give tithes, among other exhortations of a moral nature. This is for instance the case with Vercelli XX, in which the faithful are asked to leave off their heresies, adulteries, fast-breaking, drunkenness, lord-betrayals, pride, anger, gluttony, lust, disgraceful acts, wantonness, vain

---

[38] *Northumbrian Priests' Law*, c. 43, *ibid.*, i, p. 460.

[39] According to the calculation made by Kathleen Greenfield in 1981, admonitions on the payment of church dues occur in sixteen tenth- and eleventh-century homilies (K. Greenfield, 'Changing emphases in English vernacular homiletic literature, 960–1225', *Journal of Medieval History* 7 (1981), pp. 283–97, at p. 287). Although Greenfield gives the total number of relevant homilies in different collections (Blickling, Vercelli, Ælfric, Wulfstan and further anonymous ones), she does not provide any specific identification for such homilies. Using a combination of tools, such as A. diPaolo Healey and R.L. Venezky, *A Microfiche Concordance to Old English* (Toronto, 1980), the *Old English Corpus*, and R. Di Napoli, *An Index of Theme and Image to the Homilies of the Anglo-Saxon Church* (Chippenham, 1995), I have been able to identify the following late Anglo-Saxon homilies dealing with church dues: Blickling IV, X (R. Morris, ed., *The Blickling Homilies*, EETS os 73 (London, 1880)); Vercelli XVI, XX (D.G. Scragg, ed., *The Vercelli Homilies and Related Texts*, EETS os 300 (Oxford, 1992)); Ælfric's first series Homily for the First Sunday in Lent (P. Clemoes, ed., *Ælfric's Catholic Homilies: the First Series*, EETS ss 17 (Oxford, 1997), homily xi) and his homily on 'First-fruits and tithes' (see above n. 31); Wulfstan's homilies edited as Bethurum X (b and c), XIII, XIV (D. Bethurum, ed., *The Homilies of Wulfstan* (Oxford 1957, special edn 1998)), and Napier XXIII, XXXVI, L, LXI (A. Napier, ed., *Wulfstan: Sammlung der ihm zugeschriebenen Homilien nebst Untersuchungen über ihre Echtheit* (Berlin, 1883)). Among the anonymous homilies in Napier's collection those mentioning church dues are XXXV, XLIII and XLV.

speeches, uncleanness and all evils, and are also exhorted to give tithes to God from all the goods that He lends.[40]

In some other cases, however, homilies allow us to consider the payment of ecclesiastical tributes in a much better defined context. Blickling IV – written for the third Sunday in Lent – is one of the most relevant homiletic texts for our purposes, as it is entirely dedicated to the payment of tithes and first-fruits. It begins by referring to a series of biblical passages from the New Testament concerning the duty to give every twelve months the tenth part of crops and cattle. From the very beginning and throughout the whole text, the faithful are invited to give tithes and be obedient to God, so that they 'may enjoy the beauty of his glory' (*motan brucan his wuldres fægernesse*). The homily becomes particularly interesting in the passage dealing with the beneficiaries of tithe payments, as the poor appear to be the category principally entitled to receive such payments:

> Give now the tenth part of all your acquisitions to poor men, and to God's church, to the poorest of God's servants, who, with divine songs do honour the church, because the church must feed those who dwell therein (*forþon seo cyrice sceal fedan þa þe æt hire eardiaþ*).[41]

Although the first half of this passage is taken from a sermon by Caesarius of Arles, the final clause, explaining why tithes should be given to the clergy, does not seem to have been lifted from any known source.[42] Poverty appears to be the main theme here, the implication perhaps being that the servants of God who were not poor were not entitled (and maybe were not even expecting) to receive tithes.[43] The generally defensive tone of the passage suggests that the homilist was aware of some reluctance – or even resistance – to the practice of tithing and had to stress that the Church needed to feed its members. At this point the link between tithe payments and pastoral care becomes more explicit:

> No man need have any doubt of this, that the forsaken church will not take care of those that live in her neighbourhood (*seo forlætene cyrice ne hycgge ymb þa þe on hire neawiste lifgeaþ*), therefore, my dearest brethren, give your tithes to her, and for God's sake distribute them to those who observe their orders with purity of life, and will rightly be diligent about the praise of God.

In other words, the faithful should pay tithes, because, churches without financial support are incapable of providing any pastoral care.

Another very interesting and relevant homiletic text on this matter was written by Ælfric and published by Pope in his supplementary collection of Ælfric's

---

40 'Uton us nu ealle þe geornor warnian, 7 forlætan urne gedwolan 7 unrihthæmedo 7 ærætas 7 oferdruncennessa 7 hlafordswicunga 7 ofermett 7 andan 7 oferfylle 7 galnesse 7 sceandlicnessa 7 leohtbrædnessa 7 idele spræca 7 ealle unclænnessa 7 ealle yfelo, þe læs us ahwæne God for urum yfelum geearnigum ure eorðan wæstmas fram afyrre, 7 us swylce witu onasende þe we aræfnian ne magon. Ac utan symle of eallum þam godum þe us God her on worulde læne hym þa teoðunga don eadmodlice' (Scragg, ed., *Vercelli Homilies*, p. 333).

41 Morris, ed., *Blickling Homilies*, pp. 40–1.

42 Cf. the Fontes Anglo-Saxonici Project database at http://fontes.english.ox.ac.uk.

43 On this second aspect it might be interesting to point out that the *Northumbrian Priests' Law* refers to negligent priests who failed to demand church dues. See above, n. 38 and related text.

homilies.[44] It was probably intended for the harvest season and, at least in one manuscript, was added to Ælfric's homily for the twelfth Sunday after Pentecost. The homily begins with various references to biblical passages ordering men to give tithes and first-fruits. A detailed description of the division of tithes into three parts is also provided:

> Two parts of the tithes shall be given to the servants of God in the minster to which he [i.e. the payer] belongs and where he receives his Christianity [or his Christian supervision]. The third part will be divided between the poor, the widows, the orphans and the foreigners.[45]

Although minsters probably never had in Anglo-Saxon England the same type of juridical status enjoyed by *baptismales ecclesiae* on the Continent, this text allows us to observe a clearer notion of the justification behind the request for tithe payments than can be inferred from such sources as the legal codes examined above. It is mainly in Ælfric's texts that it is possible to identify specific references to the connection between the delivery of pastoral care and the duty to pay church dues in return. The most explicit examples of such a notion can be found in the Old English Letter for Bishop Wulfsige III, which has been examined above, and even more explicitly in the homily which has just been quoted. In the latter text, Ælfric had the payer in mind when he identified the church which was to receive tithe payments as being the church to which the payer belonged and where he received his Christianity, or as Pope suggests in his glossary, the church from which he received his Christian supervision, that is, his pastoral care.

It should also be noted that the majority of homilies dealing with such topics focus on tithes and occasionally on first-fruits, without even mentioning church-scot. This is probably due to the fact that the biblical passages which the homilies followed in the liturgy would have not contemplated such a due. The main exceptions concern – not surprisingly – Archbishop Wulfstan's homiletic texts, mostly because, as has often been noted by scholars of Anglo-Saxon homilies, Wulfstan's sermons, unlike Ælfric's homilies, tend to contain exhortations rather than expositions of the pericope read during the mass.[46] From our point of view Bethurum XIII is probably the most interesting text among the homilies composed by Archbishop Wulfstan, as it reproduces most of the instructions that Wulfstan gave in his law-codes. It should be noted that tithes and first-fruits are first mentioned on their own, in the same way in which they appear in other homilies commenting on biblical prescriptions. But that was obviously not going to be enough for Wulfstan, as he needed to refer to the system of church tributes in its entirety, in keeping with the instructions he put into his law-codes. Thus, the exhortation to pay tithes and first-fruits is followed by a much more detailed passage, prescribing that 'we also pay every yearly due that our elders once in the

---

[44] See above n. 31.

[45] 'Ða twegen dælas þære teoþunge man sceal betæcan Godes þeowum into þam mynstre þær þær he to hyrð, þær þær he his Cristendom hæfð, and þone þriddan dælman sceal dælan þearfum, and wuduwum, and steopcildum, and ælþeodigum mannum': Pope, ed., *Homilies of Ælfric*, ii, p. 807.

[46] Cf. D. Scragg, 'Homilies', in *The Blackwell Encyclopaedia of Anglo-Saxon England*, ed. M. Lapidge, J. Blair, S. Keynes and D. Scragg (Oxford, 1999), pp. 241–2.

past promised to God; that is, plough-alms, and "Rome-pence", and church-scots and light dues'.[47] It would seem that Wulfstan was trying to inscribe a specifically English tradition (initiated by 'our elders') into the biblical requirements upon which other homilists had previously commented. There are other Wulfstanian homilies which show a similar preoccupation with comprehensiveness; these are Napier XXIII, L and LXI, which appear to reproduce the list of dues and respective deadlines that Wulfstan also gave in VIII Æthelred.[48]

The archbishop does not seem to have been interested in providing his audience with specific reasons behind the request to pay church dues, apart from the conventional ones based on the Scriptures. However, some of the other late Anglo-Saxon homilies, including those by Ælfric, allow us to go beyond such conventional justifications. As was shown above, in these texts the laity are asked to appreciate the need on the part of the church to feed its members, especially the poorest ones. The faithful belonging to a given district served by a church from which they receive their Christian supervision (i.e. their pastoral care) are reminded that a forsaken church will not be able to take proper care of them. Therefore, although it does not seem possible to find such specific and explicit statements on the relationship between a church and its *filii* as those that we have found in Continental texts, some Anglo-Saxon sources do allow us to detect a link between the delivery of pastoral care and the need to pay church dues in return.

Wulfstan appears to have been less interested in providing direct references to such a connection. His main interests clearly centred on the need for regularisation, comprehensiveness and means to avoid possible abuses. Several scholars have pointed out how difficult it is to separate the homilist from the legislator in Wulfstan's case. His treatment of church dues is no exception. It should not be forgotten that such payments had followed different practices in different parts of the country. The archbishop's efforts, discernible both in his laws and in his homilies, aimed to systematise and extend the detailed norms which had been introduced by King Edgar in the early 960s.

What remains to be examined is the actual impact of such norms. How should one interpret the repeated occurrence of the detailed directions concerning the payment of church dues? What was the purpose of so much legislation and homiletic literature on such themes? Were the later Anglo-Saxon kings and ecclesiastics just describing the characteristics of a practice which was by then well established? Or were they trying to introduce and regulate a system which was still very idiosyncratic and differentiated throughout the country? In order to attempt a reply to such questions it is necessary to take into account some

---

[47] 'Ðonne is þærtoecan gyt to understandenne þæt we eac eadmodlice eal gelæstan on geargerihtan þæt ure yldran hwilum ær Gode behetan; þæt is ulhælmessan 7 rompenegas 7 cyricsceattas 7 leohtgescota': Bethurum, ed., *Homilies of Wulfstan*, pp. 229–30. The translation is mine.

[48] There is another Old English homily (Napier XLIII) containing a comprehensive list of ecclesiastical tributes. As Jonathan Wilcox has shown, the passage on church dues is a borrowing from Wulfstan's Napier XXIII. See J. Wilcox, 'The dissemination of Wulfstan's homilies: the Wulfstan tradition in eleventh-century vernacular preaching', in *England in the Eleventh Century*, ed. Hicks, pp. 199–217, at pp. 207–8.

documentary sources, as they may give us a better sense of the way in which such payments were treated on a local level.

FROM NORM TO PRACTICE: EARLY OCCURRENCES OF CHURCH DUES IN EPISCOPAL LEASES

There is a relatively large group of Anglo-Saxon charters dealing with church dues. The earliest ones were issued before any extensive body of legislation had been produced on the subject. When the bishops of Winchester and Worcester issued the earliest leases mentioning church dues, the only law-code which had already been promulgated on the subject was the above mentioned law of King Ine. The earliest surviving relevant charter was issued between 871 and 877 by Bishop Ealhferht of Winchester.[49] This was a lease of eight hides of land at Easton (near Winchester) for three lives in favour of a *dux* named Cuthred. The document states that the land was free from every service except the construction of bridges, military service, the payment of eight *ciricsceattan*, the priest's rights (*mæsseprestes gereohta*) and *saulsceattas* (i.e. soul-scots). The first thing to note is the correspondence between the number of hides leased and the quantity of church-scot to be paid, which appears to be a fixed quantity calculated on the number of hides held by the tenant. This document, however, also contains references to other church dues, indicating that soul-scot had already been introduced by the end of the ninth century. Even more interesting for present purposes are the so-called 'priest's rights', which in spite of their vague nature seem to hint at a form of payment due to the priest, possibly in respect of his pastoral activities. It is less easy to identify the recipient of the other church dues mentioned in this document. Were they supposed to go to the same priest? Or were they required by the bishop in return for the lease itself?

There are two slightly later leases from Winchester which are very similar to this one. They were both issued by Bishop Denewulf between 897 and 908. In the first case Denewulf leased fifteen hides at Ebbesborne (Wiltshire) to Beornwulf, his kinsman.[50] In the second case the same bishop leased forty hides at Alresford (Hampshire) to a certain Alfred.[51] Both documents mention church dues, but whereas in the latter case the actual recipient of the payments is not explicitly mentioned, in the former lease (S 1285) Beornwulf is required to contribute to the repair of the church (*cyrican bóte*) in whose jurisdiction his estate lies, and the amount of work owed by him and the rest of the population has to be proportional to the extent of the land held. As far as church-scot is concerned, the lease does not say much about the recipient, but it could be inferred that given the position of the clause dealing with church-scot, which follows immediately that on *cyrican bóte*, both dues had to be given to the same church.

---

[49] S 1275. For an edition and a translation of this lease, see A.J. Robertson, ed., *Anglo-Saxon Charters* (Cambridge, 1965), no. 14, pp. 26–7.

[50] S 1285; the lease is edited and translated in F.E. Harmer, ed., *Select English Historical Documents of the Ninth and Tenth Centuries* (Cambridge, 1914), no. 17, pp. 29–30, 60.

[51] S 1287; Robertson, ed., *Anglo-Saxon Charters*, no. 15, pp. 28–9.

If we look at other leases from the archive of Worcester, dating back to the same period, the picture becomes much clearer. In 889 Bishop Wærferth, with permission from the cathedral *familia*, leased for himself and two heirs five *manentes* of land at Elmstone Hardwicke, in Gloucestershire. The lease contains an important passage stating that the land was free from every service 'nisi tantum ut omni anno censum aecclesiae secundum rectitudinem to Clife reddantur'.[52] The same document specifies that the estate had previously belonged to the *monasterium* at *Clife* (Bishop's Cleeve). This is one of the several *monasteria* in the diocese of Worcester which by the end of the eighth century had come, together with their estates, under the control of the church of Worcester.[53] It is very interesting to note that at this stage the *census ecclesiae* (i.e. church-scot) was still being paid to the *monasterium* at Cleeve.[54] This requirement is preserved in another lease, issued by the same Bishop Wærferth between 899 and 904, through which three out of the five *manentes* at Elmstone Hardwicke were leased to a kinswoman of Wærferth's, named Cyneswith.[55] The text establishes that the estate was free from every service, except *ciricsceatte*, which again had to be paid to Cleeve.

In a slightly later lease issued in 899 in favour of a priest named Werwulf, Wærferth granted five *manentes* of land at Ablington on the Coln, in Gloucestershire. The passage on the service required states:

> Ea tamen conditione interposita atque oboedientia ut illi qui hanc terram habeant sint fideles et amici episcopo et suam rectitudinem quam circsceat et sawlsceat dici solet et to Began byrg reddant.[56]

In this case, both church-scot and soul-scot had to be paid to Bibury, the site of another *monasterium* in the diocese of Worcester, which had also come under the control of the cathedral church.

These Worcester leases open up some very important issues, as they seem to represent a crucial stage in the development of church-scot payments, at least in this area. While leasing out these estates, which had previously belonged to Bishop's Cleeve and Bibury, the bishop of Worcester was making sure that church-dues (in particular church-scot) continued to be paid to those religious houses. However, given the context in which these documents were issued, it is not entirely clear whether church-scot was originally paid to Bishop's Cleeve and Bibury from the leased estates because the latter also fell within their minster *parochiae*, or whether the allocation of church-scot was determined by the fact that the estates belonged to those minsters. In other words, was the payment of church-scot solely regulated by the system of ecclesiastical organisation, or was it also linked to the tenurial conditions of the land from which it had to be paid? The

---

[52] S 1415, B 559.

[53] P. Sims-Williams, *Religion and Literature in Western England, 600–800* (Cambridge, 1990), pp. 152, 169–70.

[54] The phrase *census ecclesiae* was frequently used to translate the Old English *ciricsceat*.

[55] S 1283; Robertson, ed., *Anglo-Saxon Charters*, no. 16, pp. 28–31.

[56] S 1279, B 580.

question remains, and will be addressed in the following pages, in connection with the evidence provided by some later episcopal leases.

Before leaving these documents aside, we should note that they all come from Winchester and Worcester. The Winchester provenance is hardly surprising, since the very first mention of church-scot is contained in King Ine's code. As far as Worcester is concerned, John Blair has suggested that the appearance of church-scot in the leases issued by Bishop Wærferth could be linked to the latter's friendship with King Alfred, who promoted a revival of Ine's laws when he decided to include them in his own code.[57] In a famous passage of the preface to his laws, Alfred says that he has chosen, among the laws issued by his predecessors, those that he finds appropriate, following the advice of some wise men.[58]

THE APPEARANCE OF TITHES IN DOCUMENTARY SOURCES

None of the leases discussed above contains any reference whatsoever to tithes, suggesting that in the regions of Worcester and Winchester tithes were not yet common, or at least that they were not required in connection with episcopal leases of this type. It was only from the reign of King Athelstan onwards that tithes became a matter for legislation. Just a few decades later tithes began to be mentioned in documentary sources as well. King Eadred issued two diplomas in 955 mentioning church dues. The first one, which has been preserved in the twelfth-century cartulary of the abbey of Peterborough, is a grant (largely in Old English) of five hides of land at Alwalton (Huntingdonshire) in favour of a thegn named Ælfsige Hunlafing.[59] The land is said to be free from every service except the three common burdens. However, as the text proceeds, a rather obscure and lacunose passage mentions church-scot, soul-scot and tithes: *geþencend londagende [. . .] ciricsceat, saulsceat, and teogeðunga*. Agnes Robertson suggested that the probably intended meaning was 'a prudent landowner [will make himself responsible for] church dues, burial fees and tithes'.[60]

Although the context in which these three church dues are mentioned is not clear because of the gap in the surviving text, Eadred's diploma remains significant in that it seems to be the earliest charter mentioning both church-scot and tithe. In another diploma that the same king issued in 955, he granted twenty hides of land at East Pennard (Somerset) to a nun named Ælfgyth in exchange for 120 *solidi*.[61] Tithe is not mentioned explicitly but Ælfgyth is asked to give to the minster at Pennard the production of two out of the twenty hides she was being granted. Further documentary sources mentioning tithes were also issued in the eleventh century. For instance, between 1016 and 1023 the abbot of Evesham

---

[57] Blair, *Church in Anglo-Saxon Society*, pp. 434–5.

[58] F. Liebermann, ed., *Die Gesetze der Angelsachsen*, 3 vols (Halle, 1903–16), i, cc. 49.9–10, p. 46.

[59] S 566; Robertson, *Anglo-Saxon Charters*, no. 30, pp. 56–9.

[60] David Dumville, who has analysed this diploma in detail, has not found this interpretation convincing; see D.N. Dumville, 'A twelfth-century English translation of a tenth-century Latin official document?', *Fedorov Readings: University Translation Studies* 3 (St Petersburg, 2001), pp. 195–215, at p. 200.

[61] S 563; B 903.

leased for three lives four and a half hides of land at Norton (Worcestershire), specifying that the lessee had to pay both his church-scot and his tithe to the minster at Evesham.[62] Later on, between 1020 and 1038, the archbishop of Canterbury leased to two of his *ministri* fifty *agri* of land belonging to the abbey of St Mary at Reculver.[63] The tenants were asked to pay tithes annually, from the estates leased, to the servants of God living in that *monasterium*.

When one compares the contents of the legislative sources of the tenth and eleventh centuries with those of the charters issued in the same period, it is clear that tithes began to assume a much more significant role in the later Anglo-Saxon period. Whereas the laws of Ine mention only church-scot, Athelstan's first code has a very long section on tithe payments and reserves only a few lines for church-scot. The same can be said for Edgar's second code, which is also the first law to demand the payment of the hearth-penny on St Peter's day (also called *Romfeoh* in some sources). With the arrival of Archbishop Wulfstan on the scene of legislative production the picture becomes much more detailed, thanks to the appearance in Æthelred and Cnut's laws of a longer list of church dues and relative deadlines. What is especially significant, however, is the fact that tithes, from the time of Athelstan's reign onwards, are given a very prominent position in law-codes, whereas church-scot, the earliest church due to appear in any Anglo-Saxon law, is listed alongside other minor dues, having apparently lost the prominence that it had had in earlier sources. However, there is another conspicuous group of documentary sources mentioning church-scot which must be analysed in this context. These are the leases issued by Bishop Oswald of Worcester in the second half of the tenth century.

CHURCH-SCOT IN BISHOP OSWALD'S LEASES

Church-scot appears in a group of fifteen late tenth-century episcopal leases from Worcester.[64] These documents are part of a larger group of seventy-four leases issued by Bishop Oswald between 962 and 990, and contained in a cartulary known as *Liber Wigorniensis* which was compiled at Worcester in the first part of the eleventh century. Most of the leases mentioning church-scot (ten out of fifteen) contain the following clause: 'Sit autem terra ista libera omni regi nisi eccelsiastici censi (sic)', in which the phrase *ecclesiasticus census* represents a literal translation of the Old English *ciricsceat*. The majority of these documents are in Latin, although the boundary clause is always in the vernacular; but in some cases the Latin formula on church-scot is inserted in texts that otherwise would have been entirely in Old English. In just one case, the Latin formula is followed by a few words which make explicit the nature and the quantity of the payment required ('Sit autem terra ista libera omni regi nisi ecclesiastici censi, id est duos

---

62 S 1423; Robertson, *Anglo-Saxon Charters*, no. 81, pp. 156–7.
63 S 1390; K 754.
64 S 1298, 1299, 1301, 1303, 1305, 1316, 1318, 1324, 1352, 1354, 1363, 1370, 1372, 1373, 1374.

modios de mundo grano').[65] This document, by which Oswald leased out two hides of land, confirms the correspondence between the amount of church-scot due and the number of hides held by the payer.

This group of leases is extremely relevant for the purposes of our analysis. Vanessa King has underlined that Oswald's leases are rather inadequate sources for the study of services due by the lessees, pointing out that at least thirty-eight out of all the leases issued by Oswald do not contain any reference whatsoever to services or rents. King has concluded that the request for service was usually implicit and that the church of Worcester probably kept 'a separate record of rents and obligations owed from tenants'.[66] If that is the case, the prominence given to church-scot is even more remarkable.

The estates leased out by Oswald in the fifteen documents under investigation were spread across four counties: Worcestershire, Gloucestershire, Warwickshire and Oxfordshire. Given this wide extent, it will appear obvious that the cathedral church of Worcester could not have acted as the minster with parochial jurisdiction over the entire area. However, these leases were issued shortly after the promulgation of Edgar's second code, which ordered church-scot to be paid to the old minster. Unlike the earlier Worcester leases examined above, mentioning Bibury and Bishop's Cleeve as legitimate recipients of church-dues, Oswald's leases do not specify any recipient, although in some cases it seems possible to identify an old minster not far from the estates which had been leased out. There is one only exception concerning an estate lying outside the diocese of Worcester. In 987 Oswald leased five hides of land at Golder (Oxfordshire) to a certain Leofward.[67] The clause requiring the payment of church-scot states:

> Et semper possessor terrae illius reddat tributum ecclesiasticum, quod circ-sceat dicitur to Pirigtune.

This is the only case among Oswald's leases in which the recipient of church-scot is explicitly mentioned. The church at Pyrton, to which church-scot had to be paid, seems to have had parochial jurisdiction over Golder (as it still does). Therefore, it would seem that outside the diocese of Worcester Edgar's law was being enforced and church-scot was being paid to the old minster with parochial jurisdiction. Within the diocese of Worcester the situation seems to have been different: it would appear that church-scot was being paid to the bishop in exchange for the leases, with no regard for the geographical position of the estates leased.

There would seem to be two possibilities to explain such an anomaly. On the one hand, we might hypothesise that, by the time Oswald became bishop, the church of Worcester no longer found it necessary to specify the location of the institution to which church-scot had to be paid. We should not forget that by this time the cathedral church had acquired control of several minster churches which

[65] S 1301; B 1087.
[66] V. King, 'St Oswald's tenants', in *St Oswald of Worcester: Life and Influence*, ed. N. Brooks and C. Cubitt (London and New York, 1996), pp. 100–16, at pp. 114–15.
[67] S 1354; K 661.

stood in its diocese, together with the estates attached to them. The identification of the ultimate beneficiary of such payments might have been regarded as an internal matter. On the other hand, however, one might wonder why such a special treatment was reserved solely for church-scot. What about the other church dues? Is it possible that at least in the area of the diocese of Worcester this church render was being treated in a way that was connected more with land-holding than with ecclesiastical organisation? In other words, is it possible that church-scot was being required by the bishop in exchange for the lease, rather than in return for pastoral care?

There is at least one important source which seems to give credit to the latter hypothesis. This is a letter, also known as *Indiculum*, that purports to have been written by Oswald for King Edgar in 964.[68] The letter lists in detail all the services owed by the tenants of the estates leased by the bishop, including riding duties, church-scot, bridge building, church building, fencing for the bishop's hunt and a variety of other things. For our purposes what is most significant about this letter is the fact that church-scot (*ciric sceott*) is mentioned alongside other types of services. Given the extent of the area in which the leased estates lay, the cathedral church of Worcester could not have been considered as the relevant old minster for all the estates leased out by Oswald. Church-scot, however, was listed among *omnia que ad ius ipsius aecclesiae iuste competunt*. This means that it had to be rendered to the church of Worcester in exchange for the lease of the estates, together with the other dues listed in the letter. Therefore, this document does not show much connection between the payment of church-scot and pastoral care.

Following the development of church-scot in this area up to the time of Domesday Book, one can find a very significant confirmation of the possibility that it was not necessarily connected with ecclesiastical organisation. The section in Domesday Book dealing with the land of the church of Worcester in Worcestershire contains the following statement:

> The Shire states that from each and every hide of land, whether free or villagers', which belongs to the church of Worcester, the bishop should have at Martinmas one pack-load of corn of the better sort which grows there.[69]

The pack-load of corn (i.e. church-scot) had to be paid to the bishop from all the land which belonged to the church of Worcester.[70] There is no reference what-

---

[68] S 1368; B 1136. The authenticity of this letter has been doubted by several historians. However, it cannot be later than the end of the eleventh century, as it was copied into Hemming's Cartulary. For a recent analysis of the cartulary, see F. Tinti, 'From episcopal conception to monastic compilation: Hemming's Cartulary in context', *EME* 11.3 (2002), pp. 233–61. According to Vanessa King, the *Indiculum* may have been composed at the time of Cnut's reign, when the church of Worcester had lost many of its estates because of the Danish settlement: King, 'St Oswald's tenants', p. 115.

[69] *Domesday Book*, i, fol. 174a (F. and C. Thorn, ed., *Domesday Book*, 16, *Worcestershire* (Chichester, 1982), 2, 80): 'Dicit uicecomitatus quod de una quaque hida terrae libera uel uillana quae ad ecclesiam de Wirecestre pertinet, debet episcopus habere in die festo Sancti Martini unam summam annonae de meliori quae ibidem crescit'.

[70] That this passage refers to church-scot is confirmed by the marginal note – reading *De ciricsceate* – appended to it in the section of Domesday Book concerning the estates of the church of Worcester copied in Hemming's Cartulary (BL, Cotton Tiberius A. xiii, fol. 140v).

soever to old minsters, pastoral care or ecclesiastical organisation here; the obligation to pay this tribute seems to be due purely to tenurial reasons.[71]

According to Domesday Book other important churches received church-scot from some very widespread areas. Pershore, in Worcestershire, was also entitled to the church-scot paid from the 300 hides which formed its ecclesiastical hundred.[72] Aylesbury in Buckinghamshire received church-scot from eight hundreds.[73] The exponents of the minster hypothesis would consider such cases as perfect examples of the way in which old minsters managed to maintain parochial rights over their ancient ecclesiastical districts up to and beyond the end of the Anglo-Saxon period.[74] The evidence for the cathedral church at Worcester, however, proves that this was not necessarily the case. Whereas such documents as the *Indiculum* or some relevant passages in Domesday Book might lead one to believe that the church of Worcester had always been entitled to receive church-scot from all the lands which it held in the late Anglo-Saxon period, there were other minsters in that region which had enjoyed that right in the past. The minsters of Bibury and Bishop's Cleeve, for instance, were still entitled to the payment of church-scot between the end of the ninth century and the beginning of the tenth.

It would seem, therefore, that by the end of the Anglo-Saxon period, at least in some areas, church-scot was being treated as a tribute not necessarily connected with the system of parochial organisation. It should also be noted that the earliest Anglo-Norman sources which mention such a due show some signs of uncertainty as to its actual nature and origin. The first example is provided by the Latin translation of a letter of King Cnut dated 1027. The Old English original has not been preserved, but its Latin translation, produced after the Conquest, was included in the Chronicle of John of Worcester. The passage in which the king asks the English people to pay church-scot at Martinmas states:

> in festiuitate sancti Martini primitie seminum ad ecclesiam sub cuius parrochia quisque deget, que Anglice ciricsceatt nominantur.[75]

In this letter church-scot appears to have been identified with first-fruits, an offering that is often mentioned in biblical texts, and in Old English homilies as well. However, we do know that church-scot was a different and very specific type of render, given that some of the homilies which refer to first-fruits also refer to church-scot as a separate due.[76] It would seem much more likely that in Cnut's

---

[71] It should be noted that, as Steve Baxter has shown, Bishop Wulfstan II of Worcester was probably responsible for the composition of the remarkably favourable section of Domesday Book concerning the estate of the church of Worcester. See S. Baxter, 'The representation of lordship and land tenure in Domesday Book', in *Domesday Book*, ed. E. Hallam and D. Bates (Stroud, 2001), pp. 73–102, 203–208.

[72] *Domesday Book*, i, fol. 175c (*Domesday Book*, 16, *Worcs.*, 9,7).

[73] *Domesday Book*, i, fol. 143d (E. Teague and V. Sankaran, ed., *Domesday Book*, 13, *Buckinghamshire* (Chichester, 1978), 3a, 1).

[74] John Blair has described the right to receive church-scot as 'the oldest and strongest sign of ancient minster status': Blair, 'Introduction: from minster to parish church', p. 12.

[75] R.R. Darlington and P. McGurk with J. Bray, ed. and tr., *The Chronicle of John of Worcester*, ii, *The Annals from 450 to 1066* (Oxford, 1995), pp. 512–19, at pp. 518–19: 'on the feast of St Martin the first fruits of the grain to the church in the parish where one lives, which are called church scot in England'.

[76] That is, for instance, the case in Bethurum XIII, discussed at pp. 40–1 above.

letter the phrase *primitie seminum* was just an incorrect translation of *ciricsceat*.[77] As a matter of fact, in Domesday Book the name of this tribute is often spelled *ciricsed*, *cirset* or *circet*, because of a probable confusion between Old English *sceat* – meaning 'tribute' – and *sæd* – meaning 'seed'. These could just be early manifestations of some uncertainty on the actual nature of this due.[78]

In spite of the confusion emerging from the above-mentioned sources, it should be pointed out that church-scot did continue to be paid after 1066, though it was not consistently named and did not necessarily follow the standard form of a pack-load of corn per hide. This is not the place to deal in detail with such survivals of Anglo-Saxon practices, but it is worth signalling the existence of several twelfth-century documentary sources referring to such a render. At Leominster the same due was called *scrifcorn* and was still being paid in the twelfth and thirteenth centuries.[79] At Lincoln the render due to the cathedral and known in the twelfth century as Marycorn is likely to be another form of church-scot.[80] There are further records, referring to the lands of other churches (such as Abingdon, Glastonbury, Gloucester, Winchester etc.), which prove that church-scot was still being paid in the twelfth and thirteenth centuries. In some cases it took the form of poultry or money, rather than grain.[81]

CONCLUSIONS

It is likely that the Normans found it difficult to understand church-scot, since they had probably never heard of it. In these circumstances it is certainly not surprising that such important churches as Worcester or Pershore managed to achieve complete control of an ecclesiastical tribute which had been paid to other minsters in the past. It should also be noted, however, that unlike other church dues, church-scot seems to have been linked to the tenurial conditions of the land, from which it was to be paid, since its very origin. After all, even the Worcester leases issued between the end of the ninth and the beginning of the tenth century, which prescribed the payment of church-scot to the minsters at Bibury and Bishop's Cleeve, dealt with estates that had previously belonged to those ecclesiastical institutions.

It would be very difficult, and probably also misleading, to draw a definite line

---

[77] For this suggestion, see Chaney, 'Anglo-Saxon church dues', p. 276, n. 6.

[78] For examples of variant spellings see *Domesday Book*, i, fols 38c (J. Mumby, ed., *Domesday Book, 4, Hampshire* (Chichester, 1982), 1, 19), and 154c (J. Morris, ed., *Domesday Book, 14, Oxfordshire* (Chichester, 1978) 1, 1–2). The confusion was probably due to the nature of this render, which consisted of a fixed amount of wheat. Various later sources refer to a tribute named *churchsed*, which they would translate with Latin *semen ecclesiae*. Cf. Neilson, 'Church rents', p. 196.

[79] See B.R. Kemp, ed., *Reading Abbey Cartularies*, Camden fourth series 33 (London, 1987), pp. 262–3, 289–92 (nos 326, 358–9) and J. Barrow, ed., *English Episcopal Acta, vii, Hereford 1079–1234* (Oxford, 1993), no. 279. Cf. B.R. Kemp, 'Some aspects of the *parochia* of Leominster in the 12th century', in *Minsters and Parish Churches*, ed. Blair, pp. 83–96, at pp. 87–8.

[80] Cf. S. Bassett, 'Lincoln and the Anglo-Saxon see of Lindsey', with an appendix, 'The name Lindsey', by Margaret Gelling, *ASE* 18 (1989), pp. 1–32 and D. Owen, 'The Norman cathedral at Lincoln', *Anglo-Norman Studies* 6 (1983), pp. 188–99. I am grateful to Julia Barrow for these references.

[81] See Neilson, 'Customary rents', pp. 194–6.

between ecclesiastical organisation and land-holding in early medieval England, given that the former would have initially depended on the estates which belonged to the old minsters. Church-scot probably represents the most tangible sign of the development of such a system, and it is clearly not by chance that the oldest English church due was calculated on the basis of the amount of land held by the payer.[82] It is also very likely that with the introduction of the tithe payment system, thanks to Continental influence, a new concept of church dues made its appearance in England. The attempts at regularisation that we find both in the late Anglo-Saxon law-codes and in Wulfstan's homilies aimed to place all church dues (including church-scot) in the same picture. However, at least in the diocese of Worcester, from which we have a substantial group of documents, the allocation of church-scot seems to have been determined through criteria other than those attached to the parochial system. Unfortunately, earlier sources are not numerous enough to allow us to come to any definite conclusion about the original nature of such a payment. What those sources do allow us to do, however, is to follow the introduction of tithes and their immediate rise to the position of principal church due in late Anglo-Saxon England. Law-codes and homilies certainly show that. Domesday Book, for its part, contains only sporadic references to tithes, but when it does refer to them, it is possible to note that they were often divided between mother-churches and dependent local churches.[83] It is very likely, as John Blair has suggested, that by this time tithes were also considered economically more convenient, given that they were proportional to the yearly produce, whereas church-scot consisted of a fixed amount of corn calculated on land-holding.[84] It was probably also for this reason that the new minor churches founded in later Anglo-Saxon times tried to secure tithe payments for themselves.[85] For its part, church-scot was still being paid to major churches, but its allocation did not necessarily depend on the system of ecclesiastical organisation. Such powerful churches as those at Worcester and Pershore seem to have been able to take advantage of the fluid nature of such an ancient tribute, although various late Anglo-Saxon kings had tried to make it part of a coherent and uniform system of ecclesiastical taxation.

Given the differences between the origins and development of tithes on the one hand, and church-scot on the other, it is probably not surprising that most – if not all – evidence concerning the relationship between the receipt of pastoral care and

---

82 It should be remembered that in 1876 Kemble had already suggested that originally church-scot was paid by tenants of ecclesiastical lands. Only later on would it have become a church due owed by all free men. J.M. Kemble, *The Saxons in England*, ii, (London, 1876), pp. 490–4.

83 An example is provided by the manor at Nether Wallop (Hampshire). Cf. *Domesday Book*, i, fol. 38c (*Domesday Book*, 19, *Hampshire* (Chichester, 1975), 1, 19).

84 John Blair has pointed out that thanks to general economic growth and the spread of more intensive field-systems, grain production per hide rose from the tenth century onwards, thus making tithes increasingly more profitable than church-scot. Blair, *Church in Anglo-Saxon Society*, p. 436.

85 Edgar's second code shows that already in the middle of the tenth century local churches had achieved important results in the allocation of tithe payments. This code says that tithes had to be paid both from the thegn's land and the land of the tenants. However, if a thegn had on his land a church with a graveyard, he was to pay the third part of his own tithe into his church; II Edgar, cc. 1.1–2, in *Councils and Synods*, i, pp. 97–8.

the obligation to pay church dues appears in connection with tithes, rather than church-scot. When tithes were introduced in Anglo-Saxon England, the English Church also imported some of the concepts which formed the basic framework of the tithe system in Continental Europe. Carolingian sources are much more explicit on the reasons why the laity were expected to pay tithes to their mother churches. However, as has been shown above, tenth- and eleventh-century English sources, especially homilies and texts for the instruction of the clergy, provide justifications of a similar nature. These indicate that in England too the laity were expected to pay their tithes in return for the pastoral care provided by the churches to which they owed their obedience.[86]

[86] I am grateful to Julia Barrow, John Blair, Nicholas Brooks, Rebecca Rushforth, Jonathan Wilcox and the late Patrick Wormald for their comments on an earlier draft of this paper.

3

Ælfric in Dorset and
the Landscape of Pastoral Care

Jonathan Wilcox

The voice of pastoral care in late Anglo-Saxon England is, to a very great extent, the voice of one single writer: Ælfric. This monk of Cerne Abbas composed a remarkably extensive and well-informed commentary on the Christian story, on the individual's responsibility to society, and on ethics and morality in sequences of homilies and saints' lives that dominate the surviving record of Anglo-Saxon preaching. In broad terms, Ælfric's works are what survive of pastoral care in action in late Anglo-Saxon England. For all that those works have been the object of much study, the very fact of one monk in a small Dorset monastery so dominating the homiletic voice of pastoral care is a phenomenon in need of explanation. In this essay I will engage this question by reconsidering Ælfric in the landscape of Dorset and show how that most local context helps to map his relation to pastoral care.

Ælfric was trained in the monastic and metropolitan centre of Winchester and would later become abbot of Eynsham, but he composed and disseminated the vast majority of his writings when he was a monk at Cerne Abbas, Dorset.[1] His pastoral programme is most fully realised in the two series of *Catholic Homilies* – two sequences of forty homilies each for Sundays and festivals through the church year, written at Cerne between 987 and 995, and disseminated massively throughout Anglo-Saxon England.[2] These innovative English homily cycles are

---

[1] For introductions to Ælfric's life, see J.R. Hurt, *Ælfric* (New York, 1972); J. Wilcox, ed., *Ælfric's Prefaces* (Durham, 1994), introduction; and M. Lapidge, 'Ælfric's schooldays', in *Early Medieval English Texts and Interpretations: Studies Presented to Donald G. Scragg*, ed. E. Treharne and S. Rosser (Tempe, AZ, 2002), pp. 301–9. On Ælfric's corpus of writings, see especially P. Clemoes, 'The chronology of Ælfric's works', in *The Anglo-Saxons: Studies in Some Aspects of their History and Culture Presented to Bruce Dickins*, ed. *idem* (London, 1959), pp. 212–47, and A.J. Kleist, 'Ælfric's corpus: a conspectus', *Florilegium* 19 (2001), pp. 1–33.

[2] P. Clemoes, ed., *Ælfric's Catholic Homilies: the First Series*, EETS ss 17 (Oxford, 1997), and M. Godden, ed., *Ælfric's Catholic Homilies: the Second Series*, EETS ss 5 (Oxford, 1979). All quotations are from these editions, referred to as CH I and CH II respectively; all translations from Old English are my own unless otherwise noted. The precise dates of composition for the two series are contested, but only within the range 987 x 995 and therefore without prejudice to the argument here; see especially the evidence presented by M. Godden, *Ælfric's Catholic Homilies: Introduction, Commentary and Glossary*, EETS ss 18 (Oxford, 2000), pp. xxix–xxxvi. For an overview, see also J. Hill, 'Translating the tradition: manuscripts, models and methodologies in the composition of Ælfric's *Catholic Homilies*', *Bulletin of the John Rylands University Library of Manchester* 79 (1997), pp. 43–65.

of obvious importance for understanding pastoral care since they make up such a large proportion of surviving preaching material – and, indeed, of surviving Old English writing of any kind.[3] Yet, for all their importance, some strikingly fundamental questions remain to be answered. How were these works and the books that contain them really used? Why were they produced in a small, newly-founded monastery in Dorset rather than in one of the Anglo-Saxon monastic powerhouses like Winchester or Canterbury? Why did this efflorescence of vernacular Christian learning occur at this particular moment in late Anglo-Saxon England? What were the circumstances that led to its successful circulation? And what effect did this systematic programme have? I will tackle these questions by placing Ælfric back in his most immediate context – the villages, towns, and settlement patterns of Dorset, where a pastoral scene dominated by large minsters was just beginning to break down due to the dual pressures of new, reformed monasteries and flourishing small churches that would soon give rise to a parish system.[4] Indeed, I will suggest it is no coincidence that the revolutionary development in pastoral care that Ælfric's standardised vernacular sequences represent came into being in the countryside where reorganisations of pastoral administration were more in evidence than in the urban centres or in the bigger monasteries. To this end, I will consider likely models for the performance of Ælfric's homilies on the ground in the vicinity of Cerne Abbas, Dorset, and correlate these, where possible, with the evidence of surviving manuscripts.

THE USES OF ÆLFRIC'S HOMILIES

To contextualise the creation of the homilies, it is first necessary to consider their performance context. While the precise use of the *Catholic Homilies* is somewhat contentious, the works themselves contain abundant markers that point to their broad intended use and expected audience. As expositions of gospel pericopes, they clearly appear to have a liturgical purpose: they provide an explanation and expansion in English of the Latin gospel reading from the mass. As such they could be read out by a priest to a congregation in the course of a church service on a Sunday or a major saint's day that was celebrated in church. Many internal references dramatise that context, as when the homiletic voice alludes to a preceding gospel reading by a deacon:

Her is geræd on ðisum godspelle þe we nu gehierdon of þæs diacones muðe . . . (CH I.x, 3–4)

---

3 Ælfric's *Catholic Homilies* occur in some 42 of the 412 manuscripts in N.R. Ker, *Catalogue of Manuscripts Containing Anglo-Saxon* (Oxford, 1957). The *Dictionary of Old English: Old English Corpus*, containing essentially all surviving Old English, comprises some 3,900,000 words of Old English, of which some 570,000 are the works of Ælfric; in other words, Ælfric wrote some 14.65% of the surviving corpus of Old English. (If one includes the Latin in the Old English corpus, these totals are 595,000 of 4,647,000 words, for some 12.8% of the corpus.) My thanks to Antonette diPaolo Healey, editor, and Xin Xiang, systems analyst, of the *Dictionary of Old English*, for those statistics from the corpus.

4 On the minsters in the area, see T.A. Hall, *Minster Churches in the Dorset Landscape*, BAR British Series 304 (Oxford, 2000). On the development of parishes throughout England, see N.J.G. Pounds, *A History of the English Parish* (Cambridge, 2000).

Here is read in this gospel which we have now heard from the mouth of the deacon . . .

Audience address within the sermons frequently alludes to a lay audience of both men and women, as would be expected at the Sunday services. Such a wide-ranging lay audience may have been inattentive at times to the preacher's message and Ælfric sometimes hints as much. In the second second series homily on Easter Day, for example, he inserts the explication of the gospel passage appropriate to Easter Wednesday (John 21:1–13):

> Sume his geswutelunge we eow sædon on oðre stowe. sume we willað eow nu secgan. nu ge her gegaderode syndon; We wenað þæt ge ealle on andwerdnysse her ne beon to ðam dæge. þe we þæt godspel rædan sceolon (CH II.xvi, 102–4)

> Some of the explanation of this we have told you in another place, some we will tell you now, now you are gathered here. We know that you were not all in attendance here on the day when we had to read that gospel.

The lay audience that is explicitly inscribed here and throughout the homilies may not be relied on to attend all services, although they are likely to turn out on Easter Day.[5] Ælfric projects, then, a broad, not especially pious, lay audience as the usual target for his homilies.

Other references, though, hint at other intended audiences. For example, in a homily that includes extensive discussion of sexual mores aimed at both secular men and women (CH II.vi), Ælfric digressively describes the duties of a priest and mentions how mass-priests and deacons should avoid all sexual intercourse or dwelling with women except relatives, citing canon law. He continues with further injunctions for such clerics, such as prohibiting them to partake in worldly affairs as reeves (CH II.vi, 136–53). The implied audience here, then, comprises both layfolk and clerics. In other instances, Ælfric includes addresses to a monastic audience. For example, a homily on St Paul (CH I.xxvii) begins by addressing a secular audience but, in an exposition of the hundredfold reward of those who turn to Christ, drawn from Matthew 19:27–29, turns explicitly to a learned and regulated audience (*ðes cwyde belimpð swiðe to munuchades mannum*, 'this text relates very much to people in monastic orders', lines 198–9). The homily, which began implying a general, biblically uneducated, audience, ends in exhortations concerning monastic conduct clearly geared towards a specialist monastic audience. At one point in CH II.vi, Ælfric claims:

> We sceolon eallum godes folce samod þa boclican lare secgan (CH II.vi, 153–7)

> We must tell written learning to all God's people together,

and the internal evidence suggests that he intended his homilies to target just such a broad audience.

Other scholars have explored the performance context of Ælfric's preaching, and Mary Clayton has been most successful in establishing the appropriate

---

5 Ælfric makes a similar comment about the audience's non-attendance on a weekday in a homily on Ash-Wednesday in *Lives of Saints*, which in one manuscript is moved to the Sunday in Quinquagessima (W.W. Skeat, ed., *Ælfric's Lives of Saints*, EETS os 76, 82, 94, 114 (London, 1881–1900; repr. as two vols, 1966 [hereafter LS]), homily xii, lines 289–92).

context.[6] She establishes Ælfric's unusual expectations in contrast with earlier Carolingian examples. As Clayton demonstrates, Carolingian homiliaries are sharply demarcated as intended for one of three distinct contexts – as collections for the monastic night office, as collections for devotional reading, or as collections for preaching – and each of these three distinct forms of homiliary had different implied audiences. Ælfric's distinctive contribution is not only his composition in the vernacular – although his systematic homiletic programme in the vernacular is, indeed, unprecedented – but also his combining characteristics of these three different types of collection. As a result, Ælfric's homilies are genuinely appropriate for the mixed audience dramatised within them.

Of course, this may not have been the only context in which the homilies were read. Malcolm Godden, who has himself amplified upon the mixed audience inscripted in the second series,[7] has recently cautioned against any too easy assumption that the homilies were intended only for their implied liturgical context. Instead, Godden plays up their potential value as reading pieces both for pious layfolk and also for monks whose access to the Latin of the liturgy may not have been as extensive as the literature of the monastic reform would suggest.[8] In serving as personal reading pieces, Godden implies, the homiletic collections may thus have functioned for layfolk in a way analogous to the later medieval phenomenon of the Book of Hours, while in the monastery they would have served as a vernacular gloss on the liturgical round, providing access to the key ideas of the liturgy for any without the ability to understand the Latin readings. Such alternative uses are clearly important in the case of Ælfric's *Lives of Saints*, since that collection provides for precisely those saints whose days were not celebrated in church services for the laity and so for whom there is no obvious liturgical use for readings in the vernacular, but such alternative models of use were probably also relevant to the Catholic Homilies.[9]

Further evidence for liturgical use of the homilies can be seen in occasional external references, including some in regulatory literature drafted by Ælfric himself. In both his Pastoral Letter for Bishop Wulfsige and his later Pastoral Letters for Archbishop Wulfstan, Ælfric lays out the duties of a priest, which include preaching in the vernacular:

> Se mæssepreost sceal secgan Sunnandagum and mæssedagum þæs godspelles angyt on englisc þam folce (Letter for Wulfsige, c. 61)[10]

---

6 M. Clayton, 'Homiliaries and preaching in Anglo-Saxon England', *Peritia* 4 (1985), pp. 207–42, which serves as a corrective to the discussion of M. McC. Gatch, *Preaching and Theology in Anglo-Saxon England: Ælfric and Wulfstan* (Toronto, 1977).

7 See M. Godden, 'The development of Ælfric's second series of Catholic Homilies', *English Studies* 54 (1973), pp. 209–16.

8 Godden, *Introduction, Commentary and Glossary*, pp. xxi–xxix.

9 I discuss the puzzle of the uses of the *Lives of Saints* and suggest a range of performance contexts in 'The audience of Ælfric's *Lives of Saints* and the face of Cotton Caligula A. xiv, fols. 93–130', in *Beatus Vir: Studies in Anglo-Saxon and Norse Manuscripts in Memory of Phillip Pulsiano*, ed. A.N. Doane and K. Wolf (Tempe, AZ, forthcoming).

10 *Councils and Synods*, i, pp. 191–226 at p. 208; cf. 'Se mæssepreost sceal mannum bodian þone soþan geleafan 7 hym larspel secgan', 'First Old English Letter for Wulfstan', c. 175, *ibid.*, i, p. 294.

The priest must tell the meaning of the gospel in English to the people on Sundays and mass-days.

Invoking the idea of the blind leading the blind from Matthew 15:14, he continues:

Blind bið se lareow, gif he þa boclare ne cann and beswicð þa læwedan mid his larleaste swa (c. 66)

The teacher is blind if he does not know book-learning and so deceives lay people through his lack of learning.

The dangers of the blind leading the blind were comically manifest to Ælfric in the example of the foolish priest who taught him in his youth, who did not understand the contemporary inappropriateness of Old Testament customs and so spoke in favour of bigamy, cited by Ælfric in the preface to his translation of Genesis.[11] Ælfric's *Catholic Homilies* provide an antidote to this literalist priest. They give the *boclare* to illuminate any priest, even a foolish one, and provide the wherewithal for telling the meaning of the gospel in English to the people.

ÆLFRIC'S HOMILIES ON THE GROUND

The Pastoral Letter for Wulfsige, Bishop of Sherborne, may provide a different kind of evidence for the use of the homilies in addition to the value of its injunctions. In this work, probably dating from the same time as the second series of *Catholic Homilies* (c. 993–5), Ælfric responded to a request from the bishop with a letter 'ventriloquising' pastoral injunctions that Wulfsige could simply read aloud to his priests. This model of delivery mirrors the use of the homilies by a priest, where the voice of Ælfric is conflated with that of the priest in front of his congregation. And Wulfsige at Sherborne provides one likely immediate user for the *Catholic Homilies* in a place where one of the mixed audiences already envisaged would have been a reality. Sherborne was an unreformed cathedral community at this time, as it had been since 705 and would remain until reformed by Wulfsige himself in 998. Here a community of secular clerics would have lived by a rule less strict than the monastic Benedictine Rule. The town of Sherborne included a substantial population of lay people – it comprised some one thousand souls a century later, by the time of Domesday Book.[12] When in residence at his cathedral, Bishop Wulfsige would have preached on Sundays and major festivals to a congregation both of clerics and of lay townsfolk. In other words, Sherborne provides precisely one of the performance contexts envisaged by Ælfric within the *Catholic Homilies*. And the town would certainly have been familiar to Ælfric: it is only some twelve miles away from Cerne along the main line of

[11] S.J. Crawford, ed., *The Old English Version of the Heptateuch*, EETS os 160 (London, 1922, repr. 1969), pp. 76–7, lines 12–36; and also Wilcox, *Ælfric's Prefaces*, preface 4, lines 11–36.

[12] A population estimate of 965 persons based on the Domesday Book is made by C. Holdsworth, 'Bishops, monasteries and the landscape, *c.* AD 600–1066', in *Landscape and Settlement in Britain, AD 400–1066*, ed. D. Hooke and S. Burnell (Exeter, 1995), pp. 27–49, at p. 36.

communication, and the pastoral letter for Wulfsige confirms Ælfric's interest in what was going on at this, his local bishop's seat. Ælfric may likely, then, have had the situation in Sherborne in mind as one performance context when he adopted the voice he chose for the *Catholic Homilies*.

But Sherborne would not have been the only place where Ælfric could imagine his works ventriloquised to a mixed audience of layfolk and clerics. He would have known other local clerical centres, albeit without a bishop. The late tenth century was probably still a time of minster churches where priests lived corporately following a rule for secular communities, such as the Enlarged Rule of Chrodegang, and whence they radiated out to provide pastoral care over a relatively large area.[13] Such minsters in Dorset are identified in a recent scholarly study by Teresa Hall, who shows that, in the vicinity of Cerne, Yetminster, Charminster, and Puddletown were certainly minster communities, while Sydling St Nicholas, Buckland Newton, and Milton may have once been.[14] Yetminster, Charminster, and Puddletown are each within ten miles of Cerne Abbas – Yetminster, with a population of 280 implied by the time of Domesday Book, is about ten miles away; Charminster, with an implied population of 150 souls, is just five miles down the River Cerne, and the present church there retains some eleventh-century material; while Puddletown is some eight miles away from Cerne down the River Piddle, with a population of perhaps 275 and a church mentioned in Domesday Book.[15] Sydling St Nicholas, with a Domesday Book population of some 205 souls, is a mere two miles from Cerne. In each of these communities, preaching on Sundays and major festivals would presumably serve a congregation both of the laity from the village and of any priests gathered in the minster church. While the vernacular sermon would be an occasion primarily for addressing the laity, the clerical audience could also be invoked at times, just as Ælfric, indeed, does in the *Catholic Homilies*. The pastoral situation in any of these churches was likely to be familiar to the preaching monk from Cerne Abbas and may well have helped inspire his work and his choice of voice.

These minster communities of secular priests also help explain what would otherwise be a conundrum concerning bookish resources. Ælfric's Pastoral Letter requires a priest to own an impressive array of books –

saltere 7 pistolboc, godspellboc 7 mæsseboc, sangbec 7 handboc, gerim 7 passionalem, penitentialem 7 rædingboc. Þas bec sceal mæssepreost nede habban, 7 he ne mæg butan beon, gif he his had on riht healdan wyle 7 þam folce æfter rihte wisigan, þe him to locað.[16]

13 See especially J. Blair, ed., *Minsters and Parish Churches. The Local Church in Transition 950–1200* (Oxford, 1988); and J. Blair and R. Sharpe, ed., *Pastoral Care before the Parish* (Leicester, London and New York, 1992). See also B. Langefeld, ed., *The Old English Version of the Enlarged Rule of Chrodegang* (Frankfurt, 2003).

14 Hall, *Minster Churches*.

15 Population estimates are made by taking the Domesday number of villagers, smallholders, and slaves, and multiplying by five to account for their households as suggested by Holdsworth, 'Bishops, monasteries and the landscape'. Original numbers are from *Domesday Book, 7, Dorset*, ed. C. and F. Thorn (Chichester, 1983). For the material remains of the parish church of St Mary at Charminster, see *An Inventory of Historical Monuments in the County of Dorset*, vol. iii (in 2 parts), *Central Dorset* (Royal Commission on Historical Monuments, 1970), i, pp. 60–3.

16 'Ælfric's Pastoral Letter for Bishop Wulfsige', cc. 52–4, in *Councils and Synods*, i, pp. 191–226 at pp.

a psalter and a book with the epistles, an evangeliary and a missal, songbooks and a manual, a computus and a passional, a penitential and a reading book. These books the priest must needs have, and he cannot be without them, if he wishes to observe his order rightly and to direct correctly the people who belong to him.

The episcopal minster community at Sherborne is a credible repository for this range of books, which could serve a number of priests working from the minster. Perhaps such a library was also feasible at the smaller local minster communities, since here resources would be pooled. A copy of Ælfric's *Catholic Homilies* would also serve each of these preaching communities well. The known distribution of manuscripts of the *Catholic Homilies* does not include small minsters, presumably because books are so unlikely to survive from such a place and would be hard to localise even if they did. It does include, though, many cathedral churches, where the chances of book survival are so much better. Although most manuscripts of the *Catholic Homilies* cannot be specifically localised, Clemoes points to their presence at the cathedral centres of Canterbury, Worcester, Rochester, Exeter, and Durham.[17]

While the late tenth century saw the continuation of minster churches – certainly retaining a clerical college at the episcopal see of Sherborne until its reform in 998 – this was also a time of competing pastoral models. The village of Cerne itself, for example, implies a special case, but one which became significant with the proliferation of reformed monasteries. At Cerne the reformed monastery was founded probably in 987 and housed a fairly small community of monks.[18] The village was similar in size or a little larger than many of the surrounding villages – Domesday Book implies a population there of some 315 souls. Later in the Middle Ages, the villagers would be served by their own parish church of St Mary, but the earliest fabric of this structure dates to about 1300.[19] Before that church was built, villagers and monks presumably shared a place of worship, with the monastic community providing pastoral care for the village. Villagers presumably came on a Sunday or major festival into the monastery's chapel to receive the word of God amidst a mixed audience of monks and laity, thus enacting precisely another kind of preaching circumstance envisaged in the

---

206–7; translation from Whitelock. Cf., also, 'Ælfric's First Old English Pastoral Letter for Wulfstan', cc. 157–8, *ibid.*, i., pp. 291–2.

[17] On the circulation of the first series, see Clemoes, ed., *First Series*, pp. 64–168, who summarises his findings at pp. 162–8.

[18] On the early history of Cerne Abbas, see K. Barker, ed., *The Cerne Abbey Millennium Lectures* (Cerne Abbas, 1988). At the time of the dissolution of the monasteries there were an abbot and sixteen monks. Comparable monasteries probably counted fewer than twenty monks, with Evesham, for example, having twelve in 1058; see D.H. Farmer, 'The progress of the monastic revival', in *Tenth-Century Studies: Essays in Commemoration of the Millennium of the Council of Winchester and 'Regularis Concordia'*, ed. D. Parsons (London and Chichester, 1975), pp. 10–19 at pp. 16–17.

[19] J. Hutchins, *The History and Antiquities of the County of Dorset*, third edn by W. Shipp and J. W. Hodson, 4 vols (1861–74), iv, p. 29, observes that the handsome large church is 'supposed to have been erected by the convent for the use of the town, about the middle of the fifteenth or beginning of the sixteenth century, at which period of time most of the great religious houses seem to have built parochial churches in the places wherein they were situated', but adds that there seems to have been a parish church here before. For a detailed account of the building, dating the earliest fabric to probably c. 1300, see *An Inventory of Historical Monuments in the County of Dorset*, i, *West Dorset* (Royal Commission on Historical Monuments, 1952), pp. 74–7.

Catholic Homilies. Nor was Cerne the only village in the vicinity with such a model. A similar pastoral circumstance would have occurred at the nearby reformed monastery of Milton (founded in 933/4 and reformed in 964), and later at Abbotsbury (founded in the second quarter of the eleventh century). In these monasteries, as in all other monasteries throughout the land where monks exercised pastoral care over a secular community, a copy of Ælfric's *Catholic Homilies* would have served well as a tool for preaching to the people with an incidental audience of monks. Two manuscript copies do, indeed, survive from Cerne, although this presents a special case as the originating scriptorium for the work.[20] Other monastic centres are likely as the place of origin or use of homiletic manuscripts, although surprisingly few can be localised to them.[21]

Even though secular minster and reformed monastery between them account for much of the likely preaching in the vicinity of Cerne Abbas, a third locus of pastoral care also probably existed in the 990s which was to become increasingly important. Minsters as mother churches had control over smaller dependent chapels. By the late tenth century, the dependent chapels were probably becoming less dependent, and a different type of small church was coming onto the scene in the form of locally owned proprietary churches.[22] As estates and villages acquired proprietary churches, those churches took over pastoral responsibilities in their immediate vicinities.[23] These churches were surely more isolated and less well-resourced than the minster communities, yet such institutions would ultimately win out and evolve into the modern system of parishes. Around Cerne Abbas, surrounding villages which had nucleated to such an extent as to be named in the Domesday Book are likely centres for these proprietary, putative-parish churches – villages like Up Cerne some two miles up the River Cerne with a population of some 90 souls; or Alton Pancras, three miles away on the River Piddle, with some 100 souls.[24] Even though Domesday Book makes no mention of churches in these villages, their development is implied by the modern layout of parishes: Alton Pancras and Up Cerne constitute two of the parishes now surrounding Cerne Abbas, along with the probably minster-derived centres of Sydling St Nicholas and Buckland Newton.

It is hard to imagine the lone priest in these little communities having the books or the book-learning that Ælfric enjoined in his pastoral letters.[25] Instead, this

---

[20] MSS London, British Library, Royal 7 C. xii and, most likely, Cambridge, University Library, Gg. 3. 28. The former is discussed and reproduced in N.E. Eliason and P. Clemoes, ed., *Ælfric's First Series of Catholic Homilies: British Museum Royal 7 C. XII*, EEMF 13 (Copenhagen, 1966).

[21] See Clemoes, ed., *First Series*, pp. 162–8. For an attempt to place one unlocalised homiliary to a fenland monastery, see my 'The compilation of Old English homilies in MSS Cambridge, Corpus Christi College, 419 and 421' (unpublished Ph.D. diss., Cambridge University, 1987).

[22] See especially J. Blair, 'Introduction: from minster to parish church', in *Minsters and Parish Churches*, ed. *idem*, pp. 1–19; and Pounds, *History of the English Parish*, ch. 1.

[23] See J. Blair, 'Local churches in Domesday Book and before', in *Domesday Studies*, ed. J.C. Holt (Woodbridge, 1987), pp. 265–78 and J. Blair, 'Secular minster churches in Domesday Book', in *Domesday Book: a Reassessment*, ed. P.H. Sawyer (London, 1985), pp. 104–42.

[24] Population estimates are made by multiplying the Domesday numbers by five to account for households, as suggested in n. 15 above.

[25] For the likely life of low learning of these local priests, see K.L. Jolly, *Popular Religion in Late Saxon England: Elf Charms in Context* (Chapel Hill, 1996).

seems a likely context for the standards implied in the ordination written about this time by Archbishop Wulfstan and circulating in association with his *Institutes of Polity*.[26] Here the would-be priest is expected to know the fundamentals of the faith and to be able to explain baptism and the mass and to know the canons *be ænigum dæle* ('to any extent'), along with enough computus to follow the calendar. There is no explicit requirement to own books; instead, there is recognition that even this lower standard may not be realistic, and the possibility for compromise is accordingly spelled out:

> 7 swaþeahhwæðere, gyf man for neode scyle gehadian samlæredne, þe ealles to lytel cann, þonne do man þæt, gyf mycel neod sy, þæs costes, ðe he him þæs borh find þæt he swa georne æfter ðam leornian wylle swa he æfre geornost mæge.[27]

> And nevertheless, if one must for necessity ordain a half-educated man, who knows all too little, one is then to do so, if there is great necessity, on condition that he find surety for himself that he will learn afterwards as eagerly as ever he possibly can.

Here is a context where Ælfric's *Catholic Homilies* would appear to be supremely useful in the field. One can imagine the lone priest being much less marked out from the surrounding community than the minster-priests and having far fewer resources. Minimal training for the priesthood included low-level literacy in Latin sufficient to conduct the mass and, perhaps, more extensive literacy in English. This local priest, barely marked out from the surrounding flock, would be a perfect user for Ælfric's homilies. Without access to a library or further learning, the priest could voice the homily, with both priest and community confident that this was legitimate wisdom delivered from a book (*þa boclican lare*). While the homiletic voice was mostly aimed at the lay congregation, the *samlæredne* priest could benefit from the wisdom alongside his congregation, occasionally even receiving the voice's direct address.

If the birth of parish churches was in progress throughout England and these parish churches represented the wave of the future, then the potential circulation for Ælfric's *Catholic Homilies* as an aid to the isolated parish priests was massive. By the late Middle Ages there were some 8,500 parishes in England, and the system was already in development in the thousands of churches present by the time of Domesday Book.[28] Here again the physical evidence from manuscripts is disappointing for correlating surviving books with likely use, although there are a few suggestive possibilities. The few incontrovertible examples of booklets that circulated separately from a codex in Anglo-Saxon England contained homilies.[29] While the two clearest examples – Oxford, Bodleian Library, Hatton

---

[26] MS Oxford, Bodleian Library, Junius 121, fols 34r–35v; K. Jost, ed., *Die 'Institutes of Polity, Civil and Ecclesiastical'*, Schweizer Anglistische Arbeiten 47 (Berne, 1959), pp. 218–22; also ed. and trans. *Councils and Synods*, i, c. 57, pp. 422–7.

[27] *Councils and Synods*, i, p. 425; translation from Whitelock.

[28] The 8,500 number is from Pounds, *History of the English Parish*, p. 3.

[29] On booklets, see P.R. Robinson, 'Self-contained units in composite manuscripts of the Anglo-Saxon period', *ASE* 7 (1978), pp. 231–8; repr. *Anglo-Saxon Manuscripts: Basic Readings*, ed. M.P. Richards (New York, 1994), pp. 25–35. For continental equivalents, see É. Palazzo, 'Le rôle des *libelli* dans la pratique liturgique du haut Moyen Age: histoire et typologie', *Revue Mabillon*, new ser. 1 (1990), pp. 9–36 (with thanks to Helen Gittos for this reference).

115, fols 140–7, and Bodleian Library, Auct. F.4.32, fols 10–18, each with a fold down the middle and soiling of the end pages – contain anonymous homilies, there is a probable separate booklet in Oxford, Bodleian Library, Junius 85, fols 18–24, of slightly larger dimensions than the surrounding book and with soiled end pages, which contains Ælfric's Homily for the First Sunday in Lent from the second series of *Catholic Homilies* (CH II.7). This may have been precisely one of those copies used in the field, although the great majority of such copies is missing. Of course, the priests' utilitarian books and booklets, carried around extensively, perhaps marked up for performance, are just the books most likely to get lost in the ravages of a millennium, particularly in view of their eventual loss of utility with the change of language, and the lack of a safe and continuous repository for collecting them.

The majority of surviving manuscripts of the *Catholic Homilies*, instead, look like clean, relatively high-status copies. These don't look like workaday priests' books – they mostly lack such signs of preparation for oral delivery as marginal notes or accents, as well as signs of wear and tear from use in the field. Instead, two uses seem more likely. These could have been the books for the pseudo-liturgical pious reading by layfolk or unlearned monastics described earlier in this essay. Such usage would likely have left fewer physical signs of use on the manuscripts. Alternatively, or in addition, these were likely exemplars, retained in monastic scriptoria, from which utilitiarian copies were made.

And multiple copies were, indeed, made. The most distinctive fact about manuscripts of the *Catholic Homilies* is that there is a great number of them – 34 of the first series with a further 50 postulated from the textual evidence. This provides an important clue about the Ælfric phenomenon. What can be recovered of the distribution of the *Catholic Homilies* shows that circulation took place on a massive scale and that Canterbury was at the heart of the operation. Clemoes demonstrates that six different phases of the texts of the first series were all circulated from Canterbury.[30] The role of Canterbury indicates that Ælfric was not alone in discerning the need for a vernacular homiletic programme. The Church hierarchy, including Sigeric, Archbishop of Canterbury, to whom the prefaces are addressed, must have seen their potential value and provided massive and official dissemination. If that included circulation to the priest in the field, it would have involved thousands of copies, perhaps written in local (minster?) scriptoria, or supplied by the scriptoria of the reformed monasteries, and deriving ultimately from copies distributed from Canterbury. The sheer number of surviving manuscripts demonstrates the official, institutionally-adopted status of these homilies. The phenomenal output of Ælfric was much more than one monk's idiosyncracy but was instead the programme of an institutional Church reacting to the pastoral needs which arose from an increasingly decentralised system of local churches and the multiple providers of pastoral care at the turn of the millennium.

---

[30] Numbers and circulation of manuscripts drawn from Clemoes, ed., *First Series*, pp. 64–168, who observes 'The leading part played by Canterbury is striking', p. 162.

CONCLUSION

Looking closely at the pastoral situation on the ground in central Dorset, then, serves to explain some of the ways in which Ælfric was the product of his age. It is easy to see one of his innovations – the use of the vernacular for the dissemination of such an ambitious programme – as the product of various larger forces, such as King Alfred's self-conscious adoption of the vernacular a century earlier, picked up by the intellectual and pastoral inventiveness of the tenth-century Benedictine reform.[31] Another innovation – the sheer scope of his pastoral programme – results from different, larger forces: the systemic needs that were emerging with the fracturing of a system of pastoral care based around large mother churches, and its replacement with small local churches that would be the foundation for the parish. It was precisely on account of this fracture that a universal pastoral programme became such a strong need for the priesthood. And the need would have been supremely visible in a quiet backwater like central Dorset with its range of pastoral models – much more so, perhaps, than in the metropolitan centre of Winchester. The result, paradoxically, is that at the moment of greatest breakdown of the old minster system, at the moment of a confusing plurality of pastoral models, at the moment of local forces acquiring most power – at just that moment, a universal pastoral system of preaching was developed. The development of that system reflects both the ambition and vision of an Ælfric and also the organisation and enthusiasm of an institutional Church that must have seized upon the project.

If Ælfric's homilies were disseminated as widely as I am suggesting, this would give flesh to the multiple fictive audiences that Ælfric himself envisages. In virtually every church, minster, and monastery throughout England, people of both sexes and all classes, in some places including among them communities of priests or monks and nuns, were assembling at the same hour on Sundays and festivals to hear the same moral, exegetical, and practical message preached at the same time. For all Ælfric's conservative orthodoxy, this achievement represents something quite revolutionary – the beginning of a form of mass communication that must have played a significant part in defining a sense of English identity at the turn of the millennium.

---

[31] Note, in this regard, Winchester's hold on standard late Old English; see H. Gneuss, 'The origin of standard Old English and Æthelwold's school at Winchester', *ASE* 1 (1972), pp. 63–83 and W. Hofstetter, *Winchester und der spätaltenglische Sprachgebrauch* (Munich, 1987). See also D.A. Bullough, 'The educational tradition in England from Alfred to Ælfric: teaching *Utriusque Linguae*', in *La scuola nell'Occidente latino dell'alto medioevo*, Settimane di studio del centro italiano di studi sull'alto medioevo 19 (Spoleto, 1972), pp. 453–94, 547–54.

4

Is there any Evidence for the Liturgy of Parish Churches in Late Anglo-Saxon England? The Red Book of Darley and the Status of Old English

Helen Gittos

O rustic priest, I suppose you do not know what an atom is.[1]

In the mid eleventh century, a substantial proportion of the population of England would have had access to a local church. Such institutions varied greatly, encompassing both the faded glory of a once great mother church which retained a small community of clerks, and the small chapel newly built by a local lord and served by a single priest.[2] If the estimates of the number of churches built (or rebuilt) in the later tenth and eleventh centuries are anything like accurate, there must have been a lot of liturgy going on.[3] What, for example, did the priest of the tiny single-cell church constructed in the tenth century immediately outside the manorial enclosure at Raunds, Northamptonshire actually do?[4]

The written and architectural sources suggest there was a demand for priests in the eleventh century and that those who supported them, whether local lords or local people, would have expected something for their money. How did these priests learn their job? Did they have any kind of education and, if not, how did they cope with the Latin of the liturgy? Presumably most of them learnt by experience, as liturgy has long been taught, and the evidence for inheritance of churches

---

[1] P.S. Baker and M. Lapidge, ed., *Byrhtferth's Enchiridion*, EETS ss 15 (1995), II.3.69–70, pp. 110–11 ('Ic wene, la uplendisca preost, þæt þu nyte hwæt beo a<tom>os'). I am indebted to Mark Atherton, Robert Hudson, Sarah Larratt Keefer and Malcolm Parkes for their advice, and to Gill Cannell of the Parker Library, Corpus Christi College, Cambridge for her help with consulting manuscripts. John Blair, Sarah Hamilton, Andy Hudson, Christopher A. Jones and Francesca Tinti kindly commented on drafts. I am especially indebted to Victoria Thompson for her assistance with Old English. Any errors which remain are my own responsibility.

[2] J. Blair, *The Church in Anglo-Saxon Society* (Oxford, 2005), chs 6–8.

[3] R. Morris, *Churches in the Landscape* (London, 1989), ch. 4; R.K. Morris, 'The Church in the countryside: two lines of enquiry', in *Medieval Villages: A Review of Current Work*, ed. D. Hooke, Oxford University Committee for Archaeology, Monograph 5 (Oxford, 1985), pp. 47–60, at pp. 49–55; R. Lennard, *Rural England 1086–1135: A Study of Social and Agrarian Conditions* (Oxford, 1959), ch. 10.

[4] A. Boddington, *Raunds Furnells. The Anglo-Saxon Church and Churchyard*, English Heritage Archaeological Report 7 (London, 1996). The dates of the phases have been revised, for which see the forthcoming report on the manor-house.

by the children of priests suggests how this could happen.[5] We will probably never know much about the rites they presided over. Even if a priest could afford to own liturgical books they are unlikely to have survived. Some may have taken the form of *libelli:* small, probably unbound, collections of rites, especially those for use in the field.[6] In any case, liturgical manuscripts were frequently discarded or dismembered as soon as they became outdated. The ones that do survive tend to be those few which were richly illustrated, or sufficiently grand to have been sent abroad as gifts.[7] It is also conceivable that local priests acquired old, second-hand books which were not designed for parish churches, and therefore difficult for them to use and for us to identify. It should not be surprising that virtually nothing survives today which is likely to have belonged to a local priest.[8] The purpose of this article is to investigate, by means of a case study, what evidence does survive, and briefly to address a larger question, that of the language of liturgical manuscripts and of the liturgy.

THE LITURGICAL DUTIES OF A PARISH PRIEST

In theory, a local priest in the late tenth and eleventh centuries was a busy man. His liturgical duties involved mass, the daily office, and occasional offices such as baptism, penance, confession, blessing marriages, visiting the sick, attending the dying, burial, perhaps ordeals, and the preparation of holy water.[9] Ælfric expected him to give sermons on Sundays,[10] and he may have been asked to officiate over ceremonies like the *æcerbot charm* for a good harvest.[11]

---

[5] Blair, *Church in Anglo-Saxon Society*, pp. 361, 493; and see J. Barrow in this volume.

[6] E. Palazzo, *A History of Liturgical Books from the Beginning to the Thirteenth Century*, trans. M. Beaumont (Collegeville, MN, 1998), pp. 189–91.

[7] D.N. Dumville, *Liturgy and the Ecclesiastical History of Late Anglo-Saxon England: Four Studies* (Woodbridge, 1992), pp. 94–5.

[8] On this topic see also Jonathan Wilcox's article in this volume.

[9] For the daily office see J. Hill, 'Monastic reform and the secular church: Ælfric's pastoral letters in context', in *England in the Eleventh Century*, ed. C. Hicks (Stamford, 1992), pp. 103–17, at pp. 106–7, 109 n. 15, the *Northumbrian Priests' Law*, c. 36 (*Councils and Synods*, i, p. 459), and J.E. Cross and A. Hamer, ed., *Wulfstan's Canon Law Collection* (Cambridge, 1999), p. 114 (Recension B, c. 2). For other duties see, for example: 'Ælfric's Pastoral Letter for Wulfsige', cc. 26–8, 84–92 (*Councils and Synods*, i, pp. 201, 213–15; B. Fehr, ed., *Die Hirtenbriefe Ælfrics in altenglischer und lateinischer Fassung*, Bibliothek der angelsächsischen Prosa 9 (Hamburg, 1914) Brief I, pp. 7–8, 19–21 (hereafter cited as Fehr with Brief number)); Ælfric's First Latin Letter for Wulfstan (Fehr, Brief 2, pp. 36–7) and Ælfric's Second Latin Letter for Wulfstan, cc. 9–18 (Fehr, Brief 3, pp. 59–60). For burial see also Blair, *Church in Anglo-Saxon Society*, pp. 463–71. In addition to the holy water required in, for example, baptism, Ælfric also thought it should be sprinkled in church every Sunday: Ælfric's Second Latin Letter for Wulfstan, c. 28 (Fehr, Brief 3, p. 61). For penance see Sarah Hamilton's article in this volume.

[10] 'Ælfric's Pastoral Letter for Wulfsige', c. 61 (*Councils and Synods*, i, p. 208; Fehr, Brief I, p. 14); Ælfric's First Latin Letter for Wulfstan, c. 159 (Fehr, Brief 2, p. 53); see also Cross and Hamer, ed., *Wulfstan's Canon Law Collection*, p. 115 (Recension B, c. 4).

[11] Blair, *Church in Anglo-Saxon Society*, pp. 483–5; K.L. Jolly, *Popular Religion in Late Anglo-Saxon England: Elf Charms in Context* (Chapel Hill, 1996). For the suggestion that *æcerbot* was intended to be used by 'a priest in the service of a secular lord' see J.D. Niles, 'The *æcerbot* ritual in context', in *Old English Literature in Context: Ten Essays*, ed. *idem* (Cambridge, 1980), pp. 44–56, at p. 50 and for a similar suggestion about the *Lacnunga* see E. Pettit, ed., *Anglo-Saxon Remedies, Charms, and Prayers from British Library MS Harley 585: The Lacnunga*, 2 vols (Lewiston, NY, 2001), i, p. liii.

A local priest may also have needed to know how to perform more complex rites at such major feasts as Candlemas, Palm Sunday and Rogationtide.[12] Where such rites were performed depended on local circumstances. When allegiances to mother churches remained strong, or when there were major monasteries and houses of secular clerks nearby, the laity (with their priest) may have visited them on such feasts. The evidence for this comes largely from the recognition processions which are mentioned in twelfth-century sources and reflect earlier traditions. Recognition processions were most often held at the dedication feast, Candlemas, the Ascension, Palm Sunday and Pentecost.[13] Two texts associated with Wulfstan's 'commonplace book' may represent an attempt by Ælfric to provide guidelines for the celebration of such feasts by secular clergy.[14] Though the sources on which these texts were based (including the *Regularis Concordia*) were adapted and often simplified,[15] they are still liturgically complex, involving stational processions between churches and the presence of a choir, deacon, and other attendants. Mother churches and others which retained a community of clergy could have used them, but a lone priest would have had difficulty.

Whether the local priest of the church at Raunds was sufficiently conscientious, and capable of performing such duties, is another matter. Of all these services, the ones most frequently mentioned are mass, the visitation of the sick, and baptism.[16] It is difficult to believe that every local priest celebrated the daily offices, especially those who had small estates to run. However, the profile that emerges from Ælfric's Pastoral Letters of avaricious, lazy, and drunken priests must be balanced by the desire of those who supported them to receive something for their money. Patrons and tithe-payers must at least have expected to attend mass now and then, to have their children baptised and their dead buried. Ælfric, following Isidore and Amalarius, repeatedly states that 'a priest who remains without a deacon has the name but has not the services'.[17] Did such priests have deacons and altar servers and, if so, who were they? Did they have choirs? To what extent were they expected to perform almost all, if not all, of the liturgy on their own? The answers to such questions must vary considerably depending on the wealth and antiquity of each church, but Ælfric's exhortations suggest that some priests did not have deacons and needed to know how to perform all the

---

12 H. Gittos, *Sacred Space in Anglo-Saxon England: Liturgy, Architecture and Place* (Oxford, forthcoming), ch. 3; Blair, *Church in Anglo-Saxon Society*, pp. 486–9 (for rogation). For the adaptation of parish churches for such services in the later medieval period: S. Helander, 'The liturgical profile of the parish church in medieval Sweden', in *The Liturgy of the Medieval Church*, ed. T.J. Heffernan and E.A. Matter (Kalamazoo, MI, 2001), pp. 145–86, at pp. 154–65.

13 Blair, *Church in Anglo-Saxon Society*, pp. 454–6; J. Blair, ed., *Minsters and Parish Churches. The Local Church in Transition 950–1200* (Oxford, 1988), pp. 11, 58, 60, 61, 66 n. 71, 93 n. 9.

14 C.A. Jones, 'Two composite texts from Archbishop Wulfstan's "Commonplace Book": the *De ecclesiastica consuetudine* and the *Institutio beati Amalarii de ecclesiasticis officiis*', *ASE* 27 (1998), pp. 233–71. For the office see J.M. Ure, ed., *The Benedictine Office: an Old English Text* (Edinburgh, 1957).

15 Jones, 'Two composite texts', pp. 249–51.

16 See, for example, Ælfric's First Latin Letter for Wulfstan, cc. 161–8 (Fehr, Brief 2, pp. 53–4).

17 'Sacerd, þe bið wunigende butan diacone, se hafað þone naman 7 næfð þa þenunga': 'Ælfric's Pastoral Letter for Wulfsige', c. 39 (*Councils and Synods*, i, p. 204; Fehr, Brief I, p. 10); Ælfric's First Latin Letter for Wulfstan, c. 123 (Fehr, Brief 2, p. 50).

parts of the liturgy which in larger communities were the responsibility of many different people.[18]

Richard Gameson has noted that one of the surviving book-lists records the possessions of a parish church,[19] albeit one in the ownership of the archbishops of York. This mid eleventh-century list records that Sherburn in Elmet (North Yorkshire) had several books for the mass (the priest's sacramentary, a gradual for the sung parts, two gospel books, and two epistolaries for the biblical lections) and for the office (a psalter, antiphonary, and hymnal).[20] This list is comparable with, though not identical to, the prescriptive lists of books which Ælfric in his Pastoral Letters and Wulfstan in the so-called *Canons of Edgar* expected all priests to own.[21] The Sherburn in Elmet list does not mention a manual or penitential, though the occasional offices could have been found in the sacramentary. Although a kalendar would have been useful, it is improbable that any parish priest would have needed to calculate the date of Easter or the other movable feasts. Byrhtferth thought he needed to teach priests enough computus to pass examination by their bishop for ordination,[22] but it is more likely that most would have known when to celebrate simply from local knowledge of what neighbouring churches were doing. As far as the books themselves were concerned, this was a period of significant development. Missals (containing everything for the mass, rather than only what was needed by the celebrant), breviaries (containing everything needed for the daily office), and manuals (containing the occasional offices) were only beginning to appear during the eleventh century. However, the lone clergymen of local churches would have found them highly desirable.

THE RED BOOK OF DARLEY

Though the surviving sacramentaries (and to some extent books for the office) may hint at how the clergy of proto-parish churches celebrated mass and office,

[18] For discussion of such questions in the later Middle Ages see Helander, 'Liturgical profile of the parish church', pp. 160–3, 175–9.

[19] R. Gameson, *The Role of Art in the Late Anglo-Saxon Church* (Oxford, 1995), p. 242. For Sherburn in Elmet: D.M. Hadley, *The Northern Danelaw: its Social Structure, c. 800–1100* (London, 2000), p. 276.

[20] M. Lapidge, 'Surviving booklists from Anglo-Saxon England', in *Learning and Literature in Anglo-Saxon England: Studies Presented to Peter Clemoes on the Occasion of his Sixty-Fifth Birthday*, ed. M. Lapidge and H. Gneuss (Cambridge, 1985), pp. 33–89, no. vi; for types of liturgical books: H. Gneuss, 'Liturgical books in Anglo-Saxon England and their Old English terminology', *ibid.*, pp. 91–141.

[21] 'Ælfric's Pastoral Letter for Wulfsige', c. 52 (*Councils and Synods*, i, pp. 206–7; Fehr, Brief I, p. 13); Ælfric's First Latin Letter for Wulfstan, c. 137 (Fehr, Brief 2, p. 51); and 'Ælfric's First Old English Letter for Wulfstan', c. 157 (*Councils and Synods*, i, pp. 291–2; Fehr, Brief II, pp. 126–7). See also the Penitential of Egbert (A.W. Haddan and W. Stubbs, ed., *Councils and Ecclesiastical Documents relating to Great Britain and Ireland*, iii (Oxford, 1878), p. 417). For discussion see Hill, 'Monastic reform and the secular church', pp. 110–11, Fehr, ed., *Hirtenbriefe*, pp. lxxxvi–xcii and C.A. Jones, 'Ælfric's pastoral letters and the episcopal *Capitula* of Radulf of Bourges', *Notes and Queries* 240 (1995), pp. 149–55.

[22] Baker and Lapidge, ed., *Byrhtferth's Enchiridion*, I.2.323–5. In the *Northumbrian Priests' Law* (c. 38), priests are to make compensation if they perform services in the wrong order: *Councils and Synods*, i, pp. 459–60.

there is nothing to suggest that any were definitely designed for that purpose. The one book that has most claim to be considered in this context is the Red Book of Darley (Cambridge, Corpus Christi College 422).[23] The manuscript is small (c. 194 x 129 mm)[24] but thick and it would readily fit in a book-satchel or roomy ecclesiastical pocket. As it now stands, it comprises two parts, the first (pp. 1–26) is a mid tenth-century copy of the Old English dialogues of Solomon and Saturn; the second part, with which we are concerned, is pp. 27–570, to which a quire was added in the twelfth century (pp. 571–86).[25] The second part was elegantly written and includes some illustrations at the beginning of the Canon of the Mass.[26] It was almost certainly produced c. 1061 because it includes paschal tables for the years 1061–98, which accords with the palaeographical evidence.[27] It is more difficult to judge where Darley was made. The strongest candidates are Sherborne (or its diocese) and the New Minster, Winchester. The Sherborne attribution rests on the presence in its kalendar of Bishop Wulfsige III, who was only otherwise celebrated at Westminster.[28] Amongst the evidence that suggests the manuscript was based on material from the New Minster, perhaps written there for use at Sherborne, is the presence of Grimbald in one of the two litanies, who is the only saint whose name is capitalised.[29] In the twelfth century, various additions were made, including the last quire (which contains various lections), and a mass for St Helen which was inserted after the computistical material. One of the scribes of the added quire was also responsible for some of the additional material in the original part of the manuscript.[30] At least by the twelfth century, the liturgical manuscript was bound together with the Solomon and Saturn dialogues because the same scribe who wrote the mass for St Helen in the second part of the manuscript also added a Latin form of excommunication in the first part.[31] By the

---

23 For some other possible candidates: Gameson, *Role of Art*, p. 243 and note his suggestion that 'books written and decorated in reformed monastic scriptoria may have been distributed to local churches throughout the south of England'.

24 M. Budny, *Insular, Anglo-Saxon, and Early Anglo-Norman Manuscript Art at Corpus Christi College, Cambridge: an Illustrated Catalogue*, 2 vols (Kalamazoo, MI, 1997), i, p. 645.

25 For descriptions of the manuscript: M.R. James, *A Descriptive Catalogue of the Manuscripts in the Library of Corpus Christi College, Cambridge*, 2 vols (Cambridge, 1912), ii, pp. 315–22; N.R. Ker, *Catalogue of Manuscripts Containing Anglo-Saxon* (Oxford, 1957), reissued with supplement 1990, pp. 119–21 (no. 70); Budny, *Manuscript Art at Corpus Christi College*, i, pp. 645–66.

26 For the illustrations, in addition to the catalogues, see Gameson, *Role of Art*, pp. 232–3; B.C. Raw, *Anglo-Saxon Crucifixion Iconography and the Art of the Monastic Revival* (Cambridge, 1990), pp. 89, 151–5 (as 'Sherborne Missal').

27 Ker, *Catalogue*, p. 120; C. Hohler, 'The Red Book of Darley', *Nordiskt Kollokvium i Latinsk Liturgiforskning* 2 (Stockholm, 1972), pp. 39–47, at p. 40; Dumville, *Liturgy and the Ecclesiastical History*, p. 74.

28 Cambridge, Corpus Christi College 422, p. 29; F.A. Gasquet and E. Bishop, *The Bosworth Psalter* (London, 1908), p. 61 n. 1; F. Wormald, ed., *English Kalendars before AD 1100*, Henry Bradshaw Society 72 (London, 1934), vi, pp. 183–95. A west country origin is further supported by the fact that it also shares a preface for one of its masses with material added to the Leofric Missal at Exeter: N. Orchard, ed., *The Leofric Missal*, Henry Bradshaw Society 113–14, 2 vols (London, 2002), i, pp. 224–5.

29 Corpus 422, p. 380; James, *Catalogue of the Manuscripts in the Library of Corpus Christi College*, ii, p. 315; but note the reservations in Dumville, *Liturgy and the Ecclesiastical History*, pp. 74–5. Both litanies are printed in M. Lapidge, ed., *Anglo-Saxon Litanies of the Saints*, Henry Bradshaw Society 106 (London, 1991), pp. 66, 125–31. See also Budny, *Manuscript Art at Corpus Christi College*, i, p. 647.

30 *Ibid.*, i, p. 646.

31 Ker, *Catalogue*, p. 121; Budny, *Manuscript Art at Corpus Christi College*, i, pp. 647–8.

sixteenth century, the manuscript was at Darley Dale, Derbyshire, as recorded by an inscription at the end of the book, and was probably owned by a local family.[32] Intriguingly, a second inscription records a tradition that oaths had been sworn upon it.[33] Since the church of Darley is dedicated to St Helen, Christopher Hohler suggested that the book had been there since the twelfth century, which would explain why the mass for St Helen was added at that time.[34] The church itself was an Anglo-Saxon foundation; it is recorded in Domesday and has several fragments of pre-Conquest sculpture.[35] It was in the gift of the king in 1086 and seems to have been granted to Lincoln Cathedral before 1105.[36] Judgements about the history of the manuscript from when it was produced until the twelfth century depend to a large extent on where the additional quire and the mass for St Helen were added. If Budny is right to suggest that the manuscript was 'refurbished' at a 'non-provincial centre', it is unlikely to have reached St Helen's, Darley Dale before the twelfth century.[37] Finally, it is worth saying that the book shows signs of having been heavily used.

The main liturgical section of the manuscript contains so much and such varied material that it is only possible to gain an idea of its contents from a summary rather than by trying to classify it as a type of book. In outline, the original part of the manuscript contains: computistical material including a kalendar and Easter tables (pp. 27–49); the Canon of the Mass (pp. 51–63); various masses – mostly votives and for the common of saints (pp. 63–268) including masses for St Olaf and St Nicholas, and for the ember Saturday in Whitweek; the *orationes pro peccatis* and *orationes matutinales* (pp. 268–76); rites for blessing a marriage (pp. 276–84), for blessing the candles at Candlemas (pp. 285–8), miscellaneous blessings, mostly of things (pp. 288–309); pages which appear to have been originally left blank (pp. 310–18); ordeals by water, fire, and bread and cheese (pp. 319–44); blessing of holy water (pp. 344–66); rites for baptism (pp. 367–93), blessing holy water (pp. 393–9), visiting the sick (pp. 399–429), burial (pp.

---

[32] *Ibid.*, i, pp. 648–9 with additions and emendations to Hohler, 'Red Book of Darley', p. 40.

[33] Both inscriptions are printed in James, *Catalogue of the Manuscripts in the Library of Corpus Christi College*, ii, p. 315 and Budny, *Manuscript Art at Corpus Christi College*, i, p. 646.

[34] The church at Darley was dedicated to Helen by at least the mid sixteenth century: D.G. Edwards, ed., *Derbyshire Wills Proved in the Prerogative Court of Canterbury 1393–1574*, Derbyshire Record Society 26 (Chesterfield, 1998), p. 230 (no. A105: will of 1558). F. Arnold-Forster, *Studies in Church Dedications or England's Patron Saints*, 3 vols (London, 1899), iii, p. 102 classifies the dedication as pre-sixteenth century, however the 1558 will is the earliest record I have found in a preliminary search.

[35] J.C. Cox, 'The church of St Helen's, Darley Dale', *Journal of the Derbyshire Archaeological and Natural History Society* 27 (1905), pp. 11–40.

[36] D.E. Greenway, *Fasti Ecclesiae Anglicanae 1066–1300*, iii, *Lincoln* (London, 1977), p. 6 (with references).

[37] The dialogues of Solomon and Saturn would not have been an inappropriate companion to what was already a compendious manuscript. They would have provided their owner with a poetic dialogue on the power of the Pater Noster, a prose section on the fight between the devil and the Pater Noster and a more traditional question-and-answer piece concerning time, nature, good and evil. In a liturgical context such as this, one could envision it fortifying the priest with knowledge, even providing him with ready answers to difficult questions. The text is printed in E. van K. Dobbie, ed., *The Anglo-Saxon Minor Poems*, Anglo-Saxon Poetic Records 6 (1942), pp. 31–48; for recent discussion see P.P. O'Neill, 'On the date, provenance and relationship of the "Solomon and Saturn" dialogues', *ASE* 26 (1997), pp. 139–68.

429–45) and burial masses (pp. 445–70); the office of the dead (470–90); offices of matins, first and second vespers, and lauds for the common of apostles, martyrs, confessors, and virgins (pp. 507–53); offices for the Triduum and Easter Sunday (pp. 555–70 and 491–506: the last quire is now displaced).

The Red Book of Darley seems to contain almost everything that the putative parish priest required. It has some computus, most importantly a kalendar and Easter tables. However, its owner would have needed a sacramentary for the Temporal and Sanctoral. It is possible that whoever commissioned this book already had a sacramentary, though without commons, votives or blessings. Perhaps it was intended as a compendium of services which could be drawn upon and adapted as need arose. It is notable that some of the masses it contains include all their various constituent parts as would be found in a missal.[38] It is not clear why some masses are treated in this way and not others. That at least some of this material was intended as an addition to what was already available is suggested by the presence of masses for Olaf and Nicholas. The cult of the latter saint was growing in popularity in the eleventh century, while the mass for Olaf seems to be the first known mass for this saint.[39] This is a peculiarly inconsistent book, as, for example, the lections for each mass are sometimes given in full, sometimes only the gospel reading is complete and the epistle given as incipit, and at other times it is the epistle which is given in full and the gospel as incipit.[40] The material for the office is even more difficult to understand. Like many of the masses, it includes everything necessary for a particular feast (except the ferial elements), but only for a limited number of occasions.[41] The offices were certainly copied from monastic material,[42] though this does not necessarily mean that it was intended to be used by a monk. Hohler resorted to suggesting that they were added later as 'a virtuous occupation'.[43] Perhaps the best that can be said about the book as a whole is that it shows a desire for completeness, for being able to perform these services on one's own if necessary, and possibly for having copied out as much information as was available from the sources to hand.

One particular element of the manuscript explains why it deserves such extended discussion here. Darley's material for the occasional offices is the most substantial that survives in any pre-Conquest book. The occasional offices, rites such as baptism and burial which would later end up collected in a manual, were the very heart of the work of a parish priest. Rites of this kind do survive from the

---

38 An idea of the relevant proportions can be gained from Budny, *Manuscript Art at Corpus Christi College*, i, pp. 651–2.

39 Hohler, 'Red Book of Darley', pp. 39–41; R.W. Pfaff, 'Massbooks', in *The Liturgical Books of Anglo-Saxon England*, ed. R.W. Pfaff, Old English Newsletter Subsidia 23 (Kalamazoo, MI, 1995), pp. 7–34, at pp. 23–4. One explanation for their odd position here is that they had been added into the part of the sacramentary from which the scribe was copying, for example as marginalia.

40 One cannot therefore assume that the priest had a separate gospel book but not an epistolary as Pfaff, 'Massbooks', p. 24.

41 A. Corrêa, 'Daily office books: collectars and breviaries', in *Liturgical Books of Anglo-Saxon England*, ed. Pfaff, pp. 45–60, at pp. 56–7.

42 *Ibid.*, p. 56.

43 Hohler, 'Red Book of Darley', p. 41.

pre-Conquest period, but often in manuscripts designed for different purposes, like pontificals and benedictionals. Some idea of the range of evidence can be gained from Sarah Keefer's brief survey.[44] Darley has the most complete and coherent collection that has survived. With this in one's satchel one would be able to perform all of the occasional offices required by a priest, except for penance and confession. This is what led Christopher Hohler to characterise it as 'the book a good, pastorally minded, monk priest is going to take with him round the villages'.[45]

THE RITE FOR BAPTISM IN THE RED BOOK OF DARLEY

It is difficult to assess for what purpose Darley was originally designed. It could have been made for someone studying at Sherborne (or the New Minster, Winchester) who was about to become the priest of a local church or household. It could also have been made for a monk who was intending to minister to the locale. One cannot be certain that it was intended to be used by a parish priest, but it is the best evidence we have for the liturgy of pastoral care in late Anglo-Saxon England. Few of its rites have been examined closely, so it is worth looking at one of the most important of them as a case study.

There is surprisingly little evidence for the liturgy of baptism in Anglo-Saxon England, presumably because these rites were most commonly located in the sorts of books (such as manuals) which have not survived. By the tenth and eleventh century infant baptism was the norm, but the rites that were used had developed from those intended for a period of instruction for adults.[46] The result was a sometimes clumsy conglomeration of actions that had taken place over a long

---

[44] S.L. Keefer, 'Manuals', in *Liturgical Books of Anglo-Saxon England*, ed. Pfaff, pp. 99–109. In addition to those mentioned by Keefer see also: for baptism, A. Davril, ed., *The Winchcombe Sacramentary (Orléans, Bibliothèque municipale, 127 [105])*, Henry Bradshaw Society 109 (London, 1995), pp. 86–94; for marriage blessings and masses, Paris, Bibliothèque nationale, Latin 943, fols 144r–v (partially printed in N.K. Rasmussen, *Les Pontificaux du haut Moyen Âge: genèse du livre de l'évêque*, Spicilegium Sacrum Lovaniense, Études et documents 49 (Leuven, 1998), p. 308), H.A. Wilson, ed., *The Benedictional of Archbishop Robert*, Henry Bradshaw Society 24 (London, 1903), pp. 55, 149–51 (a later addition); for burial, Orchard, ed., *Leofric Missal*, ii, pp. 366–74; Oxford, Bodleian Library, Laud Misc. 482, fols 67v–68v (incomplete); for ordeals, Textus Roffensis, in F. Liebermann, ed., *Die Gesetze der Angelsachsen*, 3 vols (Halle, 1903–16), i, pp. 401–9, Ker, *Catalogue*, pp. 443–7 (no. 373).

[45] Hohler, 'Red Book of Darley', p. 44.

[46] For early medieval baptismal liturgies: J.D.C. Fisher, *Christian Initiation: Baptism in the Medieval West: a Study in the Disintegration of the Primitive Rite of Initiation*, Alcuin Club Collections 47 (London, 1965); R. Cabié, 'Christian initiation', in *The Church at Prayer: an Introduction to the Liturgy*, ed. A.G. Martimort, 4 vols, translation by M.J. O'Connell of *L'Eglise en prière* (1983–84) (Collegeville, MN, 1986–88), iii, pp. 11–100; M.E. Johnson, *The Rites of Christian Initiation: their Evolution and Interpretation* (Collegeville, MN, 1999). P. Cramer, *Baptism and Change in the Early Middle Ages, c. 200–c. 1150* (Cambridge, 1993) is also useful, though less concerned with the liturgies themselves. For baptism in late Anglo-Saxon England: M.B. Bedingfield, *The Dramatic Liturgy of Anglo-Saxon England*, (Woodbridge, 2002), ch. 7; J.H. Lynch, *Christianizing Kinship: Ritual Sponsorship in Anglo-Saxon England* (Ithaca, NY, 1998). I have been unable to consult the following recent study: S.A. Keefe, *Water and the Word: Baptism and the Education of the Clergy in the Carolingian Empire* (Notre Dame, IN, 2002).

period of time. Even at this late date, the rites themselves were often located in the Temporal as part of the Easter Vigil. This is the case with the late tenth-century Winchcombe Sacramentary, the early eleventh-century sacramentary of Robert of Jumièges, and the parts of the Romano-Germanic Pontifical in Cambridge, Corpus Christi College 163.[47] However, in the early tenth-century Leofric Missal the baptismal *ordo* forms a separate rite towards the end of the book and it is also an independent service in Darley.[48]

The basic structure of Darley's rite is that of the Supplemented Hadrianum (the additions to the Gregorian Sacramentary made by Benedict of Aniane in the early ninth century),[49] but a number of features are worth noting.

- The rite begins with the priest blowing on the child three times and saying, 'Exi ab eo spiritus inmunde et da locum spiritui sancto paraclito in nomine patris et filii et spiritus sancti', and then signing him on the forehead and breast. This form of opening seems to be most common among manuscripts from north-eastern France. The exorcism found in Darley is rare in this position, though it is paralleled in the Sacramentary of Echternach (Echternach, ?895–8).[50]

- After the normal preparatory prayers, the recitation of the Pater Noster and Creed by the priest, and a Gospel lection, the priest takes the child's right hand and makes the sign of the cross in its palm, saying 'Accipe signaculum domini nostri ihesu c[h]risti in manu tua dextera ut te singnes [signes] et de aduersa parte repelles et in fide catholica permaneas et uiuas cum domino semper in secula seculorum'. This is extremely unusual and appears to be a remnant of the old tradition of the *traditio symboli*. There are a few other examples; it is also found in the Winchcombe Sacramentary (without rubric and with a slightly different version of the formula) and in an early eleventh-century manuscript from Jumièges.[51] Remarkably, it also occurs at

47 Davril, ed., *Winchcombe Sacramentary*, pp. 86–93; H.A. Wilson, ed., *The Missal of Robert of Jumièges*, Henry Bradshaw Society 11 (London, 1896), pp. 93–100; Cambridge, Corpus Christi College 163, pp. 114–19 and for this manuscript see, M. Lapidge, 'The Origin of CCCC 163', *Transactions of the Cambridge Bibliographical Society* 8.1 (1981), pp. 18–28.

48 Orchard, ed., *Leofric Missal*, ii, pp. 438–44.

49 J. Deshusses, ed., *Le sacramentaire grégorien: ses principales formes d'après les plus anciens manuscrits; édition comparative*, Spicilegium Friburgense 16, 24, 28, 3 vols (Fribourg, 1971–82), i, pp. 371–9.

50 Y. Hen, ed., *The Sacramentary of Echternach (Paris, Bibliothèque Nationale, MS. lat. 9433)*, Henry Bradshaw Society 110 (London, 1997), p. 183. Martène also prints some examples from the fifteenth to seventeenth centuries: E. Martène, ed., *De antiquis Ecclesiae ritibus*, second edn, 3 vols (Antwerp, 1736–8), i.1.7, *ordo* 1; i.1.8, *ordines* 18, 20 and for the identification of these manuscripts: A.G. Martimort, *La documentation liturgique de Dom Edmond Martène: études codicologiques*, Studi e Testi 279 (Vatican City, 1978), nos 376, 424, 426. A larger number of manuscripts have a different (or variant) exorcistic prayer, for example, Paris, BN lat. 2291 (one of the Sacramentaries from Saint-Amand, written there for Gozlinus, bishop of Paris 884–6); a sacramentary for St Maurice, Tours (s. ix²) now in two manuscripts, Tours 184 and Paris, BN, lat. 9430: Deshusses, ed., *Sacramentaire grégorien*, iii, pp. 104, 108–9 and examples printed by Martène include: *De antiquis Ecclesiae ritibus*, i.1.7 *ordines* 5, 6, 8; i.1.18 *ordines* 14, 16 (Martimort, *La documentation liturgique*, nos 371, 372, 374, 420, 422).

51 Davril, ed., *Winchcombe Sacramentary*, p. 89 (no. 425); Rouen, Bibliothèque municipale Y 127, printed in Martène, ed., *De antiquis Ecclesiae ritibus*, i.1.18 *ordo* 13 (Martimort, *La documentation liturgique*, no. 419).

the end of the rite in the late eighth-century Irish Stowe Missal and in the early printed versions of the Sarum manual.[52]

- The blessing of the font. There is nothing unusual about this in Darley except for its position in the rite. Normally the priest says the prayer *Nec te latet*, the candidate renounces the devil and is anointed with oil, they process to the font for the blessing, and then follows the affirmation of belief in the Trinity. However, Darley places the blessing earlier, immediately after the prayer *Nec te latet*. In this respect, it most resembles the somewhat muddled *ordo* in the Leofric Missal.[53]

- The distribution of the water. A common rubric from the eighth and ninth centuries onwards states that after the water has been blessed, it should be sprinkled over the people assembled around the font and that those who so desire may carry it home with them and sprinkle it wherever they wish. Darley's version reads: 'Hate her se preost helian þæt cild wið þæt halig wæter 7 sprenge se preost hine sylfne 7 þa men þe him onbutan standað. 7 nime man of ðam wætere on anum fæte ham mid þam cilde 7 sprenge þa hus 7 loc hwæt man wylle'.[54] What is clearly specified here is that it is the child who should be asperged and that the water should be sprinkled in its home. This simply seems to be a more specific version of an old rubric originally designed for use when many candidates were baptised at the same time.[55]

- Before the renunciation of the devil (or whilst it is happening), it is usual for the priest to anoint the child with the oil of exorcism by making the sign of the cross from his head and across his shoulders. This is missing from Darley, perhaps because this part of the rite (or a form of it) has been displaced to the beginning. It is notable that Ælfric specifically says, keeping closely to the normal rubrics, 'Cum oleo sancto debetis signare infantes in pectore et inter scapulas, antequam mittantur in fontem

---

[52] G.F. Warner, ed., *The Stowe Missal: MS. D. II. 3 in the Library of the Royal Irish Academy, Dublin*, Henry Bradshaw Society 31–2, 2 vols (London, 1906, 1915), ii, p. 32; A.J. Collins, *Manuale ad usum percelebris ecclesie Sarisburiensis: from the edition printed at Rouen in 1543*, Henry Bradshaw Society 91 (London, 1960), p. 30; Fisher, *Christian Initiation*, p. 84. The only other comparable rite known to me is found in a group of manuscripts written at or for the cathedral of Tours in which the priest holds the child's right hand whilst he recites the Pater Noster and Creed: Martène, ed., *De antiquis Ecclesiae ritibus*, i.1.7 *ordo* 4. For the manuscripts see Martimort, *La documentation liturgique*, no. 370 and references.

[53] For discussion of Leofric see Orchard, ed., *Leofric Missal*, i, pp. 116–17. One explanation for this would be that it results from an error some time in the distant past when the blessing of the font was integrated with the rite for baptism.

[54] Corpus 422, p. 387, printed in R.I. Page, 'Old English liturgical rubrics in Corpus Christi College, Cambridge, MS 422', *Anglia* 96 (1978), pp. 149–58, at p. 153; 'The priest at this point should command that the child be covered with the holy water and let the priest sprinkle himself and the people standing round. And let some of the water be taken in a vessel home with the child and sprinkle the house and wherever seems appropriate.' (All translations from Old English are by Victoria Thompson unless otherwise noted.)

[55] It is also worth noting that the water is distributed before the oil has been put into it rather than afterwards. The danger of being accidentally re-baptised in this way worried Ælfric (following Carolingian canonists) which is why he ordered it to be done in the order given in Darley: Ælfric's Second Latin Letter for Wulfstan, c. 8 (Fehr, Brief 3, p. 59); Ælfric's Second Old English Letter for Wulfstan, c. 8 (Fehr, Brief III, pp. 148–9). See also C.A. Jones, 'Old English *fant* and its compounds in the Anglo-Saxon vocabulary of baptism', *Mediaeval Studies* 63 (2001), pp. 143–92, esp. pp. 173–9.

baptismatis'.[56] One wonders whether Darley here preserves a version of just the sort of rite that Ælfric was trying to correct.

- The only unusual feature of the baptism itself is that after the child has been raised up from the font, the priest reiterates the baptismal formula, *In nomine patris et filii et spiritus sancti* whilst making a cross on his *hnecca* (the nape of the neck) rather than the top of his head.
- At the conclusion of the ceremony, a chrismal-cloth is laid on the child's head and a lit candle is put into its hand whilst the priest says the prayer *Accipe lampadem*. The candle is interesting because it is a relatively late and rare feature, which did not become common until the twelfth century.[57] The two earliest references known to me are Amalarius' early ninth-century *Liber officialis*, and a late ninth-century sacramentary written at Saint-Amand for Saint-Denis.[58] The practice was certainly popular in late Anglo-Saxon England: both candle and prayer appear in the Winchcombe Sacramentary and the Missal of Robert of Jumièges. Ælfric, following Amalarius, also mentions the candle in his Letter to the Monks of Eynsham.[59] Another early example is the early eleventh-century manuscript from Jumièges, which we have already encountered because it also includes the signing of the right hand.[60]

The final point that needs to be made seems more trivial than the others but is probably more significant. During the early Middle Ages, probably in eighth-century Frankish Gaul, the terms *patrinus* and *matrina* began to be used to denote godparents. *Ordo Romanus* XI uses these terms when the godparents are to bless the child but it also refers to them with the circumlocution *eos qui ipsos suscepturi sunt*. Such phrases were common before a specific vocabulary emerged, and remained in use after it had done so.[61] From the rites I have been able to examine, the new vocabulary was only rarely used in early medieval *ordines*, and periphrastic formulae based on the role of the godparents in bringing the child up from the font (and in life?) were more common. Typically, the godparents are mentioned when they either give the child to a priest or receive it from him. More interesting is the rubric in the Supplemented Hadrianum which

[56] 'You ought to sign the children on the breast and between the shoulder-blades with the holy oil before they are placed in the baptismal font': Ælfric's Second Latin Letter for Wulfstan, c. 5 (Fehr, Brief 3, p. 58).
[57] It is found in the twelfth-century Roman Pontifical: M. Andrieu, *Le Pontifical romain au Moyen-âge*, Studi e Testi 86–8, 99, 4 vols (Vatican City, 1938, 1940, 1941), i, p. 246; Cabié, 'Christian initiation', p. 69.
[58] J.M. Hanssens, ed., *Amalarii episcopi opera liturgica omnia*, Studi e testi 138–40, 3 vols (Vatican City, 1948, 1950), ii, pp. 137–8 (I.xxvi.5). This refers to the candle, but not to *Accipe lampadem*, though the antiphon is implied in the interpretation of this action in C.A. Jones, *A Lost Work by Amalarius of Metz: Interpolations in Salisbury, Cathedral Library, MS. 154*, Henry Bradshaw Society Subsidia 2 (London, 2001), pp. 137–40, 215. See also the comments in C.A. Jones, *Ælfric's Letter to the Monks of Eynsham* (Cambridge, 1998), p. 201 n. 231; Deshusses, ed., *Sacramentaire grégorien*, i, p. 695 (no. 120*).
[59] Jones, *Ælfric's Letter*, pp. 134, 201 n. 231.
[60] Rouen, BN, lat. Y 127; Martène, ed., *De antiquis Ecclesiae ritibus*, i.1.18, *ordo* 13.
[61] J.H. Lynch, '*Spiritale uinculum*: the vocabulary of spiritual kinship in early medieval Europe', in *Religion, Culture, and Society in the Early Middle Ages*, ed. T.F.X. Noble (Kalamazoo, MI, 1987), pp. 181–204, esp. pp. 183–9.

precedes the *Credo*: 'Benedicto fonte et eo tenente infantem a quo suscipiendus est, interroget sacerdos ita'.[62] Forms of this rubric survived well into the Middle Ages and this is often the only indication that it is the godparents who answer for their child, even though they have already done so in the *abrenuntio*. But Darley is different: throughout the rite, the precise role of the godparents is specified; each response, each time they tell the priest the child's name, each time they present or receive it, the rubrics make it clear what the godparents are to do, for example:

Ahsi her þ[æ]s cild[e]s [naman] þonne secge se godfæder þ[æ]s cildes naman þonne cweðe. *Abrenuntias satane.*

þa godfæderas. *Abrenuntio.*

þonne cweþe se preost. *Et omnibus operibus eius.*

Ðonne cweþe se godfæder. *Abrenuntio.*

Ðonne cweðe se preost. git þriddan siþe. *Et omnibus pompis eius.*

Ðonne andswarige se godfæder. *Abrenuntio.*[63]

One could dismiss this as being simply an urge to over-rubricate, and such may be the case, but the result is to make the structure of the rite absolutely clear. In this respect, what Darley most resembles is the early printed manuals of the late Middle Ages. It is an eminently practical document.

Darley's rite is just the sort that could have been used by a 'pastorally minded monk priest' or simply a priest. It has none of the ancient rubrics at the beginning which derive from the scrutinies (as preserved in Jumièges, for example); it always assumes the presence of one child; it runs together all the parts of the rite into one seamless action; and makes absolutely clear for the priest who should do what and when.

A full study of Darley's other rites may tell us a great deal about parochial care in the mid eleventh century. The visitation of the sick, for example, is intriguing for several reasons, but what is of most interest here is its practicality for a parochial situation. The rites for the visitation and unction of the sick in the Lanalet Pontifical, Winchcombe Sacramentary and Oxford, Bodleian Library, Laud Misc. 482 envisage the presence of a priest, deacon (or subdeacon) and other attendants.[64] The Missal of Robert of Jumièges also assumes the presence of several officiants, and the possibility of a bishop being present.[65] In contrast, in the Red Book of Darley there is no mention of anyone apart from the ministering priest.[66]

---

62 Deshusses, ed., *Sacramentaire grégorien*, i, p. 378 (no. 1084).

63 Corpus 422, pp. 388–9, printed in Page, 'Old English liturgical rubrics', p. 153.

64 G.H. Doble, ed., *Pontificale Lanaletense (Bibliothèque de la ville de Rouen A. 27. cat. 368)*, Henry Bradshaw Society 74 (London, 1937), pp. 131–9; Davril, ed., *Winchcombe Sacramentary*, pp. 249–58; Laud Misc. 482, fols 47r–67v. The latter manuscript is discussed by Victoria Thompson in this book.

65 Wilson, ed., *Robert of Jumièges*, pp. 287–95.

66 Corpus 422, pp. 399–423, partially printed in B. Fehr, 'Altenglische Ritualtexte für Krankenbesuch, heilige Ölung und Begräbnis', in *Texte und Forschungen zur englischen Kulturgeschichte: Festgabe für Felix Liebermann*, ed. H. Boehmer *et al.* (Halle, 1921), pp. 20–67, at pp. 46–64 with additions and corrections in Page, 'Old English liturgical rubrics', and T. Graham, 'The Old English liturgical directions in Corpus Christi College, Cambridge, MS 422', *Anglia* 111 (1993), pp. 439–46.

This is exactly the kind of rite, perhaps deliberately simplified, that would be expected in liturgy designed for local use. Darley's *uisitatio infirmorum* also has some relationship to the long version of this rite in Laud Misc. 482 and shares with it some potentially idiosyncratic instructions about the demeanour of the priest, about ensuring that a layman makes some form of will, and about the placing of linen gloves on the dying man's hands and linen socks on his feet.[67]

It also shares something else with Laud Misc. 482: language. The Red Book of Darley contains a substantial amount of Old English, written by the main scribes, including all the rubrics in the services for baptism and visiting the sick.

LITURGY AND THE VERNACULAR

Liturgical manuscripts provide some of the best evidence for the relative status of Latin and Old English, precisely because the language of the liturgy was Latin. When, therefore, we find the vernacular in liturgical books we are looking at the boundaries of acceptable usage. It has become increasingly clear that the vernacular was not considered a poor substitute for Latin in late Anglo-Saxon England.[68] Even vernacular medical remedies and prognostics are at last recognised as having a place in the highest churches in the land.[69] Yet one notion persists.[70] From Bede to Jane Austen, clerics (and especially parish priests) have been mocked and pilloried for their ignorance. When therefore one finds the vernacular in liturgical books, it is usually interpreted as damning testimony of linguistic incompetence.[71]

David Dumville provides the best survey yet published for the history of the vernacular in pre-Conquest English liturgy.[72] One finds occasional vernacular rubrics from the beginning of the tenth century, but it is not until the eleventh century that Old English starts appearing to any extent; by the middle of the century 'the vernacular was nibbling at the margins of the liturgy and was poised to assume a more substantial role in liturgical books'.[73] Dumville's account does

---

[67] For discussion of these parts of the rite, particularly in Laud Misc. 482 see V. Thompson, *Dying and Death in Later Anglo-Saxon England* (Woodbridge, 2004), ch. 3 and her article in this book.

[68] See for example, M. Gretsch, 'Winchester vocabulary and standard Old English: the vernacular in late Anglo-Saxon England', *Bulletin of the John Rylands University Library of Manchester* 83.1 (2001), pp. 41–87: 'It is not that the Anglo-Saxons glossed, translated and composed in English because they were too lazy and too incompetent to apply themselves to a wide-ranging study of Latin texts. What made them do it was rather an astonishing confidence in the potential of the vernacular to be developed as a medium for scholarly and religious discourse on a par with Latin' (p. 87). See also R. Stanton, *The Culture of Translation in Anglo-Saxon England* (Woodbridge, 2002).

[69] See for example, R.M. Liuzza, 'Anglo-Saxon prognostics in context: a survey and handlist of manuscripts', *ASE* 30 (2001), pp. 181–230.

[70] Though David Dumville (*Liturgy and the Ecclesiastical History*, p. 132) and even Christopher Hohler ('Red Book of Darley', pp. 42–4) have already pointed the way.

[71] For (deliberately) provocative examples: *ibid.*; C.E. Hohler, 'Some service books of the later Saxon Church', in *Tenth-Century Studies: Essays in Commemoration of the Millennium of the Council of Winchester and 'Regularis Concordia'*, ed. D. Parsons (London, 1975), pp. 60–83.

[72] Dumville, *Liturgy and the Ecclesiastical History*, pp. 127–32. P. Sims-Williams, *Religion and Literature in Western England, 600–800* (Cambridge, 1990), at pp. 273–302 is also useful.

[73] Dumville, *Liturgy and the Ecclesiastical History*, p. 132.

not quite bring out the range of occasions when Old English was used. What follows is an attempt to do so, albeit an incomplete and preliminary one.[74] My concern here is not with 'para-liturgical' texts such as translations of the gospels or glosses to hymns and psalms, or with private devotions, but with texts for the formal public liturgy. This is a difficult distinction to make; how for example to interpret an Old English prayer added into a pontifical? Or the interlinear gloss added in the late tenth century to the Durham Collectar? Both are omitted here because of the uncertainties about whether they are evidence for material which was used in the public liturgy.[75] This narrow categorisation is useful in so far as it facilitates the identification of material which appears in books most likely to have been intended for use in the liturgy.

Some manuscripts contain glosses to occasional words, for example *huslbox* above *eucharistialis vasculi* and *storcellan* above *thuribuli* in rubrics in the Anderson Pontifical.[76] There are also headings to prayers or rites, distinct from the directions for how to perform them. These are erratic, usually comprising a small number of occasional headings in Old English (not as glosses), whilst the rest of the book retains its Latin rubrics: three of the many liturgical forms added into the margins of Cambridge, Corpus Christi College 41 have Old English rubrics.[77] Also of this kind is the single vernacular rubric among many Latin ones in the surviving part of Worcester, Cathedral Library F. 173.[78] This suggests the same sort of 'casual bilingualism' noted by Susan Kelly in some leases.[79] In one case, a Latin heading *[missa pro amico fideli aut] deuoto* has had, at a slightly later date, an Old English heading placed beside it, *mæssa for wegferendum*. Here it looks as though the scribe's Latin was very bad indeed.[80] Occasionally, the Old English looks rather like an *aide-mémoire* or prompt (perhaps for an acolyte carrying the service book). For example, in the ordination rites in the Sidney Sussex Pontifical, a slightly later hand has added three notes in the margin referring to the symbols of office presented to a door-keeper, lector, and exorcist in the

---

[74] For a full survey, we await the full-length study by Sarah Keefer and Karen Jolly provisionally entitled *Two Languages at Prayer: the Vernacular in the Liturgy of Anglo-Saxon England*.

[75] Though Dumville thinks 'one is bound to suppose that this extraordinary glossing implies that the canons of Chester-le-Street were incapable of understanding their liturgical texts in the original language': Dumville, *Liturgy and the Ecclesiastical History*, p. 130.

[76] London, British Library, Add. 57337, fols 15r–v: Ker, *Catalogue*, p. 575 (no. 416); Rasmussen, *Les Pontificaux du haut Moyen Âge*, pp. 180–1. (There are four examples of this in the manuscript.) For similar examples see Cambridge, Corpus Christi College 44, pp. 114, 138, 140 where four single words are glossed in a contemporary hand: Ker, *Catalogue*, p. 46 (no. 33).

[77] Cambridge, Corpus Christi College 41, pp. 2, 21, 483; R.J.S. Grant, *Cambridge, Corpus Christi College 41: the Loricas and the Missal* (Amsterdam, 1979), pp. 56, 70, 107; Ker, *Catalogue*, pp. 43–5 (no. 32). For a similar example, see A. Corrêa, ed., *The Durham Collectar*, Henry Bradshaw Society 107 (London, 1992), pp. 227–31. In Oxford, Bodleian Library, Bodley 572, f. 40, three Latin blessings added on a blank page have vernacular headings: Ker, *Catalogue*, pp. 376–7 (no. 313).

[78] *Ibid.*, pp. 465–6 (no. 397).

[79] S. Kelly, 'Anglo-Saxon lay society and the written word', in *The Uses of Literacy in Early Medieval Europe*, ed. R. McKitterick (Cambridge, 1990), pp. 36–62, at p. 50.

[80] Oxford, Bodleian Library, Hatton 93, binding leaf: Ker, *Catalogue*, p. 390 (no. 330). The leaf comes from an eleventh-century Anglo-Saxon sacramentary, and there is good reason to think both the text and the addition (which Ker thought to be by 'a somewhat later hand') were made at Worcester. See also: F.E. Warren, 'Hatton MS. 93', *The Academy* 34 (1888), p. 242.

form *her ða rede boc* ('here the reading book').[81] Such marginal prompts are also found, mostly in Latin, throughout the Anderson Pontifical. In the rite for ordaining an acolyte, the Latin marginal prompt is partially glossed in Old English.[82] Anderson also has marginal vernacular prompts in the rite for dedicating a cemetery, some glossing Latin marginalia, others glossing rubrics in the rite itself.[83]

More intriguing, especially in relation to Darley, are the much fuller Old English rubrics supplying the directions for how something should be performed. The early eleventh-century sacramentary known as the 'Missal of Robert of Jumièges' has a rite for the visitation of the sick in which all the rubrics (save only *oratio, item, alia* and the like) are in Old English and in the hand of the main scribe.[84] After a collection of confessional and penitential material, Oxford, Bodleian Library, Laud Misc. 482 has rites for the visitation of the sick and for attending the dying with vernacular rubrics which are unparalleled in their extensiveness and sophistication.[85]

Darley displays many of these features, and the Old English headings are in the same hand as the main scribe.[86] Most of the computistical material is in Old English, which is not uncommon. Within the sacramentary/missal there are two glossed headings which may tell us more about one of its owners than he would have preferred. They are *for þone kyning* and *for flæsce costnunge þæt is idel lust* above headings to masses for a king and for the temptation of the flesh (pp. 133, 171). Are these examples of the aide-mémoire type, marking out masses which the priest used regularly? The marriage blessing has the bilingual rubric 'BLETSUNG. BENEDICTIO', and the final rubric in the burial service is in Old English (pp. 280, 444). In the offices for the common of saints the lections are headed *Ræd* or *Rædinc* though the other rubrics are in Latin (pp. 508–38 *passim*). These are examples of the occasional, casual use of Old English for headings also found in other books. The two vernacular adjurations for the ordeal (discussed below) are accompanied by Old English rubrics (pp. 330–2), though the rest of these rites are in Latin.[87] The most extensive use of Old English is in the manual section: all the rubrics for baptism, short baptism for sick children, blessing water (though the title is in Latin) and visiting the sick are in the vernacular. The rubrics in the offices for Holy Thursday to Easter are also in Old

[81] H.M.J. Banting, ed., *Two Anglo-Saxon Pontificals (the Egbert and Sidney Sussex Pontificals)*, Henry Bradshaw Society 104 (London, 1989), pp. xli–xlii, 157–8; Ker, *Catalogue*, p. 128 (no. 82).

[82] BL, Add. 57337, fol. 39; J.V. Gough, 'Some Old English glosses', *Anglia* 92 (1974), pp. 273–90, at pp. 289–90; P. Bierbaumer, 'Zu J. V. Goughs Ausgabe einiger altenglischer Glossen', *Anglia* 95 (1977), pp. 115–21, at pp. 120–1 (I am grateful to Sarah Larratt Keefer for these two references) and Rasmussen, *Les Pontificaux du haut Moyen Âge*, p. 190.

[83] British Library, Add. 57337, fols 34v–35v; Gough, 'Some Old English glosses', p. 289; Rasmussen, *Les Pontificaux du haut Moyen Âge*, pp. 187–8. In addition to the manuscripts discussed here, see also a comparable instance in Doble, ed., *Pontificale Lanaletense*, p. 121 (with illustration on pl. III).

[84] Wilson, ed., *Robert of Jumièges*, pp. 287–95; Ker, *Catalogue*, p. 449 (no. 377).

[85] See Victoria Thompson's chapter in this volume and her *Dying and Death in Later Anglo-Saxon England*, ch. 3. For an edition of the liturgical texts see Fehr, 'Altenglische Ritualtexte'.

[86] Ker, *Catalogue*, pp. 120–1 (no. 70).

[87] Printed in Liebermann, ed., *Gesetze*, i, p. 415.

English.[88] A different use of the vernacular is made in the burial service, where some of the Latin rubrics in the early part of the rite have vernacular glosses (pp. 429–35).[89] The presence of so much Old English is remarkable, but one must not lose sight of the fact that the rest of this long and complex book is in Latin.

So far, the Old English has been found in the context of liturgical books, but not actually spoken or sung in the liturgy itself. It is often said that the vernacular was never used in the liturgy but this is incorrect; there were certain specific occasions when the manuscripts suggest that Old English was spoken. In Darley's rite for the visitation of the sick, the priest's words are mostly in Latin, but sometimes in the vernacular. After the opening chant and a collect in Latin, he addresses the sick person:

To hwi gecigdest þu, broðor, us hider to þe?[90]

who should reply:

To þam þæt ge me smyrian sceoldon.[91]

The patient must then make confession and if he is in holy orders, the priest again addresses him in Old English:

Aerest þinga ðu most þa digelnysse ðines modes sefan ðurh soþe andetnisse geyppan 7 unðeawa geswicennysse behatan, 7 gif heofona wealdend þines liues dagas lengan wille, medeme dædbote underfon.[92]

If the patient agrees to confess his sins, the priest says:

Uton we nu gemænelice biddan mid eallum mode urne drihten hælend Crist, þæt he þysne his mettruman geneosnige to ðearflicere andetnisse.[93]

The remainder of the rite follows in Latin. In the visitation of the sick in Oxford, BL, Laud Misc. 482, the same parts of the rite are also in Old English together with a final long statement by the patient at the conclusion of his confession.[94] Though both manuscripts provide different directions for what is to be done for a lay man and what for a cleric, neither makes any linguistic distinction and, as we have seen, one of the vernacular statements was specifically for use with an ecclesiastic.

The Old English elements in these two ceremonies are witnesses to the presence of the vernacular in confessional and penitential contexts from at least the

---

[88] Graham, 'Old English liturgical directions in Corpus Christi College, Cambridge, MS 422', pp. 445–6.

[89] Partially printed in Fehr, 'Altenglische Ritualtexte', pp. 65–7.

[90] 'Why did you summon us here to you, brother?': Corpus 422, pp. 400–1. The text is printed in Fehr, 'Altenglische Ritualtexte', pp. 49–51, with minor corrections by Graham, 'Old English liturgical directions in Corpus Christi College, Cambridge, MS 422', p. 444.

[91] 'In order that you might anoint me'.

[92] 'First of all, you must reveal the secrets of your mind's understanding through true confession and promise abstinence from vices, and if the ruler of heaven desire to lengthen the days of your life, undertake appropriate penance'.

[93] 'Let us now pray all together with whole heart to our Lord Saviour Christ, that he visit this his sick person with needful confession'.

[94] Laud Misc. 482, fols 50–1, 54. This prayer is discussed by Victoria Thompson in her chapter in this book.

mid tenth century. As Dumville notes, this is where Old English is most frequently found: 'in the area of penitential discipline for the laity where it was necessary for the unlatinate (both laity and, no doubt in part, clergy) to participate more fully in spoken rather than merely physical aspects of the liturgy'.[95] Other versions of the visitation omit such directions, so for example Jumièges simply says at this point: 'siððan fra þan untruman beo his andytnys gecyd. 7 æfter þon letania'.[96] The spoken vernacular elements in Darley and Laud 482 are present because they incorporate directions for confession (drawn from English vernacular traditions) at the appropriate position.[97]

Confession was not the only occasion when the vernacular could be used. At the coronation of either Edward the Martyr (975) or Æthelred (979) at Kingston, the coronation oath was read out by the king in Old English, and the text of it then placed on the altar. Following the oath, Dunstan, archbishop of Canterbury spoke, again in the vernacular, about the responsibilities of the king and urged him to keep his promises. This at least is the evidence provided by the oath found in two manuscripts.[98] Whether this was an innovation, and whether the tradition of vernacular oath-swearing continued is not known, but it is salutary to note that no hint of these vernacular elements of the rite can be found in the relevant *ordines*, which suggests the practice may have been more common than the surviving evidence indicates. Several manuscripts contain vernacular adjurations for the ordeals, including two for cold water at the end of the rite in Darley.[99] There is also one Old English excommunication formula preserved in a mid twelfth-century manuscript. It follows a Latin excommunication text which it closely parallels, though it is not an exact translation. In her discussion, Elaine Treharne was understandably cautious about suggesting that it would have been used in the liturgy, but in the context of the other evidence presented here, this looks more plausible.[100] The common characteristic of the instances where the

---

[95] Dumville, *Liturgy and the Ecclesiastical History*, pp. 131–2. See also A.J. Frantzen, *The Literature of Penance in Anglo-Saxon England* (New Brunswick, NJ, 1983), chs 5 and 6, and Sarah Hamilton's article in this volume.

[96] 'Then let his confession be declared by the sick man, and then afterwards a litany [should be sung]': Wilson, ed., *Robert of Jumièges*, p. 287 (translation p. lxxi).

[97] For the penitential material see A.J. Frantzen, 'The tradition of penitentials in Anglo-Saxon England', *ASE* 11 (1983), pp. 23–56; *idem, Literature of Penance.*

[98] BL, Cotton Cleopatra B. xiii and BL, Cotton Vitellius A. vii. The text of the former is printed in W. Stubbs, ed., *Memorials of Saint Dunstan Archbishop of Canterbury*, Rolls Series (London, 1874), pp. 355–7. For discussion see J.L. Nelson, 'Ritual and reality in the early medieval *Ordines*', *Studies in Church History* 11 (1975), pp. 41–51, repr. in her *Politics and Ritual in Early Medieval Europe* (London, 1986), pp. 329–39, at pp. 336–8 and P.E. Schramm, *A History of the English Coronation*, trans. L.G. Wickham Legg (Oxford, 1937), pp. 179–85.

[99] Corpus 422, pp. 330–2; Liebermann, ed., *Gesetze*, i, pp. 409–15; Keefer, 'Manuals', pp. 108–9; *eadem*, '*Ut in omnibus honorificetur Deus*: the *corsnæd* ordeal in Anglo-Saxon England', in *The Community, the Family and the Saint: Patterns of Power in Early Medieval Europe*, ed. J. Hill and M. Swan, International Medieval Research 4 (Turnhout, 1998), pp. 237–64. Keefer notes that the adjuration for the ordeal by bread and cheese 'which is intended for the clergy only, is invariably found in Latin while other ordeal adjurations for the laity frequently appear in Old English' (*ibid.*, p. 247 n. 49).

[100] Cambridge, Corpus Christi College 303, p. 339; E.M. Treharne, 'A unique Old English formula for excommunication from Cambridge, Corpus Christi College 303', *ASE* 24 (1995), pp. 185–211. For excommunication more generally, see Sarah Hamilton, 'Remedies for "great transgressions" ', below.

vernacular is found in a liturgical context is that they are direct addresses by a priest to an individual (not necessarily a layman) in circumstances in which it is critical that he understands what is happening.[101] In the case of the coronation, they were direct addresses by Dunstan to the king and by the king to his people.

What conclusions can be drawn? On the one hand, Old English was not considered out of place even in the grandest liturgical books, if the original owner of the Missal of Robert of Jumièges was content with the book written for him.[102] The pages of a liturgical manuscript did not need to be kept untainted by the vernacular, which was sometimes used casually in place of Latin. On the other hand, the presence of Old English in the liturgy itself was restricted to a few specific contexts suggesting that each language was considered to have a certain range of functions. At times one could choose which was most appropriate, especially when comprehension was vital for the well-being of the soul.

It seems to me that the problem with the argument that Old English in liturgical texts implies their users were poor Latinists is that it relies on the assumption that the vernacular was present because they *needed* it. A better explanation for unsystematic translation or 'casual bilingualism' is that the vernacular was simply a perfectly normal language for writing as well as speech. Victoria Thompson's studies of the vernacular rubrics for the visitation of the sick and for attending the dying in Laud Misc. 482 have demonstrated that Old English rubrics (and occasionally Old English in the liturgy) were not the preserve of Byrhtferth's 'backwoods' priests.[103] And we can be as sure as we can of anything that Jumièges's first owner had no problems with his Latin. One thinks here of the point made by Roy Liuzza about Ælfric railing against prognostics, whilst Ælfwine, abbot of New Minster, Winchester had plenty of them in his own prayerbook.[104] For Ælfric, Wulfstan and Æthelwold (as Bede before them), a sound knowledge of Latin was the ideal but it is likely that for most men, even those with good Latin, their standard language was Old English. By the eleventh century, translation of texts of all kinds was commonplace in England and it is worth remembering that, though rare, translation of the liturgy was not entirely unknown in the early and central Middle Ages.[105]

It is difficult to assess how much Latin was known by the man for whom Darley was made. As pre-Vatican II generations know, it is possible to have a familiarity with Latin sufficient to follow various masses and parts of the office without actually being able to comprehend long passages of prose. The partial

---

[101] Given that excommunication and ordeal are closely associated with legal procedures, I also wonder whether this may reflect legal procedure and, in the case of the coronation, traditions associated with swearing oaths.

[102] A point made by Hohler, 'Red Book of Darley', p. 44.

[103] See n. 85.

[104] Liuzza, 'Anglo-Saxon prognostics in context', pp. 196–200.

[105] In 880 Methodius received papal approval for celebration of the liturgy in Slavonic and the Cathars in the Languedoc also used a vernacular liturgy; J. Shepard, 'Slavs and Bulgars', in *The New Cambridge Medieval History, ii, c.700–c.900*, ed. R. McKitterick (Cambridge, 1995), pp. 228–48, esp. pp. 242–5; B. Hamilton, 'Wisdom from the East: the reception by the Cathars of Eastern dualist texts', in *Heresy and Literacy, 1000–1530*, ed. P. Biller and A. Hudson (Cambridge, 1994), pp. 38–60. See also Sarah Hamilton's article in this volume, n. 19.

Old English gloss to the rubrics in the burial service may suggest that in this case the book's owner did need the vernacular, but other Latin texts were transmitted with vernacular glosses. It is possible that this could also be the case here.[106] What the evidence indicates is that by the eleventh century Old English was a perfectly respectable language for the rubrics of the liturgy and even on occasion for the liturgy itself. The extant manuscripts do not suggest that Old English was always employed specifically because a certain priest would not be able to decipher the Latin. In their interpretation of the status of Old English historians seem to have been influenced by anti-clerical rhetoric as well as by the idealism of writers like Ælfric, who felt the need to apologise for the act of translation even while they performed on such a grand scale.

Nevertheless, the rites which have the most extensive Old English passages are those for occasional offices not reserved for bishops – the pastoral duties that were the main responsibility of the priest. The possibility must therefore be considered that such cases are indicative of poor latinity. Most of the surviving manuscripts containing lengthy rubrics (where Old English is most often found) are pontificals and benedictionals for bishops or the sacramentaries of major monasteries and cathedrals. One would expect such books to be conservative and traditional in their use of language. If more books for priests like Darley and Laud Misc. 482 survived, their Old English would probably look less out of place.

One potential explanation for the presence of Old English in these rites turns on what Ælfric would have made of this, especially if Darley was produced at Sherborne, only ten miles from Cerne Abbas and for whose bishop he wrote the first of his Pastoral Letters. Ælfric was pre-eminently interested in the education and training of the clergy in their duties and in the liturgy they had to perform. He produced vernacular preaching material, a grammar, glossary and colloquy, pastoral letters for the instruction of priests, and perhaps a consuetudinary for secular clergy.[107] The only element missing for a truly comprehensive reform is accessible, authoritative texts of the liturgy itself. Some of Ælfric's homilies discuss liturgical texts in some detail; the step-by-step explication of infant baptism in the second series Epiphany homily is a prime example.[108] This suggests a detailed and keen interest in the liturgy, and Ælfric may well have fostered the production of rites for pastoral care with clear, explicit rubrics in Old English which explained how they should be performed. The late eighth-century Irish Stowe Missal, with its occasional Old Irish rubrics for baptism, and the early tenth-century Durham collectar show that this insular tradition did not begin with the second generation of reformers. Yet it is only in the second quarter of the eleventh century that Old English is found in liturgical contexts to any degree. Might we see in the Red Book of Darley remnants of a liturgical

---

[106] For an example: M. Gretsch, 'The Roman Psalter, its Old English glosses and the English Benedictine Reform', in *The Liturgy of the Late Anglo-Saxon Church*, ed. H. Gittos and M.B. Bedingfield, Henry Bradshaw Society Subsidia (London, 2005), pp. 13–28.

[107] See n.14 above and Jonathan Wilcox's chapter in this volume.

[108] M. Godden, ed., *Ælfric's Catholic Homilies: the Second Series*, EETS ss 5 (Oxford, 1979), no. 3 (esp. pp. 27–8).

counterpart to the corpus of vernacular homilies?[109] The 'English books' in which Ælfric 'saw and heard much error' may have included service-books as well as homiliaries.[110] One argument against this would be the occasions when Darley's baptismal *ordo* includes some of the very practices that Ælfric had been railing about sixty years before.

It may be simpler to see the presence of the vernacular in the liturgy, unparalleled in western Europe at that date, as a natural consequence of the long-standing relationship between the Church and the vernacular in England. Bede, Alfred, Æthelwold and Ælfric all thought it more important that God's word be understood than that it should be understood in Latin, however desirable that was: 'It certainly cannot matter by what language a man is acquired and drawn to the true faith, as long only as he comes to God'.[111] In this context, Darley and Laud Misc. 482 look almost inevitable, and the pontificals and benedictionals deliberately conservative. Rather than interpreting the presence of the vernacular in the liturgy as testament to the lack of latinity amongst the clergy, it may be better to see it as evidence for the high status accorded to Old English in the late pre-Conquest period.

There is very little evidence for the liturgy of parish churches in late Anglo-Saxon England, though Darley brings us as close to it as we may ever get. A consideration of the liturgy of parish churches forces one to look again at familiar questions: who staffed local churches; were they, and if so where were they, educated; where did they get their knowledge of the liturgy from, and how was it transmitted? This preliminary survey of the presence of the vernacular in liturgical contexts warns that we should not assume that the amount of Old English in Darley is necessarily indicative of an incompetent, ignorant priesthood. But it might just hint at how the priest who served the chapel at Raunds, and so many others like him, was able to perform the liturgy in the eleventh century.

---

[109] This was at least implied as long ago as 1972, though has been little noticed: Hohler, 'Red Book of Darley'.

[110] 'ac for ðan ðe ic geseah 7 gehyrde mycel gedwyld on manegum engliscum bocum': P. Clemoes, ed., *Ælfric's Catholic Homilies: the First Series*, EETS ss 17 (Oxford, 1997), p. 174.

[111] 'Wel mæg dug[an hit naht] mid hwylcan gereorde mon sy gestryned 7 to þan soþan geleafan gewæmed, butan þæt an sy þæt he Gode gegange': 'King Edgar's Establishment of Monasteries', *Councils and Synods*, i, pp. 151–2.

5

Remedies for 'Great Transgressions': Penance and Excommunication in Late Anglo-Saxon England

Sarah Hamilton

The act of penance, in Burchard of Worms' words, both corrects the bodies of sinful men, and acts as medicine for their souls.[1] The tension between its disciplinary and curative aspects will be explored in this two-part study, focusing firstly on the attempts by the higher clergy in the late Anglo-Saxon Church to ensure that devotional penance played a regular part in the life of every Christian, and secondly on the provisions made for those contumacious sinners who refused to come to penance.

PENANCE

Penance is a vague term, and what is meant by *paenitentia* is not always clear. The clergy of late Anglo-Saxon England knew and repeated the penitential dichotomy first articulated by the early ninth-century Carolingian reformers: in Ælfric's words 'secret sins shall be expiated secretly, and open openly, that those may be edified by his repentance who had previously been seduced by his sins'.[2] Secret

---

[1] Burchard describes book xix, *De poenitentia*, of his *Decretum* as 'the Corrector and the Medicus since it contains ample correction for bodies and medicines for souls' ('Liber hic Corrector uocatur et Medicus, quia correctiones corporum et animarum medicinas plene continet'): *PL* 140, col. 949.

[2] 'Þa diglan gyltas man sceal digelice betan, and ða openan openlice, þaet ða ær wæron þurh his mandæda geæwiscode': B. Thorpe, ed., *The Homilies of the Anglo-Saxon Church: the First Part Containing the 'Sermones Catholici' or Homilies of Ælfric*, 2 vols (London, 1844–6), i, pp. 498–9 (Sermon for the seventeenth Sunday after Pentecost). That the dichotomy was possibly known to Wulfstan may be inferred from its inclusion in a collection of penitential canons found in one manuscript of his canon law collection, Cambridge, Corpus Christi College 190 (s. xi[1], Worcester hand?, provenance: Exeter s. xi[2]), p. 238: 'Qui publice peccauerit arguatur et publica paenitentia purgabitur. Et si hoc occulte fecerit occulte ad confessionem uenerit, occulte ei penitentia imponatur', B. Fehr, ed., *Die Hirtenbriefe Ælfrics in altenglischer und lateinischer Fassung*, Bibliothek der angelsächsischen Prosa 9 (Hamburg, 1914), p. 243. On the manuscript see: N.R. Ker, *Catalogue of Manuscripts Containing Anglo-Saxon* (Oxford, 1990), no. 45, pp. 70–3; H. Sauer, 'Zur Überlieferung und Anlage von Erzbischof Wulfstans "Handbuch" ', *Deutsches Archiv für Erforschung des Mittelalters* 36 (1980), pp. 341–84 at p. 383, where he ascribes it to block III; C.A. Jones, 'Two composite texts from Archbishop Wulfstan's "Commonplace Book": the *De ecclesiastica consuetudine* and the *Institutio beati Amalarii de*

penance could be administered by any priest at any time, as long as he followed the guidance on tariffs for individual sins set out in a penitential, but public penance remained an episcopal prerogative; entry into public penance was restricted to a public service on Ash Wednesday, in which the penitent was expelled, physically and metaphorically, from the Church, whilst on Maundy Thursday he was reconciled with and re-entered the Church.[3] This division was never in practice as straightforward as the Carolingian legislation suggested it should be, but nevertheless there has been a tendency amongst historians of penance, both for Anglo-Saxon England and the Continent, to concentrate on 'secret' penance and ignore the evidence for its public counterpart.[4] This bias is in large part a consequence of the confessional debates following the Reformation, when a key issue of the Protestant critique was the absence of Biblical authority for the medieval penitential system. In the sixteenth century debate focused on auricular confession and has continued to do so ever since.[5]

Encouraging frequent penance

In the case of England this bias is especially understandable in the light of the wealth of material.[6] The survival of a substantial body of evidence in the form of penitentials and confessional rites, in both Latin and Old English, reflects the considerable effort made by the higher clergy of the late Anglo-Saxon Church to

---

ecclesiasticis officiis', *ASE* 27 (1998), pp. 233–71 at p. 236. Cyrille Vogel articulated the Carolingian dichotomy in *Le pécheur et la pénitence au moyen âge* (Paris, 1969), pp. 24–7; this distinction is first found in the *Paenitentiale Remense* (c. 800), iv.50–1: 'Si publice peccauerint, publice peniteant. Si occulte peccauerint, occulte peniteant', F. Asbach, ed., *Das Poenitentiale Remense und der sogen. Excarpsus Cummeani: Überlieferung, Quellen und Entwicklung zweiter kontinentaler Bussbücher aus der 1. Hälfte des 8. Jahrhunderts* (Regensburg, 1975), p. 30; it was repeated by the Council of Rheims (813): 'Ut discretio seruanda sit inter paenitentes qui publice et qui absconce paenitere debent', *MGH Legum* 3, *Concilia aevi Karolini*, i, ed. A. Werminghoff (Hanover-Leipzig, 1906), i, no. 35, c. 31, p. 256.

3   On the rituals of public penance see C. Vogel, 'Les rites de la pénitence publique aux Xe et XIe siècles', *Mélanges René Crozet* (Poitiers, 1966), pp. 137–44, reprinted *idem, En rémission des péchés. Recherches sur les systèmes pénitentiels dans l'Eglise latine*, ed. A. Faivre (Aldershot and Brookfield, Vermont, 1994), no. VIII; S. Hamilton, *The Practice of Penance, 900–1050* (London, 2001), pp. 108–21, 150–66.

4   For example, H.C. Lea, *A History of Auricular Confession and Indulgences in the Latin Church* (London, 1896); O.D. Watkins, *A History of Penance* (London, 1920); T.P. Oakley, *English Penitential Discipline and Anglo-Saxon Law in their Joint Influence* (New York, 1923); J.T. McNeill and H.M. Gamer, ed., *Medieval Handbooks of Penance* (New York, 1938); R. Mortimer, *The Origins of Private Penance in the Western Church* (Oxford, 1939); B. Poschmann, *Penance and the Anointing of the Sick* (Freiburg-London, 1964) (trans. by F. Courtney of *Busse und letzte Ölung* (Freiburg, 1951)); Vogel, *Le pécheur*; A.J. Frantzen, *The Literature of Penance in Anglo-Saxon England* (New Brunswick, NJ, 1983). There are two recent exceptions for continental penance: M.C. Mansfield, *The Humiliation of Sinners: Public Penance in Thirteenth-Century France* (Ithaca and London, 1995); M. de Jong, 'Power and humility in Carolingian society: the public penance of Louis the Pious', *EME* 1 (1992), pp. 29–52; *eadem*, 'What was public about public penance? Paenitentia publica and justice in the Carolingian world', in *La Giustizia nell'alto medioevo (secoli IX–XI)*, Settimane di studio del centro italiano di studi sull'alto medioevo 44, (1997), pp. 863–902.

5   A. Murray, 'Confession before 1215', *Transactions of the Royal Historical Society*, sixth series 3 (1993), pp. 51–81; A.T. Thayer, *Penitence, Preaching and the Coming of the Reformation* (Aldershot, 2002); Hamilton, *Practice*, pp. 9–13.

6   For survey and analysis: Frantzen, *Literature of Penance*.

encourage the practice of penance and confession amongst all Christians.[7] The pastoral literature of late Anglo-Saxon England includes several exhortations by the higher clergy to the lower clergy to encourage the widespread practice of penance amongst the laity. According to the tenth-century *Ecclesiastical Institutes*, in the week preceding the beginning of Lent the priest should call his flock together, settle all their quarrels and award penances to those who confess their sins.[8] Like the rest of this collection, this instruction was taken directly from Theodulf bishop of Orléans' highly influential early ninth-century *capitula*.[9] Members of the laity were also encouraged to 'form the habit of frequent confession' and prepare themselves 'often and frequently' to receive communion.[10] Not only should priests encourage the laity to make regular or annual confession, they should, according to Wulfstan's *Canons of Edgar* (1005 x 1008), encourage the dying to make a last confession.[11] These sorts of prescriptions, recorded in the legislation from the mid tenth century onwards, reaching a climax under Archbishop Wulfstan, co-exist with the recording at the same time of penitentials, confessional rites, prayers and other instructions in both Latin and Old English. A substantial body of these texts survives, leading their most recent historian, Allen Frantzen, to suggest they reflect the attempts by the higher clergy of the late Anglo-Saxon period to give some substance to their aspirations for a more universal penance amongst both the clergy and the laity.[12] For the world these authors aspired to was one in which penance played a regular part in lay lives.

Their aspirations are outlined in various vernacular instructions, to both the laity and clergy, on how they should observe the Lenten penance. One text in a mid eleventh-century pastoral collection (London, British Library, Cotton Tiberius A. iii) admonishes its audience to 'repent, confess and fast in Lent in order to atone for misdeeds committed during the year'.[13] Collective fasting was combined with individual penance and confession in an act whose significance was as much devotional as disciplinary. This particular text makes provision for

---

[7] The early eleventh-century promotion of penance has traditionally been placed in a political context, as part of an attempt by the early eleventh-century reformers to reform the Church in order to alleviate the external attacks which they viewed as God's punishment for their sins, but the interest in penance can be traced back to the tenth century: S. Keynes, *The Diplomas of King Æthelred 'the Unready': a Study in their Use as Historical Evidence* (Cambridge, 1980), pp. 217–19; P. Wormald, *The Making of English Law: King Alfred to the Twelfth Century*, i: *Legislation and its Limits* (Oxford, 1999), pp. 331–2, 455.

[8] H. Sauer, ed., *Theodulfi Capitula in England: Die altenglischen Übersetzungen zusammen mit dem lateinischen Text*, Münchener Universitäts-Schriften. Institut für englische Philologie. Texte und Untersuchungen zur englischen Philologie 8 (Munich, 1978), pp. 376–7, c. 36.

[9] Theodulf I, c. 36, *MGH Capitula episcoporum*, i, ed. P. Brommer (Hanover, 1984), pp. 133–4.

[10] V Æthelred, c. 22, in *Councils and Synods*, i, p. 355. On the connection between communion and confession see J. Avril, 'Remarques sur un aspect de la vie paroissale: la pratique de la confession et la communion du Xe au XIVe siècle', in *L'Encadrement religieux des fidèles au moyen-âge et jusqu'au Concile de Trente: la paroisse – le clergé – la pastorale – la dévotion: actes du 109e congrès national des sociétés savantes. Dijon 1984: section d'histoire médiévale et de philologie* (Paris, 1985), i, pp. 349–50; R. Meens, 'The frequency and nature of early medieval penance', in *Handling Sin: Confession in the Middle Ages*, ed. P. Biller and A.J. Minnis (York, 1998), pp. 37–8.

[11] *Canons of Edgar*, c. 68, in *Councils and Synods*, i, pp. 335–6.

[12] Frantzen, *Literature of Penance*.

[13] *Ibid.*, p. 164. The text is edited by H. Sauer, 'Zwei spätaltenglische Beichtermahnungen aus Hs. Cotton Tiberius A. iii', *Anglia* 98 (1980), pp. 1–33 at pp. 21–3.

two different audiences as it includes endings in the first person plural, suggesting a collective clerical audience joined together in an act of devotional atonement, and a set in the second person plural, which suggests disciplinary instruction to a lay audience. But too much should not be made of this difference, for the collusive nature of Lenten penance was made clear in the words attributed to the priest in the vernacular instructions added to a pontifical at Salisbury (after the see's transfer there from Sherborne in 1075) in the late eleventh century: 'And do not think that I am telling you to do things that I have not done and do not do myself. That may be. I may do worse than you. But do as I teach you and not as I do . . . May God grant us both, if it be His will, to receive the Holy Sacrament at Easter with clean body and soul.'[14] The use of the second person singular implies one-to-one instruction of a layman by a priest, but the priest acknowledges his own sinfulness and need to atone in terms which echo a prayer found in many rites for confession from the ninth century onwards in which the priest prepares to hear confession by asking for God's mercy on his own sinfulness.[15] Another text recorded in a different hand, also late eleventh-century, in the same manuscript ends, after a series of detailed instructions on how the congregation should observe the Lenten fast: 'This is the time when we should go to our spiritual teachers and confess our sins and do as they direct us. I earnestly beseech anyone in this congregation who knows he has done wrong to go to his confessor and tell him and ask for his intercession and prayers . . . Fasting is nothing without confession, confession nothing without repentance, and repentance nothing without abstention from sin. If anyone cannot bring himself to go to one teacher let him go to another.'[16] This provision, encouraging the penitent to go elsewhere to confess if he cannot face his own priest, ensures that the emphasis of the text is on voluntary devotional confession rather than disciplinary penance.[17] It is not about the priest, or even perhaps the bishop – for the same scribe also copied into this manuscript a confession prayer in Old English which could only be spoken by a bishop – asserting his right of jurisdiction over particular forms of behaviour and particular rites, but rather about confession as part of the spiritual preparations, during Lent, for Easter.[18]

---

[14] N.R. Ker, 'Three Old English texts in a Salisbury Pontifical, Cotton Tiberius C.i', in *The Anglo-Saxons: Studies in Some Aspects of their History and Culture Presented to Bruce Dickins*, ed. P. Clemoes (London, 1959), pp. 262–79 at p. 275. On the general context to these additions see T. Webber, *Scribes and Scholars at Salisbury Cathedral c. 1075–c. 1125* (Oxford, 1992).

[15] For example, see the prayer beginning 'Domine deus omnipotens, propitius esto mihi peccatori' to be said by the priest before hearing the penitent's confession included in both the *ordo* at the beginning of book vi of Halitgar's penitential and in the *ordo* for penance 'in the usual way' ('qualiter sacerdotes suscipere debeant poenitentes more solito') in the Romano-German Pontifical: H.J. Schmitz, ed., *Die Bussbücher und die Bussdisciplin der Kirche* (Mainz, 1883), p. 472; C. Vogel and R. Elze, ed., *Le Pontifical romano-germanique du dixième siècle*, 3 vols (Vatican City, 1963–72), ii, cxxxvi. 2–3, p. 234. On the role of the priest in confession see Victoria Thompson's article in this volume

[16] Ker, 'Three Old English texts', pp. 277–9.

[17] This provision also casts an interesting sidelight on the lack of privacy within small communities, and a reluctance on the part of penitents to visit certain priests, perhaps because they knew too much or were too involved in the life of that community to act as a neutral observer, although Allen Frantzen views such provisions as ensuring that members of the laity could provide a check on the behaviour and honesty of corrupt priests: *Literature of Penance*, p. 173.

[18] This prayer is edited by H. Logeman, 'Anglo-Saxonica Minora', *Anglia* 11 (1889), pp. 102–3; M.

Administering frequent penance

In Anglo-Saxon England, as in the post-Carolingian Frankish kingdoms, churchmen made provision for hearing confessions in the vernacular.[19] Old English texts of penitentials, rites for administering confession, and confession prayers all survive from the late tenth and eleventh centuries.[20] Three vernacular texts of penitentials have been identified: the *Scrift boc* (also known as the *Confessional*), the *Penitential* and the 'late Old English Handbook for the use of a confessor'.[21] The earliest is the first, the *Scrift boc*, a tenth-century compilation, whose principal source is the Penitential of Theodore; it shares a common manuscript tradition with the *Penitential*, a tenth-century abbreviated version of books III–V of Halitgar of Cambrai's early ninth-century Frankish collection, to which was added part of the *Scrift boc* as a fourth book.[22] Both the *Scrift boc* and the *Penitential* survive in three eleventh-century manuscripts with Worcester connections: Cambridge, Corpus Christi College 190, Oxford, Bodleian Library, Junius 121 and Oxford, Bodleian Library, Laud Miscellaneous 482.[23] The most recent of the three is the so-called 'Handbook for use of a confessor' which dates from the late tenth or early eleventh centuries and which enjoys a different manuscript tradition. Unlike the two earlier texts, it is not just grounded in the ninth-century Frankish material, but derived in large part from the *Penitential*; it

---

Förster identified the fact that it also occurs in Cambridge, Corpus Christi College 190: 'Zur Liturgik der angelsächsischen Kirche', *Anglia* 66 (1942), pp. 1–51 at pp. 12–20; on the script see Ker, 'Three Old English texts', p. 272.

[19] For Old High German texts of confession prayers recorded in early medieval manuscripts see E. von Steinmeyer, ed., *Die kleineren althochdeutschen Sprachdenkmäler* (Berlin, 1916), pp. 309–61. Two tenth-century rites for penance 'in the usual way' (i.e. non-public penance) recorded in German manuscripts refer to vernacular confession: that in the mid tenth-century Romano-German Pontifical instructs the penitent 'Deinde fiat confessio peccatorum rusticis uerbis': Vogel and Elze ed., *Le Pontifical romano-germanique*, ii, cxxxvi.23, p. 242; that in the Fulda Sacramentary, c. 980, includes the text of a vernacular confession prayer: G. Richter and A. Schönfelder, ed., *Sacramentarium Fuldense saeculi X: Cod. Theol. 231 der K. Universitätsbibliothek zu Göttingen* (Fulda, 1912), repr. Henry Bradshaw Society 101 (1972–7), p. 282, which is also found in a later Fulda manuscript, Ms Vat. lat. 3548 (c. 1015–25); on the Fulda tradition see the discussion and notes in Hamilton, *Practice*, pp. 144–5, 147–8. A late eleventh- or early twelfth-century South Italian manuscript includes a confession prayer in Old Italian: Rome, Biblioteca Vallicelliana, Cod. B. 63, fol. 231v: P. Pirri, ed., *L'abbazia di Sant'Eutizio in Val Castoriana presso Norcia e le chiese dipendenti*, Studia anselmiana 45 (Rome, 1960), p. 47.

[20] For a listing see R. Frank and A. Cameron, ed., *A Plan for a Dictionary of Old English* (Toronto, 1973), no. 11, pp. 123–6. For a detailed consideration of the use of the vernacular in the liturgy see Helen Gittos' essay, above.

[21] A.J. Frantzen, 'The tradition of penitentials in Anglo-Saxon England', *ASE* 11 (1982), pp. 23–56; *idem, Literature of Penance*, pp. 122–50.

[22] C. Vogel, revised by A.J. Frantzen, *Les 'Libri paenitentiales'*, Typologie du moyen âge occidental 27 (Turnhout, 1985), pp. 39–40. The *Confessional* is edited by R. Spindler, *Das altenglishe Bussbuch* (Leipzig, 1934); the *Penitential* is edited by J. Raith, *Die altenglische Version des Halitgar'schen Bussbuches*, Bibliothek der angelsächsichen Prosa 13, repr. (Darmstadt, 1964).

[23] Frantzen, 'The tradition of penitentials', pp. 40–5; *idem, Literature of Penance*, pp. 133–9. For the Worcester connection of Cambridge, Corpus Christi College 190 see D. Dumville, *English Caroline Script and Monastic History: Studies in Benedictinism, A.D. 950–1030*, (Woodbridge, 1993), p. 52 n. 228; on the Worcester provenance of Bodleian Library, Laud Misc. 482 (s. xi^med): *idem, Liturgy and the Ecclesiastical History of Late Anglo-Saxon England* (Woodbridge, 1992), pp. 131, 133, and Ker, *Catalogue*, no. 343, pp. 419–22; on the Worcester script of Oxford, Bodleian Library, Junius 121 see *ibid.* no. 338, pp. 412–18.

is, however, more independent of its sources than the other two, and begins with an *ordo confessionis* in Latin.[24] The 'Handbook' is also the shortest of the three vernacular penitentials; as well as the rite for the administration of confession it includes instructions as to whom the priest should administer penance, especially to the sick and 'men of substance' who could afford to commute their penance, and, as Frantzen has noted, in tariffs borrowed from the *Penitential* which made provision for different penances according to the rank of the sinner, bishops are omitted from the list, suggesting the text was intended for use by a priest, rather than a bishop, in the delivery of pastoral care to his flock.[25] The 'Handbook' is briefer and less comprehensive in its textual coverage than the other two texts, confirmation perhaps that it was intended for use by a primary deliverer of pastoral care rather than as a reference text.

Although the text of the 'Handbook' is, perhaps, the most practical of the three vernacular penitentials, the evidence from individual manuscripts suggests that specific attempts were made to provide textual support for the exhortations to administer frequent confession prescribed by the higher clergy in the laws. Oxford, Bodleian Library, Laud Miscellaneous 482, for example, is an eleventh-century handbook containing a mixture of legal and liturgical texts in Old English and Latin, including the two longer, more comprehensive and episcopal vernac-ular penitentials, the *Scrift boc* and the *Penitential*, as well as several parts of the 'Handbook', instructions on how to hear confession and give penance, together with Latin rites for the sick and the dying in which the introductions and rubrics are in Old English.[26] These are exactly the sort of texts a priest seeking to fulfil Wulfstan's instructions that every priest should 'shrive and impose penance on him who confesses to him and also help to make atonement and give the sacra-ment to sick men when they have need of it, and also anoint them if they ask for it, and after the death readily see to the funeral' would need.[27] The codex's dimen-sions support this conclusion: it is a narrow, thin book, 202 x 91 mm, sixty-seven folios in length, and therefore eminently portable.[28] It was produced at Worcester in the second half of the eleventh century.[29] Whilst combinations of penitential and canon law with liturgy are often classified as episcopal handbooks, this manuscript was probably made, as Helmut Gneuss suggests, for the use of a priest

[24] Frantzen, 'The tradition of penitentials', pp. 45–9; *idem*, *Literature of Penance*, pp. 139–41; on its manuscript history see R. Fowler, ed., 'A late Old English handbook for the use of a confessor', *Anglia* 83 (1965), pp. 1–34 at pp. 1–4. The Latin *ordo* was based on that in the Enlarged Rule of Chrodegang: Förster, 'Zur Liturgik', pp. 22–3.

[25] Frantzen, *Literature of Penance*, pp. 139–40; Fowler, 'Old English Handbook', pp. 32–4.

[26] Ker, *Catalogue*, no. 343, pp. 419–22; fols 46–7 (art. 17): directions for a confessor; fols 47–68v (art. 18): rites for the sick and dying in Latin with introduction and rubrics in Old English. For a more detailed consideration of this manuscript see Thompson in this volume.

[27] *Canons of Edgar*, c. 68, in *Councils and Synods*, i, pp. 335–6.

[28] S.J.P. Van Dijk and J. Hazelden Walker suggest a height of 20 cm as the boundary between portable and non-portable: *The Origins of the Modern Roman Liturgy*, (Westminster, MD, 1960), p. 32.

[29] Ker, *Catalogue*, no. 343, pp. 419–22. Whilst Ker's attribution to Worcester was somewhat tentative, more recently Dumville has suggested a Worcester provenance for it, see n. 23 above, as has Richard Gameson in 'Book production at Worcester in the tenth and eleventh centuries', in *St Oswald of Worcester: Life and Influence*, ed. N. Brooks and C. Cubitt (London and New York, 1996), pp. 194–243 at p. 241.

in the delivery of his pastoral services.[30] Here it is perhaps worth noting that this combination of confessional with death rites is also found on the Continent, where two such collections have been associated respectively with the late ninth-century monastic community at Lorsch and an early eleventh-century community of canons in Rome.[31] In both cases it has been suggested that these collections were made for the regular clergy to support their work in administering pastoral care to the laity outside their house. As Victoria Thompson has suggested for Laud Miscellaneous 482, such collections were intended not so much as tools for the direct ministry, as to educate the clergy in the significance of such rites.[32] The Red Book of Darley is another text apparently made for use by a priest, which contains Old English rubrics to the Latin pastoral rites for baptism, as well as the visitation of the sick.[33] By the sixteenth century the manuscript was at Darley Dale in Derbyshire, but current opinion suggests it was probably made at Sherborne in the mid eleventh century, reaching Derbyshire later, perhaps as early as the twelfth century.[34] The Red Book is a relatively humble book – Christopher Hohler suggested it was for the use of 'a good, pastorally minded, monk priest . . . to take with him round the villages' – but vernacular rubrics for the visitation of the sick were also included in the prestigious service book, the Missal of Robert of Jumièges [Rouen, Bibliothèque Municipale, Ms Y6 (274)].[35] As Helen Gittos shows in her article, there is a good deal of evidence that eleventh-century churchmen were happy to use Old English in a variety of contexts; there is however, only one example of an Old English title for a Latin form of confession, which is found in a mid tenth-century collection, London, British Library, Cotton Vespasian D. xv, which contains other texts dealing with confession and penance, including a Latin text of the penitential of Theodore.[36]

[30] H. Gneuss, 'Liturgical books in Anglo-Saxon England and their Old English terminology', in *Learning and Literature in Anglo-Saxon England: Studies Presented to Peter Clemoes on the Occasion of his Sixty-Fifth Birthday*, ed. *idem* and M. Lapidge (Cambridge, 1985), pp. 91–141 at p. 135.

[31] F. Paxton, '*Bonus Liber*: a late Carolingian clerical manual from Lorsch (Biblioteca Vaticana, MS Pal. lat. 485)', in *The Two Laws: Studies in Medieval Legal History Dedicated to Stephan Kuttner*, ed. L. Mayali and S.A.J. Tibbetts (Washington, DC, 1990), pp. 1–30. For the description and attribution of Biblioteca Apostolica Vaticana, Ms Archivio S. Pietro H. 58 to the early eleventh-century community of the basilica of SS. XII Apostoli in Rome by Pierre Salmon, 'Un "libellus officialis" du XIe siècle', *Revue Bénédictine* 87 (1977), pp. 257–88; *idem*, 'Un témoin de la vie chrétienne dans une église de Rome au XIe siècle: le *liber officialis* de la basilique des Saint-Apôtres', *Rivista di storia della chiesa in Italia*, 33 (1979), pp. 65–73.

[32] For a similar suggestion about the educational purpose of Vatican, Ms Archivio S. Pietro H. 58, see S. Hamilton, 'The *Rituale*: the evolution of a new liturgical book', in *The Church and the Book*, ed. R.N. Swanson, Studies in Church History 38 (Woodbridge, 2004), pp. 74–86 at pp. 80–81.

[33] For a detailed consideration of the use of Old English in this manuscript in particular, and a description of the manuscript, see Helen Gittos, above.

[34] *Ibidem.*

[35] B. Fehr, 'Altenglische Ritualtexte für Krankenbesuch, heilige Ölung und Begräbnis', in *Texte und Forschungen zur englischen Kulturgeschichte: Festgabe für Felix Liebermann*, ed. H. Boehmer *et al.* (Halle, 1921), pp. 20–67; R.I. Page, 'Old English liturgical rubrics in Corpus Christi College, Cambridge, Ms 422', *Anglia* 96 (1978), pp. 149–58; C. Hohler, 'The Red Book of Darley', *Nodiskt Kollokvium i Latinsk Liturgiforskning* 2 (Stockholm, 1972), pp. 39–47, quote at p. 44; Hohler dates the manuscript to the 1060s on the basis of the dates in the Easter table.

[36] Fol. 68: *þis siondon ondetnessa to gode seolfum*: ed. F. Holthausen, 'Anglo-Saxonica', *Anglia* 11 (1889), p. 172; Ker, *Catalogue*, no. 211, pp. 277–8.

The episcopal bias of the evidence

Unfortunately practical manuscripts such as these are all too rare; the practicalities of preservation favoured large institutions at the expense of rural churches.[37] Although there is ninth-century evidence that rural churches in East and West Frankia had copies of penitentials, the manuscript evidence for both England (and also East and West Frankia) in the tenth and eleventh centuries is biased towards episcopal and monastic libraries.[38] For example, Oxford, Bodleian Library, Bodley 718 is seemingly an English copy of a Carolingian handbook; it includes Gerbald of Liège's episcopal *capitula* interpolated between the preface and a penitential ascribed to Egbert, *ordines* for both confession and reconciliation, and the canonical collection known as the *Quadripartitus*.[39] Bodley 718 was copied in the second half of the tenth century by the same scribe who copied the Dunstan Pontifical, for which David Dumville has suggested a Canterbury origin.[40] Its provenance remains unclear but Dorothy Bethurum suggested Wulfstan used it to compose his own canon law collection, and Patrick Wormald's more recent analysis has shown that it was certainly an important source for three manuscripts of Wulfstan's so-called 'commonplace book', which all appear to have a Worcester connection.[41] One of these manuscripts, Cambridge, Corpus Christi College 190, displays an especial interest in penance. It has a complicated codicology: Part A, in Latin, was written in a Worcester hand in the first half of the eleventh century,[42] and includes the Penitential of Egbert together with Ælfric's two Pastoral Letters for Wulfstan, some liturgical and penitential directions and Latin sermons on the penitential significance of Ash Wednesday and Maundy Thursday; Part B was written at Exeter in the middle of the eleventh century, with additions made later in the century, and includes the Old English *Scrift boc* and *Penitential*, together with the Old English version of Ælfric's two Pastoral Letters for Wulfstan, as well as the abbot's Pastoral Letter for Wulfsige and an Old English *ordo* for confession and absolution.[43] This codex is almost

---

[37] On this topic see also Jonathan Wilcox and Helen Gittos' articles in this volume.

[38] C. Hammer Jr, 'Country churches, clerical inventories and the Carolingian Renaissance in Bavaria', *Church History* 49 (1980), pp. 5–17; Y. Hen, 'Knowledge of canon law among rural priests: the evidence of two Carolingian manuscripts from around 800', *Journal of Theological Studies* 50 (1999), pp. 117–34; R. Meens, 'Priests and books in the Carolingian era', unpublished paper delivered at the Leeds International Medieval Congress, July 1998; for his identification of thirty-two early medieval manuscripts containing penitentials for use in a pastoral setting, see *idem*, 'Frequency', pp. 42–3, 56–8, although this sample shows a bias towards the ninth century. Tenth-century manuscripts containing penitentials from the post-Carolingian kingdoms show a bias towards the higher clergy: *ibid.*, pp. 45–6; Hamilton, *Practice*, pp. 44–50.

[39] F. Kerff, *Der Quadripartitus. Ein Handbuch der karolingischen Kirchenreformen. Überlieferung, Quellen und Rezeption* (Sigmaringen, 1982), pp. 20–4; Wormald, *Making of English Law*, p. 216.

[40] Dumville, *Liturgy and the Ecclesiastical History*, pp. 82–6.

[41] These are London, British Library, Nero A. i, Cambridge, Corpus Christi College 265 and Cambridge, Corpus Christi College 190: Wormald, *Making of English Law*, pp. 210–24, esp. p. 223 n. 240. For this description see D. Bethurum, 'Archbishop Wulfstan's commonplace book', *Publications of the Modern Language Association* 57 (1942), pp. 916–29 at p. 928, and Wormald's critique, *Making of English Law*, p. 218.

[42] Dumville, *English Caroline Script*, p. 52 n. 228; Wormald, *Making of English Law*, pp. 220–4.

[43] Ker, *Catalogue*, no. 45, pp. 70–3.

certainly that bequeathed by Leofric to the Exeter chapter in 1072 as *canon on leden 7 scriftboc on englisc*.[44]

Bodley 718 and Cambridge, Corpus Christi College 190 were both apparently compiled within an episcopal context, and intended as reference texts for use by the higher clergy rather than as manuals for use by a priest in the confessional. They are just two examples amongst the penitential manuscripts surviving from late Anglo-Saxon England which show a similar bias towards the higher clergy.[45] Oxford, Bodleian Library, Bodley 311 (s. x) contains copies of Cummean's Penitential, the *Canones Gregorii*, a tripartite penitential, and some canons.[46] British Library, Royal 5 E. xiii is a ninth-century Breton manuscript, which includes apocrypha as well as a version of the Penitential of Bede and the *Collectio Hibernensis*.[47] The inclusion of an Old English gloss in late Anglo-Saxon hands in both these continental manuscript collections of penitential and canonical material testifies to their having been in England from the tenth century onwards and reflects the values of English high clerical culture; they contain such a variety of texts that they are unlikely to have been of particular use to the rural clergy, or within reach of their pockets.

Not all the manuscripts associated with Anglo-Saxon penance show the same legal bias of those noted above. In London, British Library, Cotton Vespasian D. xv – a mid tenth-century text – a long confession prayer with an Old English rubric was combined with various extracts on penance, and a version of Theodore's Penitential.[48] London, British Library, Cotton Vespasian D. xx is a small codex from the mid tenth century, written in large Anglo-Saxon minuscule, which is made up of series of Latin texts for the practice of penance.[49] The collection begins with instructions to the priest on the importance of giving penance to those who seek it, followed by a rite for giving penance to be administered, according to its rubric, by either a bishop or a priest.[50] This rite is similar to both that in Halitgar's Penitential and the rite for giving penance in the ordinary way in the mid tenth-century Romano-German Pontifical, and concludes with the absolution of the penitent; provision is also made for the absolution of an

---

[44] *Ibid.*, p. 73.

[45] See also Cambridge, Corpus Christi College 320, an English copy of a continental handbook, copied in s. x², which includes *Poenitentiale Sangermanense*, Penitential of Theodore, Penitential of Bede and an *ordo* for confession based on Halitgar: Ker, *Catalogue*, pp. 105–6.

[46] Ker, *Catalogue*, no. 307, p. 360: two glosses were added, possibly at Exeter, in the tenth or eleventh centuries. Meens, however, classifies as a manuscript with a pastoral purpose because its primary interest is in penance: 'Frequency', p. 55.

[47] G.F. Warner and J.P. Gilson, *Catalogue of Western Manuscripts in the Old Royal and King's Collections*, 4 vols (London, 1921), i, p. 116. Glossed at Worcester in the tenth century: Frantzen, *Literature of Penance*, p. 130; H. Gneuss, *Handlist of Anglo-Saxon Manuscripts. A List of Manuscripts and Manuscript Fragments Written or Owned in England up to 1100* (Tempe, AZ, 2001), no. 459, p. 80; Dumville, *English Caroline Script*, p. 48.

[48] Fols 68r–101v: Ker, *Catalogue*, no. 211, pp. 277–8. Fols 102r–120v – extracts from Amalarius of Metz – have been attributed to an early eleventh-century Worcester hand: Dumville, *English Caroline Script*, p. 149 n. 49, *idem, Liturgy and the Ecclesiastical History*, p. 136.

[49] Ker, *Catalogue*, no. 212, p. 278; Frantzen, *Literature of Penance*, p. 132; Dumville, *Liturgy and the Ecclesiastical History*, p. 130. The written space measures 152 x 95 mm with 15 lines to a page.

[50] 'Incipit ordo ad dandam paenitentiam qualiter episcopus uel presbiteri paenitentis suscipere debeant': fol. 4r.

excommunicant, suggesting an episcopal audience for the text, as absolution was reserved to the bishop at this time for both penance and excommunication.[51] This *ordo* is followed by a *missa pro penitentie*, a feature of contemporary continental pontifical rites, and a series of confession prayers.[52] An Old English confession prayer was added in the same script at the end of the codex.[53] Although Frantzen viewed this manuscript as intended for 'devotional rather than judicial or disciplinary purposes', the parallels between this text and those of pontifical services suggest that this text was intended primarily as a liturgical text for the administration of penance, probably by a bishop given the reference to the absolution of both penitents and excommunicants.[54]

It is hard to see therefore how scholars can move any further forward from Allen Frantzen's defeatest view, written twenty years ago: 'We do not have a full understanding of how the penitential was used, how widely penance was practiced or how the penitential interacted with other kinds of pastoral literature.'[55] As this review of manuscript evidence demonstrates, the evidence for penance in the ordinary way remains largely episcopal and monastic, despite the efforts made by bishops to promote its practice amongst the rural clergy, perhaps because more practical manuscripts are much less likely to have survived. Further, the wealth of material for penitentials, and *ordines* for hearing confession, in both Latin and especially Old English, has obscured the picture of penitential practice in late Anglo-Saxon England. There is considerable evidence that the practice of public penance flourished in East and West Frankia in the tenth and eleventh centuries.[56] Wulfstan by contrast claimed that the practice of public penance was little known in his own land.[57] But work in the past five years has shown Wulfstan's views to be unnecessarily pessimistic: the evidence of tenth-century laws and the inclusion of rites peculiar to England in the late tenth- and early eleventh-century Anglo-Saxon pontificals suggest that the practice of public penance was known in England from the time of the tenth-century reformers, and in particular that bishops sought to retain control over the rite for the reconciliation of penitents on Maundy Thursday.[58] The English experience therefore conforms to that on the Continent.

But what was to be done in the case of those men 'disobedient to God or evilly

---

[51] Fols 54r–57r.

[52] Fol. 68 seq. For an example of the mass following a penitential rite, see 'missa post confessionem', Vogel and Elze ed., *Le Pontifical romano-germanique*, ii, cxxxvii, p. 245.

[53] Fols 87–92v. Ed. Logeman, 'Anglo-Saxonica minora', pp. 97–100.

[54] Frantzen, *Literature of Penance*, p. 132. Neils Rasmussen has suggested that pontificals have their origins in collections of *libelli* devoted to particular rites; this collection appears to conform to this ideal of a *libellus*: *Les Pontificaux du haut Moyen Âge: genèse du livre liturgique de l'évêque* (Louvain, 1998).

[55] Frantzen, *Literature of Penance*, p. 4. The current University of Utrecht project, *Building a Christian society: penitentials of the tenth and eleventh centuries*, will do much to illuminate this area: http://www.let.uu.nl/ogc/ucms/penitentials.html.

[56] Hamilton, *Practice, passim*.

[57] D. Bethurum, ed., *The Homilies of Wulfstan* (Oxford, 1957), pp. 234–5.

[58] B. Bedingfield, 'Public penance in Anglo-Saxon England', *ASE* 31 (2002), pp. 223–55; S. Hamilton, 'Rites for public penance in late Anglo-Saxon England', in *Ritual and Belief: the Rites of the Anglo-Saxon Church*, ed. H. Gittos and M.B. Bedingfield, Henry Bradshaw Society Subsidia (Woodbridge, 2005).

fallen into deadly sins', whom the priest could not 'turn to repentance or dare not because of worldly power'?[59] Wulfstan encouraged the reporting of such cases by priests to the diocesan synod: 'it is right that every priest announce in a synod if he knows in his parish' of such a man.[60] For in the case of recalcitrant sinners, those who refused to accept the authority of the bishop by coming to penance and atoning for their sins, the ultimate sanction was excommunication from the Christian community and the rites of the Church.

EXCOMMUNICATION

It is therefore necessary to examine the evidence for excommunication in late Anglo-Saxon England in more detail, for it was the stick to the carrot of penance. Although public penance implies temporary excommunication from the Church, it should not be confused with the anathema, for the penitent was exiled from the Church for only a set time, usually Lent, and provision was made to allow him (or her) to receive the last rites if necessary and be reconciled with the Church. By contrast, excommunication placed the sinner outside the Church for ever, and it was up to the excommunicant to seek reconciliation with the Church and enter voluntarily into penance.[61] Medieval churchmen sought strenuously to distinguish excommunication from penance. It had a long history going back to the early Church (and even beyond that to the Old Testament) which was reflected in the body of church law inherited by the Anglo-Saxons and continuously refined and developed; ninth-century Frankish churchmen were particularly concerned with the legal definition and regulation of excommunication.[62] Excommunication had its own rites, recorded by Regino of Prüm in the early tenth-century collection he compiled for the archbishop of Trier.[63] It also had its own laws: Burchard of Worms devoted book XI of his early eleventh-century law collection to excommunication, book XIX to penance.[64] There were degrees of excommunication, ranging from temporary excommunication to total social exclusion, referred to from the ninth century onwards as anathema, in which anyone having contact with an excommunicant was threatened with divine punishment.

It was only in the years around 900, however, that excommunication *formulae*

---

[59] *Canons of Edgar*, c. 6, in *Councils and Synods*, i, p. 317. Cf. Theodulf I, c. 28, *MGH Capitula episcoporum*, i, ed. Brommer, p. 125; *Northumbrians Priests' Law*, c. 42: 'If a priest conceals what wrong is rife among men in his parish he is to compensate for it', in *Councils and Synods*, i, p. 460.

[60] *Ibid.*, i, p. 317.

[61] On excommunication in general see E. Vodola, *Excommunication in the Middle Ages* (Berkeley, Los Angeles and London, 1986); D. Logan, *Excommunication and the Secular Arm in Medieval England* (Toronto, 1968).

[62] Vodola, *Excommunication*, pp. 1–20; R. Hill, 'The theory and practice of excommunication in medieval England', *History* 42 (1957), pp. 1–11. Both also deal with the pre-Christian history of the practice.

[63] Regino of Prüm, *Libri duo de synodalibus causis et disciplinis ecclesiasticis*, ed. F. Wasserschleben (Leipzig, 1840), ii.412–18, pp. 369–75. As Wasserschleben's edition is not widely available, in places I have had to make use of the problematic edition in Migne's *Patrologia Latina*: ii.407–14 (note different numbering), *PL* 132, cols 358–63.

[64] *PL* 140, cols 855–76, 949–1014.

were first recorded.[65] In West Frankia a lengthy maledictory *formula* was added to the Sens Pontifical now in St Petersburgh. ' "We excommunicate and strike them with anathema . . . may they be cursed in the town, may they be cursed in the field . . . in [their] homes . . . in [their] waters . . .". They are forbidden from entering church, hearing mass, contact with their fellow Christians, receipt of the Last Rites and Christian burial.'[66] In Lotharingia at around the same time, c. 906, Regino of Prüm set out a hierarchy of four excommunication formulae in the collection he compiled for the archbishop of Trier; these ranged from the *excommunicatio breuis* to the *terribilior excommunicatio* which was aimed at notorious criminals – profaners, violators of property, and murderers – who were cursed with a series of maledictions.[67] The rites in Regino's *Libri duo* were adopted by the compilers of the Romano-German Pontifical; composed in Mainz c. 960, the Pontifical circulated widely within East Frankia and beyond the boundaries of the Reich in the late tenth and eleventh centuries, and was to be an important influence on the later development of the Roman liturgy.[68] Both the *Libri duo* and the Romano-German Pontifical also included a rite for the reconciliation of excommunicants, for the purpose of excommunication was to coerce opponents of the clergy into settlement with them at a time when secular justice was simply not effective.[69] This growth in the records for the rites for excommunication only slightly precedes that for texts of the monastic clamour; Lester Little's searching analysis suggests that the 'heartland of ecclesiastical cursing' lay in the monasteries of northern France, in the period 990–1250.[70] Episcopal excommunication and monastic clamour are, of course, as Little showed, closely related, although the appearance of records of excommunication rites preceded those for the monastic clamour by almost a century;[71] both are also symptoms of what Patrick Geary has described as a ritual war, mounted by the clergy against their opponents when royal justice disappeared with the breakup of the Carolingian Empire in the late ninth century.[72]

Pronouncing excommunication: the evidence of the Anglo-Saxon formulae

Set against this Frankish background it is perhaps surprising to realise that there is very little secure evidence for any Anglo-Saxon excommunication *formulae*. This is despite the fact that in 1903 Felix Liebermann edited and published

---

[65] L.K. Little, *Benedictine Maledictions. Liturgical Cursing in Romanesque France* (Ithaca and London, 1993), pp. 30–44.

[66] Saint Petersburg, Public Library, Ms lat. 4° v.I.35, fols 105v–107r, as transcribed by L. d'Achery, *Spicilegium sive Collectio Veterum Aliquot Scriptorum qui in Galliae bibliothecis delituerant*, revised by S. Baluze, E. Martène and L.F.J. De La Barre, 3 vols (Paris, 1723; repr. London, 1967), iii, pp. 320–1. Little, *Benedictine Maledictions*, p. 35.

[67] Regino, *Libri duo*, ii.409–13, *PL* 132, cols 360–2.

[68] Vogel and Elze, ed., *Le Pontifical romano-germanique*, i, lxxxv–xc, pp. 308–17.

[69] *Ibid.*, i, pp. 317–21; Regino, *Libri duo*, ii.418, ed. Wasserschleben, p. 375; ii.414, *PL* 132, cols 362–3.

[70] Little, *Benedictine Maledictions*, p. 186.

[71] *Idem*, 'La morphologie des malédictions monastiques', *Annales: Economies, Sociétés, Civilisations* 34 (1979), pp. 43–60 at pp. 49–53.

[72] P.J. Geary, 'Living with conflicts in stateless France: a typology of conflict management mechanisms, 1050–1200', in his *Living with the Dead in the Middle Ages* (Ithaca and London, 1994), pp. 147–9.

thirteen *formulae* from ten Anglo-Saxon manuscripts which he identified as dating to the tenth and eleventh centuries.[73] This corpus has been extended by Hans Sauer's 1996 edition of the *formulae* in two manuscripts of Wulfstan's canon law collection, Cambridge, Corpus Christi College 265 and Oxford, Bodleian Library, Barlow 37, and also by Elaine Treharne, who published the Latin *formula* for which Liebermann gave only the Old English text.[74] These *formulae* are listed in the appendix to this chapter; as Treharne herself pointed out in 1995 there is no Anglo-Saxon *formula* recorded in any manuscript before the mid eleventh century. Out of twenty *formulae*, only three (Appendix, nos 1, 2, and 11) are found in manuscripts dating from the mid eleventh century, in London, British Library, Cotton Tiberius C. i – a German manuscript – and Cambridge, Corpus Christi College 422. A further six *formulae*, found in three manuscripts, can be dated to the late eleventh and early twelfth century (nos 3, 5, 6, 7, 8, 9 in Appendix below).

That Liebermann attributed so many *formulae* found in later manuscripts to the late Anglo-Saxon period is due to his editorial method. He dated these *formulae* on the grounds that comparable rites were recorded in continental manuscripts of an earlier date. But Liebermann used the continental rites edited by Edmond Martène in the early eighteenth century and relied on Martène's dating for his conclusions.[75] Since Adriaen Martimort's 1978 study of Martène's sources it is clear that in many cases Martène's datings need to be revised as he was often too early in his manuscript dating.[76] For example, Martène dated the *formula* in the Lanalet Pontifical (Rouen, Bibliothèque Municipale, Ms A.27) to c. 900, whereas the codex is now dated to the early eleventh century; in any case the excommunication *formula* contained in it was added in a slightly later hand.[77]

The earliest manuscript evidence for rites for excommunication in Anglo-Saxon England are the two examples recorded on fols 195v–197r of London, British Library, Cotton Tiberius C. i (Appendix, nos 1 and 2).[78] This manuscript is a copy of the Romano-German Pontifical made in Germany in the mid eleventh century, which was at Sherborne by 1070.[79] Whilst at least two other copies of the Romano-German Pontifical were known in England by the mid eleventh century

---

73 F. Liebermann, ed., *Die Gesetze der Angelsachsen*, 3 vols (Halle, 1906), i, pp. 432–41.

74 H. Sauer, 'Die Exkommunikationsriten aus Wulfstans Handbuch und Liebermanns Gesetze', in *Bright is the Ring of Words. Festschrift für Horst Weinstock zum 65. Geburtstag*, ed. C. Pollner, H. Rohlfing, and F-R. Hausmann, Abhandlungen zur Sprache und Literatur 85 (Bonn, 1996), pp. 283–307; E.M. Treharne, 'A unique Old English formula for excommunication from Cambridge, Corpus Christi College 303', *ASE* 24 (1995), pp. 185–211.

75 E. Martène, *De antiquis Ecclesiae ritibus*, second edn, 3 vols (Antwerp, 1736–8), ii, pp. 904–11.

76 A.G. Martimort, *La documentation liturgique de Dom Edmond Martène: études codicologiques*, Studi e Testi 279 (Vatican City, 1978).

77 Martène, *De antiquis Ecclesiae ritibus*, ii, pp. 904–5; Martimort, *La documentation liturgique*, p. 420; G.H. Doble, ed., *Pontificale Lanaletense (Bibliothèque de la ville de Rouen, A. 27 Cat. 368)*, Henry Bradshaw Society 74 (1937); for the date of the Pontifical, see D. Dumville, 'Liturgical books for the Anglo-Saxon episcopate', in his *Liturgy and the Ecclesiastical History* (Woodbridge, 1992), pp. 86–7.

78 Cotton Tiberius C. i is a composite manuscript: fols 2–42 comprise twelfth-century computistical treatises, fols 43–203, the Romano-German Pontifical.

79 J.L. Nelson and R.W. Pfaff, 'Pontificals', in *The Liturgical Books of Anglo-Saxon England*, ed. R.W. Pfaff, Old English Newsletter Subsidia 23 (Kalamazoo, MI, 1995), pp. 96–7.

(Cotton Vitellius E. xii and Cambridge, Corpus Christi College 163), Cotton Tiberius C. i is the only example to contain the rites for excommunication.[80] The forms it contains do not, however, seem to have influenced any of the other English examples.

As is clear from the list in the Appendix below, *formulae* were often added to earlier manuscripts, such as that on fol. 1v of the Dunstan Pontifical, Paris, Bibliothèque Nationale, Ms lat. 943 (Appendix, no. 7). Whilst the Pontifical's main text was probably written at Canterbury for Dunstan's use before being taken to Sherborne in the late tenth century, this *formula* was added by a north French hand in the second half of the eleventh century.[81] It is therefore probably post-Conquest, and was perhaps, although it is by no means certain, added after the book was taken to Jumièges. In any case it is evidence for practice in the Anglo-Norman rather than Anglo-Saxon Church. It is quite a short text but is typical of the material:

> By the authority of God the Almighty Father, Son and Holy Spirit, and Holy Mary, Mother of Our Lord Jesus Christ, and St Michael, archangel of the angels and St Peter, Prince of the Apostles, and all the saints of God we excommunicate and we anathematize and we bar N. from the thresholds of the holy Church of God. May part of him burn in the lake of fire with Satan and his angels and unless he repents and decides to come to do satisfaction and make amends, may the lamp be extinguished in his heart for ever. Amen.[82]

Despite its brevity, this *formula* is unique although many of its constituent elements can be found in other examples. The initial invocation of God's authority, and the appeal to the saints, is very characteristic of many of the *formulae* identified by Liebermann in late eleventh-, twelfth- and early thirteenth-century manuscripts (his III, IV, V, VIII, IX, X, XI and XII, of which only two – his IX and XII – omit the 'ex'). But the Dunstan formula is unique amongst English *formulae* in invoking both St Michael and St Peter. The second clause beginning 'we excommunicate', is a variant on a standard clause, and the reference to the thresholds of the holy Church is also found in many examples.[83] The next clause, 'May he burn in the lake of fire with Satan and his angels', is unique: it is more usual in the Anglo-Saxon and Frankish material to find a reference to a list of evil men, beginning with Dathan and Abyron.[84] The only parallel for this text is in Regino where the excommunicant is damned with the devil and his

---

[80] M. Lapidge, 'The Origins of CCCC 163', *Transactions of the Cambridge Bibliographical Society* 8 (1981), pp. 18–28; *idem*, 'Ealdred of York and Ms. Cotton Vitellius E. XII', *The Yorkshire Archaeological Journal* 55 (1983), pp. 11–25.

[81] For date of the main text see Dumville, *Liturgy and the Ecclesiastical History*, pp. 82–4; I would like to thank Simon Keynes for sending me a copy of fol. 1v.

[82] 'Auctoritate dei omnipotentis patris et filii et spiritus sanctus. et sanctae mariae genitricis domini nostri ihesu christi. et sancti michaelis angelorum archangeli. et sancti petri apostolorum principis. et omnium sanctorum dei. exconmunicamus et anatematizamus et a liminibus sanctae dei aecclesiae sequestramus. N. Sit pars eorum cum sathana et angelis eius. in stanno ignis ardentis. Et nis resipuerint. et ad satisfactionem et emendationem uenire seuduerint. sic extinguatur lucerna cordis in secula seculorum. amen.', fol. 1v.

[83] E.g. Appendix nos 9 and 10; Regino, *Libri duo*, ii. 409, *PL* 132, col. 360.

[84] E.g. Appendix nos 9, 10, 11, 15, 17 and 18.

angels and all the reprobates in eternal fire.[85] Similarly there is no reference to the lake of fire in other *formulae*. The next clause, that the excommunicant is damned unless he repents and decides to do satisfaction and make amends, is standard to all *formulae*, English and continental. The final clause – 'may the light be extinguished in his heart forever' – is also very common and finds an echo in the ceremony recorded in the East Frankish material, in which after reading the excommunication *formula* the bishop, with twelve bishops surrounding him, threw to the ground the candles they had been holding and stamped them out.[86] Like most *formulae*, that in the Dunstan Pontifical appears to have been a one-off, composed from standard phrases. Many *formulae*, indeed, appear to have been composed for specific occasions. But, as one would suspect, this particular *formula* is closest to others recorded in the north French tradition. In particular it is almost identical to one recorded from Compiègne in an early thirteenth-century missal.[87] It seems at least possible therefore that all English *formulae* beginning 'ex auctoritate dei patris omnipotentis et filii et spiritus sancti' may have a West Frankish origin.

Excommunication: the evidence of the laws

Most of these *formulae* therefore belong to a post-Conquest milieu but they need not, however, necessarily have been a Norman 'invention'. Elaine Treharne's analysis of the Old English *formula* in Cambridge, Corpus Christi College 303 suggests that an earlier, pre-Conquest, text underlies this twelfth-century copy. Hans Sauer has shown the similarity in the rites recorded in two Worcester manuscripts of Wulfstan's 'commonplace book': Cambridge, Corpus Christi College 265 (s. xi$^{3/4}$) and Oxford, Bodleian Library, Barlow 37 (s. xii^{ex}/s. xiii^{in}) (Appendix, nos 3, 4, 5 and 6), suggesting perhaps an earlier tradition at that see. And there are other indications which suggest that excommunication was practised in late Anglo-Saxon England. The most explicit piece of evidence is that in Wulfstan's early eleventh-century synodal *Injunctions on the Behaviour of Bishops*,

> It befits bishops that they never pronounce a curse [i.e. sentence of excommunication] on any man, unless they must of necessity. If anyone does so of necessity for great transgressions, and the man still will not submit to right, it is then to be announced to all colleagues and they are all then to pronounce the same on him, and announce that to him. Then let him submit afterwards and atone the more deeply, if he cares about God's mercy and blessing.[88]

---

85 Regino, *Libri duo*, ii.409, *PL* 132, col. 360: 'et damnatum cum diabolo et angelis eius et omnibus reprobis in igne aeterno judicamus nisi forte a diaboli laqueis resipiscat et ad emendationem et poenitentiam redeat et Ecclesiae Dei, quam laesit, satisfaciat'.

86 *Ibid.*; Vogel and Elze ed., *Le Pontifical romano-germanique*, i, lxxxv.5, pp. 310–11.

87 Paris, BN lat. 17319, fols 216r–v; Little, *Benedictine Maledictions*, p. 41.

88 'Biscepoum gebyreþ þaet hi æfre on ænine man curs ne settan, butan hy nyde scylan. Gyf hit þonne ænig for micclum gewyrhtum nyde gedo, 7 man gebugan nelle þonne gyt to rihte, þonne cyðe hit man eallum geferum, 7 hi calle þonne settan on þaet ylce 7 him þæt cyðan. Gebuge þonne syððan 7 gebete þe deoppor, gif he Godes miltse 7 bietsunge recce': c. 12, in *Councils and Synods*, i, p. 412. The text is preserved in Oxford, Bodleian Library, Junius 121, fols 15v–17 and London, British Library, Cotton Nero A. i, fols 99–100, and was probably drafted by Wulfstan.

This injunction to use excommunication only as a last resort is also recorded in Wulfstan's own canon law collection.[89] But this is only one of several references to excommunication in the Anglo-Saxon legislation of the tenth and eleventh centuries.

Alfred's late ninth-century laws enjoin a sentence of forty-day imprisonment on anyone who fails to perform a pledge, but if he escapes 'he is to be outlawed and to be excommunicated from all the churches of Christ'.[90] Similar penalties were enjoined on those guilty of perjury in II Athelstan (926–30): 'And he who swears a false oath and it becomes known against him is never afterwards to be entitled to an oath, nor is he to be buried in a consecrated cemetery when he dies, unless he has the witness of the bishop in whose diocese he is that he has done penance for it as his confessor has prescribed for him.'[91] According to I Edmund, anyone who refused to pay his tithe is to be excommunicated.[92] Those who commit perjury and practice sorcery are for ever to be cast out from any share in the Church of God unless they more eagerly turn to true penance.[93] This particular injunction was repeated in the early eleventh-century so-called 'Laws of Edward and Guthrum': 'If wizards or sorcerers, perjurers or murderers or foul, polluted, manifest whores are caught anywhere in the land they are to be driven from this country and the nation is to be purified, or they are to be completely destroyed in this country unless they desist and atone very deeply.'[94] V Æthelred enjoins that all excommunicants should not remain in the king's neighbourhood, on pain of death and loss of all their possessions unless they submit to ecclesiastical penance.[95] VIII Æthelred (1014) enjoins that anyone who protects 'God's outlaw' does so at the possible expense of his life and certainly of all his property.[96] I Cnut enjoined excommunication on anyone who married a nun.[97] II Cnut enjoined exile on contumacious homicides, perjurers, injurers of the clergy and adulterers, and repeated VIII Æthelred's injunction against all those who maintain and keep a fugitive from God.[98] Throughout the tenth and eleventh centuries, therefore, bishops sought the support of the crown in imposing the sentence of excommunication against certain types of serious sinner: perjurers, sorcerers, murderers, and also those who refuse to pay their tithes. The injunction in VIII Æthelred and II Cnut against all those who protect and maintain an excommunicant comes directly from canon law.[99]

As Treharne suggested, much of the evidence for codification of excommuni-

---

[89] J.E. Cross and A. Hamer, ed., *Wulfstan's Canon Law Collection* (Cambridge, 1999), Recension A, c. 22, p. 75.

[90] Liebermann, ed., *Gesetze*, i, cc. 1.2 (imprisonment), 1.7 (excommunication), pp. 48–9.

[91] II Athelstan, c. 26, *ibid.*, pp. 164–5.

[92] I Edmund, c. 2, *ibid.*, pp. 184–5.

[93] I Edmund, c. 6, *ibid.*, pp. 186–7.

[94] 'Laws of Edward and Guthrum', c. 11, in *Councils and Synods*, i, p. 312.

[95] V Æthelred, c. 29, *ibid.*, i, p. 359.

[96] VIII Æthelred, c. 42, *ibid.*, i, p. 401.

[97] I Cnut, c. 17, *ibid.*, i, p. 440; The *Northumbrian Priests' Law* anathematized a priest who left a woman and took another: c. 35, *ibid.*, i, p. 459.

[98] II Cnut, cc. 6, 66, *ibid.*, i, pp. 489, 500–1.

[99] Cf. texts collected in Burchard, *Decretum*, xi.31–44, *PL* 140, cols 866–8. The view of excommunicants as contagious goes back to the third century: Vodola, *Excommunication*, pp. 16–17.

cation under Æthelred and Cnut can be associated with Wulfstan.[100] To the evidence already cited should be added the injunctions to priests in Wulfstan's *Canons of Edgar* to 'announce in a synod if anything is harming them and if any man has seriously ill-used them. They are then all to take it on as if it were done to them all, and to give their help that it may be amended as the bishop directs', and to report to the synod 'any man disobedient to God' whom he 'cannot turn to repentance or dare not because of worldly power'.[101] The legal evidence, much of which was compiled or redacted by Wulfstan, thus both presages and echoes the interest in excommunication displayed by the archbishop elsewhere in his writings. The inclusion of five excommunication *formulae* in three Worcester manuscripts from the second half of the eleventh century testifies at the very least to a continuing interest in excommunication in that see.[102] If one accepts Patrick Wormald's argument that Cambridge, Corpus Christi College 265 repesents an early stage in the evolution of Wulfstan's 'commonplace book', then the inclusion of excommunication *formulae* in that manuscript, next to a copy of the royal law-code IV Edgar, is evidence for interest in excommunication at Worcester in the early eleventh century.[103]

This secular legal evidence has already been reviewed by Elaine Treharne, but she did not examine the evidence of the penitential and canonical collections. As Carole Hough has shown, there is a good deal of overlap between the penitentials and secular law in this period, reflecting Wulfstan's role in the making of royal law.[104] The evidence of the canon law recorded in the manuscripts associated with Wulfstan's 'commonplace book' suggests that excommunication was sometimes viewed ambiguously in the early eleventh century, being only partially distinguished from public penance. Two of these manuscripts, Cambridge, Corpus Christi College 190 and London, British Library, Nero A. i, cited a canon concerning those penitents who, through having sinned publicly, are excommunicated until they repent, and included instructions on how the penitent should behave in this situation, and how those around the penitent should avoid all contact until the completion of penance.[105] It concludes with a text attributed to Basil: 'Basilus episcopus dicit: Cum excommunicato neque orare neque loqui neque uesci cuique licebit'.[106] This text was generally attributed to Isidore of Seville by various Frankish authors including Smaragdus, Regino of Prüm and Burchard of Worms.[107] This text highlights the monastic flavour of the law on

---

100 Treharne, 'A unique Old English formula', esp. p. 199. The fundamental role played by Wulfstan in the redaction of royal law codes is shown by Wormald, *Making of English Law*, ch. 5.

101 *Canons of Edgar*, cc. 5–6, in *Councils and Synods*, i, pp. 316–17. Cf. *Northumbrian Priests' Law*, c. 42: 'if a priest conceals what wrong is rife among men in his parish, he is to compensate for it', *ibid.*, i, p. 460.

102 Cambridge, Corpus Christi College 265 and 146; London, British Library, Cotton Tiberius A. xiii; Appendix nos 3, 5, 6, 8, 9, 22.

103 Wormald, *Making of English Law*, pp. 211–19.

104 Summarised by C. Hough, 'Penitential literature and secular law in Anglo-Saxon England', *Anglo-Saxon Studies in Archaeology and History* 11 (2000), pp. 133–41.

105 Fehr, ed., *Hirtenbriefe*, p. 246: 'Incipit exemplum de excommunicato pro capitali crimine'.

106 *Ibid.*, p. 246.

107 Smaragdus, *Expositio in regulam B. Benedicti*, c. 26, *PL* 102, col. 851; Regino, *Libri duo*, ii.392, *PL* 132, col. 357; Burchard, *Decretum*, xi.31, *PL* 140, col. 866.

excommunication, and also the ambiguity between public penance and excommunication. The canons which refer to excommunication in Recension A of Wulfstan's own canon law collection are similarly ambivalent.[108] But that a distinction was made between penance and excommunication is clear from the description of the service for 'those who after excommunication come to reconciliation with the grief of penance' recorded both in Cambridge, Corpus Christi College 265 (s. xi³/⁴ Worcester), and in the first part of London, British Library, Cotton Vespasian D. xv, a twelfth-century pontifical.[109] It describes a service in which 'those who have been excommunicated come to correction' with a contrite heart, and with their intercessors come to the gate of the cemetery, barefoot and clad in sackcloth; their intercessors act as intermediaries between the penitent excommunicant and the bishop, who receives them in a formal service in which he leads each by the hand through the door of the church, and absolves them on behalf of St Peter the Apostle. They then proceed outside and put on their best clothes before returning to the bishop to seek his blessing in a communal service during which the antiphon is sung, followed by preces and a formal absolution. This service has no parallel with those recorded in either the major continental liturgical or the canon law collections, and thus appears to be unique to eleventh-century England.[110] In the light of Wormald's arguments for the early origins of the section of the Wulfstan 'commonplace book' in which this text is found in Cambridge, Corpus Christi 265, this service is apparently further evidence for the existence of a rite of excommunication in early eleventh-century England, and the prayer for the absolution of an excommunicant in British Library, Cotton Vespasian D. xx, suggests that there was a rite for excommunication being practised in the mid tenth century.[111]

Excommunication: the evidence of the charters

There is, however, one further piece of evidence, which has not yet been investigated by scholars interested in the history of excommunication and penance in Anglo-Saxon England: the testimony of the sanction clauses in Anglo-Saxon charters. Whilst spiritual sanctions are a commonplace of tenth and eleventh-century charters, they usually take the form of rather general dire threats, such as that against anyone who has been tempted to infringe this gift that he should be anathematized before the tribunal of our lord Jesus Christ, unless he first makes amends.[112] There is, however, one anathema *formula*, common to at least sixteen Anglo-Saxon charters, which threatens the attacker with excommunication:

[108] A. 78, A. 80: Cross and Hamer, ed., *Wulfstan's Canon Law Collection*, pp. 99–100. Excommunication should not be confused with public penance as it was by Treharne, who erroneously refers to the entry into excommunication on Ash Wednesday and reconciliation on Maundy Thursday, when both church law and liturgy clearly regarded these days as reserved for the rites of public penance: 'A unique Old English formula', p. 192.

[109] London, Cotton Vespasian, D. xv, fols 57r–61v, Cambridge, Corpus Christi College 265, pp. 213–15; the text in CCCC 265 is edited in Sauer, 'Die Exkommunikationsriten', pp. 293–4.

[110] Cf. Regino, *Libri duo*, ii.414, *PL* 132, cols 362–3; Burchard, *Decretum*, xi.8, *PL* 140, cols 860–1; Vogel and Elze ed., *Le Pontifical romano-germanique*, i, xci, pp. 317–21.

[111] See n. 51 above.

[112] 'Sin autem quod non optamus infringere temptauerit predictum donum nouerit se esse anathema-

may he be alienated from the fellowship of the holy Church of God and also from participation in the sacred body and blood of Jesus Christ, son of God, through whom the whole
earth was liberated from the ancient enemy, and since Judas the betrayer of Christ was
cut off on the left part, unless he does penance through humble satisfaction, because he
presumed to rebel against the holy Church of God, may he obtain rest neither in practice
nor in theory in this life, but may he be pushed into the abyss of eternity and most miser-
ably tortured.[113]

Susan Kelly has identified this *formula* in sixteen Anglo-Saxon charters, at least
nine of which are now accepted as genuine. It first appears in the charters of
Eadwig and Egar for Abingdon in 959: a grant by Eadwig to Abingdon in 959
confirming the abbey's privileges and lands, and a grant by Edgar in late 959
confirming the abbey's privileges and restoring various lands in Berkshire.[114] It is
also used in Edgar's grant of privileges and restoration of lands to Pershore
Abbey in 872, and Edgar's confirmation of land in Hampshire to Eadgifu, 959 x
961 and also his confirmation of the privileges of Romsey Abbey, 959 x 975.[115] It
was repeated in three charters from Æthelred's reign which all survive in contemporary or original copies: Æthelred's confirmation of the privileges and freedom
of Abingdon in 993, his grants of privileges to Ealdred, bishop of Cornwall in
994, and a grant of land forfeited by Wistan for murder to Leofwine, *dux*, in
998.[116] To this group should be added Æthelred's 980 grant to the Old Minster of
Winchester which contains a variation on this clause which nevertheless
threatens any rebel against the power of the holy and individual Trinity with
alienation from the communion of the holy Church.[117] Finally this sanction clause
is found in Cnut's grant of land at Stoke Canon in Devon to Hunuwine, *minister*,
in 1031 which Pierre Chaplais identified as original.[118]

Five of this group, including the two earliest examples, belong to the group
known as the 'orthodoxorum' charters after the first word in the proem of most of
these texts, which begins with Creation and the Fall of man, before mentioning
the Incarnation and that Mary's virtue has cancelled Eve's sins.[119] The 'orthodoxorum' charters have been the subject of much debate; Simon Keynes suggested

---

tizatum ante tribunal domini nostri Iesu Christi, nisi prius digna satisfactione emendare maluerit'. This
formula is used in three charters from the 940s: S 488, S 512 and S 522a. It was identified by S. Kelly,
Formulas in Anglo-Saxon Diplomas (privately circulated pamphlet, 1993), p. 46, but the formula can
also be found by interrogating the on-line *Regesta Regum Anglorum* (http://www.anglo-saxons.net/
hwaet/?do=show&page=Charters, accessed 8 September 2004).

113 'sit ipse alienatus a consortio sancte Dei ecclesie necnon et a participatione sacrosancti corporis et
sanguinis Iesu Christi filii Dei, per quem totus terrarum orbis ab antiquo inimico liberatus est, et cum
Iuda Christi proditore sinistra in parte deputatus, ni prius hac digna satisfactione humilis penituerit,
quod contra sanctam Dei ecclesiam rebellis agere presumpsit, nec in uita hac practica ueniam nec in
theorica requiem apostata obtineat ullam, sed eternis barathri trusus iugiter miserrimus crucietur':
Kelly, *Formulas in Anglo-Saxon Diplomas*, p. 50.

114 S 658 and S 673; S.E. Kelly, ed., *Charters of Abingdon Abbey*, 2 vols, Anglo-Saxon Charters 7
(Oxford, 2000), nos 83 and 84, ii, pp. 337–48.

115 S 786; S 811; S 812.

116 S 876, Kelly, ed., *Charters of Abingdon*, no. 124, ii, pp. 477–83; S 880; S 892.

117 S 836.

118 S 971: P. Chaplais, 'The authority of the royal Anglo-Saxon diplomas of Exeter', *Bulletin of the Institute of Historical Research* 39 (1966), pp. 1–34.

119 *Orthodoxorum* charters: S 658; S 673; S 786; S 812; S 876.

that the early examples were forgeries based on Æthelred's 993 grant to Abingdon (S 876), but Susan Kelly's recent edition of the Abingdon charters suggests that the earlier examples should be accepted as genuine.[120] She has also shown how the use of the *orthodoxorum* proem was initially recorded only with charters associated with the Benedictine reform whose 'primary function . . . is the royal acknowledgement of the right of free election of abbots and confirmation of ancient freedoms enjoyed by communities'.[121] The exception, that of Edgar for his grandmother, Eadgifu (S 811), should be read in a reform context as she was a supporter of Æthelwold and Dunstan.[122] Kelly suggests that the earliest example, Eadwig's grant to Abingdon (S 658), was probably drawn up by Æthelwold himself, and 'that Æthelwold and his fellows' turned to weighty *formulae* to give these important royal privileges, which 'guaranteed the status' of their foundations and refoundations, more authority.[123] In these circumstances it is easy to see why this sanction clause, threatening the separation of the offender from the company of the Church and participation in the sacrosanct body and blood of Christ would have appealed to these reformers, and why it was used initially only in royal charters associated with the restoration of lands and privileges to monastic houses.

There are no direct verbal parallels between this tenth-century charter *formula* and the language of the eleventh-century English excommunication rites, nor with that of the major continental rites. Further investigation of the influence, if any, of West Frankish liturgical and charter material on this aspect of the Benedictine reform might prove fruitful. Without such an investigation, it is still possible to conclude that the charter material provides a firm basis for Wulfstan's own interest in excommunication and reinforces the suggestion of the laws and of the manuscripts of Wulfstan's 'commonplace book' that the practice of excommunication was well known in tenth-century England.

CONCLUSIONS

But if the Anglo-Saxons attached importance to excommunication, why did the clergy of the late Anglo-Saxon Church, unlike their Frankish counterparts, seemingly not think it worth recording rites of excommunication? It is important to realise that such texts were often very ephemeral, composed for specific occasions, such as that in the St Petersburg Sens Pontifical, which specifically names those being excommunicated.[124] The list of people to be summoned for

---

[120] S. Keynes, *The Diplomas of Æthelred 'the Unready' 878–1016: A Study in Their Use as Historical Evidence* (Cambridge, 1980), pp. 98–101; Kelly, ed., *Charters of Abingdon*, pp. lxxxiv–cxxv. See also Eric John who argued for the authenticity of the five charters: *Orbis Britanniae* (Oxford, 1966), pp. 181–209.

[121] Kelly, ed., *Charters of Abingdon*, p. lxxxvi.

[122] *Ibid.*, p. xci.

[123] *Ibid.*, p. xciii.

[124] 'Igitur cognoscat uniuersalis ecclesia hostes saeuissimos et tyrannos improbos aduersarios et persequutores pessimos sanctae Dei Ecclesiae Gauzfridum atque Geilonem, Rangenardum, Erodmundum eius filium, eorumque commilitories (?sic), ecclesiasticarum rerum peruasores, canonicos praeceptorum dei contemptores sanctorum canonum transgressores . . .': L. d'Achery,

excommunication added in a late eleventh-century hand to the *Benedictional of Archbishop Robert of Jumièges*, seemingly composed for use at the time of the unrest in Normandy which followed William the Conqueror's death, shows the further development of this process.[125] One of the rites in Cambridge, Corpus Christi College 265 rages against 'those rebels against holy Christianity who with madness in their heart came at the start of Lent to the land of St Mary *quae æt Christes hala alioque uocabulo æt ontelawe uocatur*, and burnt it, afflicting some men with blows, killing others, and carrying off the goods of all inhabitants of that estate who still persist in malice and disdain to come to penance'.[126] It is, however, of relevance to note that no Carolingian *formulae* survive, yet we know from an incidental reference in one of Archbishop Hincmar of Rheims's letters that the reading of the excommunication sentence was a normative practice: he suggested to his parish clergy that the excommunication sentence should be read before the Gospel, and not after as was general practice, because malefactors usually left Mass immediately after the Gospel, and therefore avoided hearing the sentence.[127] Excommunication rites only began to be recorded in both the East and West Frankish kingdoms in the early tenth century. It has been suggested that their sudden appearance, together with the increase in references to excommunication in the sanction clauses of West Frankia in the tenth century, should be attributed to the efforts made by West Frankish bishops to assert their authority in the wake of the collapse of royal authority.[128] The increase in records of excommunication rites is, however, part of a general increase in the recording of episcopal rites which coincides with the evolution of the pontifical in the late ninth and tenth centuries in East as much as in West Frankia.[129] The West Frankish model does not offer therefore a wholly satisfactory explanation, for the recording of excommunication rites in both pontificals and law collections in East Frankia, which did not witness a collapse in royal authority, occurs from the early tenth century onwards. In late Anglo-Saxon England, despite the fact that it was the Norman bishops, rather more than their Anglo-Saxon predecessors, who chose to record excommunication rites, it appears that excommunication, like its counterpart penance, was an important aspect of the pastoral life of the Church.[130]

Spicilegium siue Collectio Vetetum Aliquot Scriptorum qui in Galliae Bibliothecis Delituerant, rev. S. Baluze, E. Martène, L.F.J. De La Barre (Paris, 1723), iii, pp. 320–21.

125 *The Benedictional of Archbishop Robert*, ed. H.A. Wilson, Henry Bradshaw Society 24 (London, 1903), p. 166.

126 'Ex illorum consortio quidam rebelles sancte christianitati existentes corde amenti in capite sancti quadragessimalis ieiunii terram beatae Mariae adierunt, quae æt Christes hala alioque uocabulo æt Ontelawe uocatur, illamque combusserunt, homines quoque quosdam flagris adfecerunt, quosdam occiderunt substantiamque omnium terre illius habitatorum secum asportauerunt et adhuc in sua persuerantes malitia ad penitentiam uenire dedignantur': p. 209, ed. Sauer, 'Die Exkommuniktionsriten', p. 294; for translation see Wormald, *Making of English Law*, pp. 211–12.

127 *PL* 126, col. 101; Little, *Benedictine Maledictions*, p. 34.

128 In addition to the work of Geary and Little cited above see M. Frassetto, 'Violence, knightly piety and the Peace of God movement in Aquitaine', in *The Final Argument: The Imprint of Violence on Society in Medieval and Early Modern Europe*, ed. D.J. Kagay and L.J.A. Villalon (Woodbridge, 1998), pp. 13–26.

129 Rasmussen, *Les Pontificaux des haut Moyen Âge*.

130 I would like to thank Julia Crick, Helen Gittos, Stephen Lee and Francesca Tinti for their assistance with this paper.

Sarah Hamilton

Appendix:
Manuscripts Containing Excommunication *formulae*
Attributed to late Anglo-Saxon England

Abbreviations:

Liebermann F. Liebermann, ed. *Die Gesetze der Angelsachsen*, 3 vols (Halle
1903–16); excommunication *formulae* at i, pp. 432–41.

PRG C. Vogel and R. Elze, ed., *Le Pontifical romano-germanique du
dixième siècle*, 3 vols (Vatican City, 1963–72).

Sauer H. Sauer, 'Die Exkommunikationsriten aus Wulfstans Handbuch und
Liebermanns Gesetze', in *Bright is the Ring of Words. Festschrift für
Horst Weinstock zum 65. Geburtstag*, ed. C. Pollner, H. Rohlfing and
F.-R. Hausmann (Bonn, 1996), pp. 283–307.

Treharne E.M. Treharne, 'A unique Old English Formula for excommunication
from Corpus Christi College 303', *ASE* 24 (1995), pp. 185–211.

(1) London, British Library, Cotton Tiberius C. i, fols 195v–197r (pontifical),
s. xi[med], Prov.: Germany, then Sherborne. Textual parallel: *PRG, ordo* xc, i, pp.
315–17.

(2) London, British Library, Cotton Tiberius C. i, fols 197r–199r (pontifical),
s. xi[med], Prov.: Germany, then Sherborne. Textual parallel: *PRG, ordo* lxxxv, i,
pp. 308–11. Ed. Liebermann I.

(3) Cambridge, Corpus Christi College 265, pp. 211–13 (Law and liturgy;
Wulfstan's 'commonplace book'), s. xi[3/4], Prov.: Worcester. Textual parallel:
similar but not identical to (2) above. Ed. Sauer (1).

(4) Oxford, Bodleian Library, Barlow 37, fols 40v–41r (Law and liturgy;
Wulfstan's 'commonplace book'), s. xi[ex]/sxiii[in], Prov.: Worcester. Textual
parallel: (3) above. Ed. Sauer (1).

(5) Cambridge, Corpus Christi College 265, p. 215 (Law and liturgy; Wulfstan's
'commonplace book'), s. xi[3/4], Prov.: Worcester. Ed. Sauer (3).

(6) Cambridge, Corpus Christi College 265, p. 209 (Law and liturgy; Wulfstan's
'commonplace book'), s. xi[3/4], Prov.: Worcester. Ed. Sauer (5).

(7) Paris, Bibliothèque Nationale, Ms lat. 943, fol. 1v (Dunstan Pontifical), s. x[2],
Prov.: Canterbury, Sherborne. Text added in a north French hand, s. xi[2].

(8) Cambridge, Corpus Christi College 146, p. 329 (Samson supplement to pontifical), s. xi[ex], Worcester. Ed. Liebermann IV.

(9) Cambridge, Corpus Christi College 146, p. 329 (Samson supplement to pontifical), s. xi[ex], Worcester. Ed. Liebermann V.

(10) Cambridge, Corpus Christi College 190, p. 364 (Law and liturgy; Wulfstan's
'commonplace book'), s. xi[med], Prov.: Exeter. Text added in s. xi[ex]/s. xii[in]
hand. Ed. Liebermann III.

(11) Cambridge, Corpus Christi College 422, p. 310 ('Red Book of Darley',
sacramentary), s. xi[med] (1060s), Prov.: variously attributed to the scriptoria of
Westminster, Sherborne, and Winchester, subsequently at Darley in Derbyshire. Ed. Liebermann VI.

(12) Cambridge, Corpus Christi College 422, p. 14 (sacramentary, as (11) above),
addition in s. xii hand (Ker). Ed. Liebermann V (NB only minor differences
from (9)).

(13) Cambridge, Corpus Christi College 303, p. 339 (Ælfric's homilies and *vitae*), s. xii$^{1/4}$, Prov.: Rochester. NB Added to text. Ed. Treharne.

(14) Cambridge, Corpus Christi College 303, p. 339 (Ælfric's homilies and *vitae*), s. xii$^{1/4}$, Prov.: Rochester. NB Added to text; this is a version of (13) in Old English. Ed. Treharne and Liebermann VII.

(15) Textus Roffensis, fol. 98 (Legal collection), 1123–4, Prov.: Rochester. Ed. Liebermann VIII.

(16) Textus Roffensis, fol. 99v (Legal collection), 1123–4, Prov.: Rochester. Ed Liebermann IX.

(17) London, British Library, Cotton Vespasian D. xi, fol. 108v, *c.* 1200. Ed. Liebermann X.

(18) London, British Library, Cotton Vitellius E. xvii, fol. 252v, s. xiv, Prov.: Evesham. Ed. Liebermann XI.

(19) London, British Library, Cotton Vespasian D. xv, fol. 3v, 1130. Ed. Liebermann XII.

(20) Cambridge, University Library, Ee 4.19, p. 122, c. 1350, 'York manual'. Ed. Liebermann XIII.

(21) Rouen, Bibliothèque municipale, Ms 368, fol. 183r (Lanalet Pontifical), s. xi addition for use at Lanalet. G.H. Doble, ed., *Pontificale Lanaletense*, Henry Bradshaw Society 74 (1937).

(22) London, British Library, Cotton Tiberius A. xiii, fol. 190 (early addition to s. xi^{ex} Worcester cartulary), s. xi^{ex}/s. xii^{in}, Prov.: Worcester.

6

The Pastoral Contract in Late Anglo-Saxon England: Priest and Parishioner in Oxford, Bodleian Library, MS Laud Miscellaneous 482

Victoria Thompson

In the mid eleventh-century manuscript, Oxford, Bodleian Library, MS Laud Miscellaneous 482, vernacular confessional and penitential texts are juxtaposed with the *ordines* for the sick and dying, a unique combination in the surviving Anglo-Saxon material.[1] Although in themselves most of these texts are conventional, their combination is not, and furthermore the *ordines* have exceptionally long and detailed vernacular rubrics.[2] The present discussion asks whether this manuscript, written (probably in Worcester) by a single scribe, can tell us anything particular about pastoral care in the late Anglo-Saxon Church. Laud Misc. 482 refers to the priest-parishioner relationship many times, in many contexts and from many perspectives. By combining confessional and penitential texts with the rites for visiting the sick (*uisitatio infirmorum*) and attending the dying (*ordo in agenda mortuorum*) the manuscript's compiler allows us to see confession and penance in context, and our attention is drawn to some of the most challenging encounters a priest is likely to have with the souls in his charge. This suggests that the penitentials were still seen as important aids to successful confession as late as the period at which Laud Misc. 482 was made. For reasons outlined below the manuscript demands to be evaluated as a unified whole, an anthology of purposefully chosen and authoritative quotations which underpin and give force to the performative language of the liturgy.

Laud Misc. 482 is considered here as a text of both literary and historical

---

[1] There is no complete edition of Laud Misc. 482. It is described in N.R. Ker, *A Catalogue of Manuscripts containing Anglo-Saxon* (Oxford, 1957), no. 343, pp. 419–22. The *ordines* are edited by B. Fehr, 'Altenglische Ritualtexte für Krankenbesuch, heilige Ölung und Begräbnis', in *Texte und Forschungen zur englischen Kulturgeschichte*, ed. H. Boehmer *et al.* (Halle, 1921), pp. 20–67. The longer English *Penitential* ('Pseudo-Egbert') is edited by J. Raith, *Die altenglische Version des Halitgar'schen Bussbuches* (Hamburg, 1933). The shorter penitential (*Scrift Boc* or *Confessional*) and some of the brief penitential texts are edited by R. Spindler, *Das altenglische Bussbuch* (Leipzig, 1934). Some of Laud Misc. 482's confessional material is also edited by R. Fowler, 'A late Old English handbook for the use of a confessor', *Anglia* 83 (1965), pp. 1–34.

[2] As Sarah Hamilton points out (see her article above), there are two continental manuscripts which similarly combine confessional/penitential material with the liturgy for the dying, but to the best of my knowledge the essay-length rubrics of Laud Misc. 482 are not paralleled.

status, although it is neither narrative nor documentary. Its claims to literary status rest on its use of dramatic metaphor and heightened, sometimes alliterative, language. Palaeographical evidence points strongly to its origin in mid eleventh-century Worcester, and the capitalisation of St Peter's name in the litany for the visitation rite suggests more specifically Worcester Cathedral as the likely provenance.[3] The episcopate of either Ealdred (1046–62) or St Wulfstan (1062–95) would be an attractive context for its production. Both of these men were committed to a high standard of pastoral care, with the latter particularly noted for his skill and sympathy in hearing confessions, and this manuscript's complex combination of penitential and liturgical material is likely to tell us something about the ideals promulgated within Worcester's episcopal *familia*.[4]

Laud Misc. 482 contains one comparatively simple penitential (the *Scrift Boc* or *Confessional* on fols 30–40) and another more complex penitential including much theoretical material on the administration and purpose of penance (the *Penitential* on fols 1–19, sometimes referred to as the 'Penitential of Pseudo-Egbert'). Frantzen has suggested that the compilation and translation of the shorter and simpler text may have Alfredian origins, while the second has been ascribed to the Worcester or Ramsay circles of Bishop Oswald in the mid-to-late tenth century. Laud Misc. 482 also contains several sections of the group of texts that Fowler has called a 'Handbook for the use of a confessor', which, he suggests, was compiled in the circle of Archbishop Wulfstan II of York (1002–1023), who was also Bishop of Worcester.[5] All of these texts occur elsewhere in a small group of eleventh-century manuscripts, with the *Scrift Boc* and *Penitential* always found together, and often in company with some of the texts from the 'Handbook'.[6] This consistency may point to an intentional compilation of these texts, perhaps in Worcester, perhaps with the aim of promulgating them as the 'standard set texts'.

Although Laud Misc. 482's various images of the obligations mutually sustained by the priest and his flock are conventional enough, taken cumulatively they provide a rounded picture not only of the theory of perfect Christian living but also of the many pitfalls that all parties might encounter when attempting to put theory into practice. These texts are undoubtedly derivative, but this means no more than that they are backed by the weight of tradition, and it certainly does not mean that they cannot inform us about the late Anglo-Saxon Church in action.

---

[3] R. Gameson, 'Book production at Worcester in the tenth and eleventh centuries', in *St Oswald of Worcester: Life and Influence*, ed. N. Brooks and C. Cubitt (London and New York, 1996), pp. 194–243, at p. 241; D. Dumville, *Liturgy and the Ecclesiastical History of Late Anglo-Saxon England* (Woodbridge, 1992), pp. 131 and 133.

[4] F. Barlow, *The English Church 1000–1066* (London, 1963), p. 269.

[5] A. Frantzen, 'The tradition of penitentials in Anglo-Saxon England', *ASE* 11 (1982), pp. 23–56; Raith, *Die altenglische Version des Halitgar'schen Bussbuches*, pp. xxxviii–xxxix; Spindler, *Das altenglische Bussbuch*, pp. 111–25; Fowler, 'Old English Handbook'.

[6] The *Confessional* and the English *Penitential* (also known as 'Pseudo-Egbert') are also found in Cambridge, Corpus Christi College 190; Oxford, Bodleian Library, Junius 121; Brussels Bibliothèque Royale 8558–63 (2498); London, British Library, Cotton Tiberius A. iii; Cambridge, Corpus Christi College 265 and Cambridge, Corpus Christi College 201. With the exception of CCCC 190 each of these manuscripts also contains some of the texts in Fowler's postulated 'Handbook'.

Their nature as texts translated from Latin originals also enables a comparison with those sources; this comparison reveals omissions, divergences and rephrasing, which in turn show something of the particular interests of their translators.

THE MANUSCRIPT

Laud Misc. 482 is a small narrow manuscript (202 x 91mm), consisting of sixty-seven folios and written in one hand. The first forty-three folios contain the compilation of confessional and penitential material translated from various sources, and they conclude with the words 'FINITUM EST' in red rustic capitals. There was then originally a blank folio (now containing later medieval material), and the same scribe resumes his work on folio 45. Folios 45–7 contain more material on confession, and this then leads seamlessly into introductory rubrics for the *ordines* for anointing the sick and attending the dying. The manuscript now ends on folio 67v, breaking off mid-collect during the prayers to be said if the sufferer should be taking a long time to die. The final folios are missing.

Table 1: CONTENTS OF BODLEY LAUD MISC. 482

PART ONE, PENITENTIAL AND CONFESSIONAL: fols 1–43

	Folios	Contents
1	fols 1–19	Vernacular *Penitential* in four books. I is a series of authoritative quotations about the meaning of penance and confession. II and III (fols 5r–14r) are a conventional list of tariffs; IV is a summary of the major points of the preceding three books. This text is also known as the 'Penitential of Pseudo-Egbert'
2	fols 19–20	'12 things through which God forgives men their sins' (repeated in an abbreviated form as no. 10 below)
4	fols 20–1	Canons 1–11 of the Synod of Rome, 721
5	fols 21–7	Penitential material
6	fols 27	A computistical note on ember days
7	fols 27–8	Extracts from penitential material
8	fol. 28	Passage on confession
9	fols 28–30	Texts on confession, particularly on ways of commuting penance, concluding with a repetition of no. 3 above
10	fol. 30	A briefer version of the '12 things through which God forgives men their sins' (see no. 2 above)
11	fols 30–40	Vernacular short penitential (*Confessional* or *Scrift Boc*)
12	fols 40–2	Passage on penance and confession
13	fols 42–3	Commutation of penance, ending FINITUM EST

PART TWO, LITURGICAL: fols 45–67

14	fol. 44	BLANK
15	fols 45–6	Passages on penance and confession
16	fols 46–7	Formula for absolution following confession
17	fols 47–67	*Ordines* for visiting the sick, celebrating mass in a sick person's house, attending the dying, and burying the dead, extensively rubricated in English. The final folios are missing.

Other than the Latin of the *ordines*, the entire manuscript, including the exten-sive rubrics supplied for those *ordines*, is in English. While there are a few other eleventh-century English liturgical books with vernacular rubrics, those of Laud Misc. 482 are by far the longest, and they are unparalleled in their detail and preci-sion.[7] These rubrics are also remarkable for the amount of direct speech they put into the mouth of the parishioner as well as the priest, and for their repeated insis-tence that these rites are for both the ordained and the lay, even those members of the laity who have hitherto had no knowledge of Creed or Paternoster. Laud Misc. 482 has been examined as a liturgical manuscript, and as a penitential manuscript, but it does not fit neatly under either heading, and it is possible that neither is entirely appropriate.[8]

Elsewhere I have argued that this manuscript is an anthology compiled with the primary aim of teaching priests the meaning of their ministry to the sick and dying, and that the texts were chosen, according to this underlying principle, to explicate the centrality of confession and penance in the challenging environ-ments of sickbed and deathbed.[9] The present argument focuses in detail on one aspect of this: the way in which these texts explore the close personal and recip-rocal bond between the priest and parishioner in this life and the next, and in particular the idea that the priest's own spiritual well-being depends on his ability to minister adequately to the souls in his care. Through the repetition of this idea in a variety of forms and contexts, Laud Misc. 482 establishes a model of what might be best called a *contractual* bond between these two parties, and it does this in two main ways. One is through its explorations of the meaning and purpose of confession, and the other is by its considerations of the three-way encounter of priest, parishioner and Christ at the Last Judgement.

As noted above, very little of Laud Misc. 482 is unique to this manuscript. However, the lengthy vernacular rubrics commenting on the *ordines* for the sick and dying are exceptional (though they draw on many sources), and in these we can see the compiler's aims most clearly.[10] Although they come at the end of the manuscript we will therefore begin with them, before going on to see how they are contextualised by association with, reference to, and quotation from the English confessional and penitential material also found elsewhere.

---

[7] The other relevant books with comparable but briefer English rubrics are the Red Book of Darley (Cambridge, Corpus Christi College 422) and (to a lesser extent) the Missal of Robert of Jumièges. H.A. Wilson, *The Missal of Robert of Jumièges*, Henry Bradshaw Society 11 (London, 1986); R.I. Page, 'Old English liturgical rubrics in Corpus Christi College, Cambridge, MS 422', *Anglia* 96 (1978), pp. 149–58; T. Graham, 'The Old English liturgical directions in Corpus Christi College, Cambridge, MS 422', *Anglia* 111 (1993), pp. 439–46; H. Gittos, this volume.

[8] D. Dumville, *Liturgy and the Ecclesiastical History of Late Anglo-Saxon England* (Woodbridge, 1992), p. 133; S.L. Keefer, 'Manuals', in *The Liturgical Books of Anglo-Saxon England*, ed. R. Pfaff, Old English Newsletter Subsidia 23 (1995), pp. 99–109, 104; H. Gneuss, 'Liturgical books in Anglo-Saxon England and their Old English terminology' in *Learning and Literature in Anglo-Saxon England: Studies Pres-ented to Peter Clemoes on the Occasion of his Sixty-Fifth Birthday*, ed. M. Lapidge and H. Gneuss (Cambridge, 1985), pp. 91–142, at 134–5; A. Frantzen, 'The tradition of penitentials', pp. 23–56.

[9] V. Thompson, *Dying and Death in Later Anglo-Saxon England* (Woodbridge, 2004), ch. 3 *passim*.

[10] The rubrics to the *ordo* for the sick in CCCC 422 (The Red Book of Darley), while clearly related to those of Laud Misc. 482, go into much less detail and lack many of the features analysed here, such as the compendium of scriptural reference and quotation.

Liturgical rubrics are idiosyncratic, their phrasing and emphases vary from *ordo* to *ordo* and manuscript to manuscript, but as a genre they are usually terse and pragmatic. This cannot be said of the rubrics of Laud Misc. 482, which are often longer (sometimes much longer) than the prayers they introduce, and contain much of cultural interest. These expanded rubrics constitute an extensive essay on best ritual practice for the sick and dying, paying close attention to questions of timing, gesture and location, vestments and liturgical equipment, and frame of mind, although the different *ordines* have different foci of interest. The rubrics to the *ordo* for the sick are overwhelmingly concerned with confession and the material culture of unction, whereas those for the *ordo in agenda mortuorum* are much more interested in the dying man's grasp of the basic principles of faith, and in the proper treatment of the corpse.

THE PRIEST/PARISHIONER RELATIONSHIP IN THE VERNACULAR RUBRICS TO THE *VISITATIO INFIRMORUM*

The rubrics for the *ordo* for anointing the sick take care, to an unusual degree, to emphasise the need for gentle and humble behaviour on the part of the priest. While rubrics in other manuscripts of these *ordines* refer to this subject once or twice at most, Laud Misc. 482's references are much more frequent. Before the priest enters the sick person's house he is warned to behave *mid incundre eadmodnesse, butan æghwylcere modes toþundenesse* ('with inward humility and without any arrogance of spirit'). After the collect he is reminded to conduct himself *mid gelimplicre 7 mid mycelre eadmodnesse* ('with suitable and great humility'), *mid ealre liðnesse* ('with all gentleness') and *mid ealre eadmodnesse* ('with all humility'). After the sick person has made his confession he is to be treated *mid mycelre liðnesse* ('with great gentleness'). Finally, in a parenthetical note on proper practice for a confessor, embedded in the rubric, the priest is warned against arrogance because *he hine ne ofersyme ne on orwennesse ne bringeð* ('he [the priest] should not overwhelm him [the parishioner] nor bring him into hopelessness'). Does this repeated emphasis on humility suggest that the author was worried that priests might be tempted to self-aggrandisement and to claim as their own the healing powers that they ascribe to God? Indeed, this may be a kind of malpractice against which the rubricator is also warning when he reiterates that the priest can only perform the rite *mid Godes fultume*, with God's support. The priest's spiritual condition is thus established as a major concern, on a par with the spiritual and physical welfare of the patient to whom he is attending. It is noteworthy that no such phrases appear in the equally complex rubric for the *ordo in agenda mortuorum* a few folios later, where the focus of detailed attention is last-minute instruction in the basic tenets of faith and the proper laying-out of the corpse. The deathbed seems to have offered less scope for abuse of the priestly function than did the sickbed.

Again, it is only the *ordo* for anointing the sick that is expanded with a compendium of quotations and paraphrases from the prophets, psalms and gospels, intended primarily for the priest to introduce when appropriate as a source of reproof or comfort for the sick person. These scriptural passages appear in two places in the rubrics, first when the priest is asking the sick person to confess, and then when confession has been made but before the sick person is invited to repeat a formulaic confessional prayer (which will be further discussed below).

The priest's invitation to confession is given in reported speech and followed by a direct quotation from the Gospel of Matthew, which the priest is to use in response to a patient who refuses to confess his sins and be reconciled with those against whom he has trespassed:

> se hælend cwæð on his godspelle: Gif ge mannum heora synna nyllað forgifen, se heofonlica fæder eowra synna eow ne forgifð
>
> (the Saviour says in his Gospel, If you will not forgive men their sins, the heavenly father will not forgive you your sins. Matthew 6:15).

The rubric then continues *gyf he thonne cwyð þæt he . . . wylle ge his synna andettan* ('if he then says that he . . . is willing to confess his sins to you'), in which *he* could refer to the formerly recalcitrant parishioner, who has now repented and agreed to confess, or to someone else, who welcomes the priest and is unproblematically willing to confess. In the case of those who continue to refuse, the priest is unable to administer unction. Where more compliant parishioners are concerned, the priest is to hear confession *geornlice mid gesceade 7 mid mycelre liðnesse* ('keenly, with discernment and with great gentleness'). It is in this context that the second quotation applies, and it is directed at the priest rather than the parishioner:

> 7 understand se sacerd hwæt se hælend þurh þone witegan cwæð: Gif þu þam unrihtwisan nylt his unrihtwisnesse gecyðan, hwæt, ic his blod æt þinum handum befrine
>
> (and let the priest understand what the Saviour says through the Prophet: if you will not tell the unrighteous man of his unrighteousness, lo, I will require his blood at your hands. Ezekiel 3:18, cf. Ezekiel 33:6–8).

These two quotations extend and expand the theme already noted, that the priest and parishioner are *both* flawed and vulnerable souls, in need of support. Indeed, the quotations balance each other, both are presented as the words of the *hælend*, and the juxtaposition of the two demonstrates the collaborative effort expected of both parties.

While both these passages are taken directly from the Bible, the remaining passages conflate, summarise or allude to the Scriptures rather than quoting them verbatim. One reiterated *sententia* is the inability of the priest to know God's mind, while other references emphasise the availability of mercy and forgiveness even to the sinner who repents at the last minute:

> se hælend þurh þone witegan cwæð: Gif hwa geuntrumege, he his synna behreowsige, 7 se ðe nolde on gesundfulnesse, huru þinga do hit on wanhalnesse; for þan þe Godes mildheortnes is swa mycel swa nis nan eorðlic man þæt mæge oðrum his mildheortnesse areccan
>
> (the Saviour said through the prophet: If any one should fall sick, let him repent his sins,

111

and that which he would not do in health, let him indeed do it in sickness; for God's mercy is so great that there is no man on earth who can assess His mercy to another)

eft he cwæð: Ðonne se synfulla his synna begeomrað, þonne wurð he gehealden. 7 þy dæge þe se synfulla gecyrð fram his synnum to dædbote, þy dæge he leofað and nane sweltað

(again He said, When the sinful man laments his sins, then he becomes healed, and on that very day that the sinful man turns from his sins to repentance, he lives and in no way dies)

gyt he cwyð: Andette þe sylf þine unrihtwisnessa, þaet þu mæge beon gerihtwisod

(furthermore He said: Confess you yourself your unrighteousness, so that you may be healed)

for þam þe se sealm scop cwyð, þæt mid heofena waldend is mænigfeald mildheortnys 7 unarimedlicu alysednes

(because the Psalmist said that there is manifold mercy and immeasurable redemption with the Lord of Heaven).

Biblical allusions on this scale are extremely unusual in liturgical rubrics, whether Latin or vernacular, and they support the hypothesis that this manuscript was compiled primarily as an educational tool and reference guide (which does not, of course, preclude the possibility that it may have been used in the field). To this end the rubric provides a compendium of authoritative statements about the validity of repentance in the face of death, the importance of confession, and the infinite nature of God's mercy; and it represents a solemn warning to the priest not to assume that even the worst of sinners is damned. It is noteworthy that almost every one of these texts stresses comfort, reassurance and the possibility of last-minute redemption; only the first, to be said to the person who refuses to confess, allows for the possibility of damnation. The section of rubric containing these passages ends with the assertion that repentance (*behreowsunge*) and the healing of holy unction (*haliges smyrelses lacnung*) are as important for salvation as baptism and confirmation (*bisceopunga*), and this is followed by the confessional prayer spoken by the sick man.

NIS NAN MAN LEAHTERLEAS: THE PRIEST/PARISHIONER RELATIONSHIP AS CONSTRUCTED IN THE CONFESSIONAL AND PENITENTIAL MATERIAL

The passage from Ezekiel inserted into the rubrics (quoted above) underlines the idea that at the end of time Christ Himself will hold the priest responsible for the ultimate well-being of his flock, and that this is the issue on which his own salvation will depend. This is a significant theme not only in Laud Misc. 482's rubrics but also in the confessional and penitential material. Immediately before the *ordines*, beginning at the bottom of fol. 46r, there is a short advisory essay on good confessional practice, one of the few of Laud Misc. 482's texts that have no precise parallels, though similar texts exist. It starts by reminding the priest of the chief sins against which the parishioner must be warned to defend himself, and it then goes on to give the priest a direct speech (in the first person singular throughout). This begins:

> Ic þe halsige 7 beode 7 hate þæt þu gode ælmihtigum hyrsumige for þan me is neod þearf þæt ic þe riht lære 7 þe is neod þearf þæt þu riht do

> (I entreat and bid and command you that you obey God Almighty, because it is necessary for me that I teach you properly and it is necessary for you that you act properly).

For þan me is neod þearf . . .: the words that are here put into the mouth of the priest explicitly establish a reciprocal and mutually-dependent relationship in which his own needs and responsibilities are presented as being as important as those of the parishioner, and indeed take syntactic priority. The priest goes on to put the confession which he is about to hear into its broadest context, embedding it in the anticipation of death and Judgement, although the confessional encounter here is not explicitly presented as being in the context of serious illness (as it is to be when it appears in the *ordo* for the sick which begins on the next folio). The priest first reminds his listener that he will leave the world as naked as he came into it, except for those good deeds he may have done. He then stresses the always potentially imminent moment of death:

> 7 geþenc þæt þe is seo tid swiðe uncuð 7 se dæg þe þu scealt þas lænan woruld forlætan. 7 to godes dome gelæded beon

> (and remember that the time and the day are utterly unknown to you on which you must leave this fleeting life and be led to God's Judgement).

The priest is also cast as Christ's representative, with the confessional encounter here and now a rehearsal of the coming trial of the soul at the Last Judgement. No sin *ne to þon mycel ne eft to þon lytel* ('neither the great nor the small') is to go unconfessed, in anticipation, as it says, of the great Doom, when everything, good or evil, that the parishioner has ever done will be revealed to God:

> þonne bið nan wiþ þæs þe þu æfre gedydest godes oððe yfeles. godes ælmihtiges eagum bemiðen

> (then will none of the things that you ever did, for good or evil, be hidden from Almighty God's eyes).

The parishioner needs the priest to teach him how to be saved, but the priest also needs the parishioner to be open and obedient to his words.

While this prayer does not mention the roles that the priest himself is to play at the Last Judgement, other texts in Laud Misc. 482 do just this in some detail. There are two functions for the priest at Doomsday: he is to act as a privileged intercessor for his flock (an image considered in detail below), and he is also of course himself a soul on trial. This latter image, which we have already noted in the *uisitatio* rubrics, is found in the first chapter of the manuscript's first item, the longer and more complex of the two vernacular penitentials, translated and adapted from the Carolingian Penitential of Halitgar.[11] Its opening paragraph

---

[11] A. Frantzen, 'The tradition of penitentials'; R. Meens, 'The frequency and nature of early medieval

instructs priests not to hold back (*wandige*) from prescribing appropriate penance to the powerful and great, in accordance with the book's instructions, because

> se hælend cwæð gif se sacerd nolde þam synfullan his synna bote tæcan þæt he eft þa sawle æt him secean wolde

> (the Saviour says if the priest does not wish to prescribe to the sinful man a cure/penance for his sins, then He in turn will seek the soul from him).

This *sententia*, like that in the *uisitatio* rubric quoted above, draws on the imagery in Ezekiel, but the language of the biblical text has here been adapted closely to its cultural context. While the rubric used the more general *ge* (you), *synna* (sins) and *forgifen* (forgive) to describe the actions that the priest must do to ensure his own salvation, the penitential has *sacerd* (priest), *bote* (cure/penance) and *tæcan* (prescribe). This, with the further substitution of *sawle* for *blod*, rewrites the biblical passage to make it refer specifically (and anachronistically) to confession and penance.

The image of the pastor leading his flock to Judgment occurs again in the *Penitential*, in Book III, chapter 16, a passage that also draws extensively on the dramatic narrative in Ezekiel of the sheep devoured by wolves due to the neglect of the shepherds. God's accusations about the 'scattered flock' (*min heord tosceacred*) are given verbatim, followed by the exegetical comment that

> Eall þis is gecweden be biscopon 7 be mæssepreoston þe godes folc on domesdæg to þam dome lædan sceolon: ælc þæne dæl þe him her on lif ær betæht wæs

> (All this is said about bishops and mass-priests who must lead God's people to the Judgement at Doomsday: each to get the portion that was prescribed to him here previously when alive).

Halitgar has no passage exactly equivalent to this, and the English adaptor draws particular attention to the issue of priestly accountability by his closing remark regarding the story's relevance.

Although the text of the English *Penitential* has Halitgar as its main source, the passage just quoted shows that the Anglo-Saxon translator felt at liberty to rearrange, abbreviate and interpolate his original. This is also evident in Book III, chapter 15, which reiterates the admonition that priests should not fail (*wandige*) to criticise the deeds of high-ranking parishioners, whether from fear, affection or embarrassment, nor should they accept bribes to do so. The implication is that once a priest has forcefully brought their sins to the sinners' attention, he has done all he can. Here the *Penitential* differs significantly from its source. This chapter is derived from a much longer passage in Halitgar, which concludes with the warning that unless the priest not only *teaches* (*annuntiaueris*) but also successfully *reforms* (*ut ab impietate sua conuertatur, et uiuat*) such a wayward member of his congregation, both priest and parishioner will be damned (*et te . . . et ipsum . . . flammis perennibus perdam*).[12] The Anglo-Saxon text is thus both an edited-

---

penance', in *Handling Sin: Confession in the Middle Ages*, ed. P. Biller and A.J. Minnis (York, 1998), pp. 35–61.

[12] *PL* 105, cols 691–2.

down and rewritten version of its model, representing a considerable softening of its message. It concludes with a clause not to be found in Halitgar, saying that priests must

> bodian ælcon men hwæt him sy to donne 7 hwæt to forganne, gif hy sylfe wyllað þæt heom be geborhgen on domesdæg beforan gode sylfe

> (command every man what is to be done and what is to be foregone, if they themselves want themselves to be protected at Doomsday before God Himself).

The translator has thus avoided any direct mention of the pains of Hell, redirecting attention to Doomsday rather than what comes after. This suggests that he has faced up to the inevitable and implicitly conceded that some people are unlikely to pay attention even to the most dedicated of spiritual advisers. Instead he appeals directly to the priests' instincts for self-preservation. It is they (*hy sylfe . . . heom*) who need protection 'on Doomsday before God', protection afforded by the knowledge that they have done their best to instruct their flocks properly, even if some of the sheep have gone subsequently astray. The texts anthologised in Laud Misc. 482 thus construct the priest both as a figure wielding extraordinary power and as someone who is burdened with extraordinary responsibility, who is himself as needy as the souls he tends. This image of the vulnerable priest has scriptural authority, particularly from Hebrews 5:1–3, where St Paul discusses the fallibility of human nature in connection with the priestly office:

> qui condolere possit his qui ignorant et errant quoniam et ipse circumdatus est

> (he is able to deal gently with the ignorant and wayward, since he himself is subject to weakness).

The sense that he shared in general human weakness brought a priest closer to his parishioners, as well as to Christ, whose human infirmities Paul goes on to consider.

Nonetheless, while a priest's awareness of his part in fallen humanity was clearly something to be commended, it was possible to go too far. Penitentials in general suggest that priests who transgressed the boundaries of acceptable behaviour were a perennial problem to those in authority. Such transgressions need not fall into the penitentials' more sensational categories of murder or adultery, and the texts in Laud Misc. 482 suggest that spiritual pride was among the major sources of anxiety. As we saw above, the *uisitatio* rubrics express great concern that a priest should be humble and reluctant to prejudge the fate of other sinners. Precisely this theme is also explored in the first book of the English *Penitential* (I, 9), which considers the dangers posed by bishops and priests who are too judgemental, in a passage worth quoting in full, since it demonstrates the very close interconnexion between the penitential and liturgical material in this manuscript:

> Nis þam biscope ne þam sacerdan þam men to for wyrnenne scriftes þe him þæs togyrnð þeah he mid þære mænigfealdnesse þære synne bisgung abisgod sy. For þam godes mildheortnes is swa mycel swa nis nan eorðlic man þæt mæge oðrum his mildheortnesse areccan 7 eac se witega cwyð þurh þone halgan gast gif se synfulla man gehwyrfð fram his synnum to bote þonne bið he hal. 7 eft he cwyð andette þe sylf þine unrihtwisnesse

þæt þu beo gerihtwisod 7 se sealm sceop cwyð þæt mid drihtne sy unarimedlicu
mildheortnes þy sceal se bisceop 7 se sacerd mildheortlice þam synfullan deman for þam
nis nan man leahterleas

(It is not for the bishop or the priest to refuse confession to a person who desires it
although he be contaminated with manifold committing of sins. Because the mercy of
God is so great that there is no earthly man who may assess His mercy for another and
also the prophet says through the Holy Ghost 'if the sinful man turns from his sins to
penance then he is whole'. And also he says 'confess yourself your unrighteousness that
you be made righteous' and the Psalmist says that with God mercy is immeasurable.
Therefore the bishop and the priest must mercifully judge the sinful person for no one is
without blemish).

This passage adduces several of the same scriptural references which we have
also seen embedded in the rubrics for the *uisitatio* at the other end of the manuscript, one of many places where these different genres cross-refer in Laud Misc.
482. It identifies the two main pitfalls which the confessor might encounter as
presumption to second-guess the mind of God, and as vainglory concerning his
own soul. Several additional passages stress that the worst of all sins is to believe
that one's sins are so terrible that they cannot be forgiven. It is thus the priest's
challenging responsibility to find the right balance, to make sure that confession
of sins is comprehensive, but at the same time to guard against plunging the
parishioner into despair by overstressing the seriousness of those sins he
confesses. These detailed passages focusing on the priest-parishioner relationship
at confession need to be put in the context of the numerous passages within the
penitential tariffs specified for priests who themselves sin. The aim of these
repeated messages is to awaken and refine the priest's awareness of what it means
to sin, and to enable him to hear confession and tend the sick and dying in the most
successful way, for the good of his own soul as well as those of his flock.

THE VOICE OF THE PARISHIONER IN LAUD MISC. 482

Laud Misc. 482's rubrics are also exceptional for the amount of direct speech put
into the mouth of the patient in the rubric of the *ordo* for the sick, which incorporates a confessional prayer. (The prayer in itself is not unusual and there is a close
parallel in London, British Library Cotton, Tiberius A iii (fols 45v–46r), but its
insertion here into the rubrics is noteworthy.) After the priest has strengthened the
sick person's faith with the scriptural quotations and heard his confession, the
patient himself concludes this part of the ritual with a prayer designed to cover
anything with which the confession may not have dealt. (Presumably the priest
would read the prayer aloud and the parishioner repeat each clause.) He starts

Geþæf 7 gecnæwe ic eom, þæt ic on mænigfealdum synnum bewyled eam, þeah hy ne
me namcuðlice nu to mynde cuman ne magon. Nu andette ic minum drihtne 7 eallum his
halgum 7 þe, þe min gastlice scrifte eart, þæt ic gesyngod hæbbe on manigfalde wisa

(I agree and acknowledge that I am wrapped around with manifold sins, although they
do not all come to mind now, known by name. Now I confess to my Lord and to all His
saints and to you, who are my spiritual confessor, that I have sinned in many ways ...).

He then briefly cites the ways in which he has sinned and promises repentance *æfter þinre tæcinge* ('in accordance with your instruction'), should God grant him life, and he concludes with

> And ic bidde þe, þe min gastlica lareow eart, þæt þu me foreþingie ⁊ beforan mines drihtnes þrym-setle on domes dæge minre andetnesse gewita sy.

> (And I pray you, who are my spiritual teacher, that you intercede for me and, in front of God's throne on Judgement Day be a witness to my confession).

This prayer for intercession is directed to the priest at the bedside and casts him as the representative of 'my Lord and all His saints'. It demonstrates once more the strength of the relationship between supplicant and priest. Their reciprocal connection is not to end at death. The priest will have to testify to the validity of the parishioner's confession, serving as a character witness in God's court and thereby attesting to the quality of his own teaching as well as to the sincerity of his pupil.

THE PROBLEMATIC PARISHIONER

The texts we have considered so far have shown an awareness of the complex and fallible nature of the priest, but the parishioner, up to this point, has appeared primarily as a compliant puppet, content to mouth the words the priest supplies. This, however, is very far from the picture given in Laud Misc. 482 as a whole, as we saw with the figure of the man who rejects the priest's invitation to confess and thereby makes himself ineligible for unction. Taken in its entirety the manuscript paints a complex picture of human error. The penitentials, of course, here as elsewhere give an exhaustive list of sins, with their tariffs often graded, increasing in severity in accordance with whether the sinner is a layman, in minor orders, a deacon, a priest or a bishop. The sins they list belong to fallen human nature, however, rather than being culturally specific, and it is not part of the present argument to maintain that they can tell us anything particular about late Anglo-Saxon England (although a preliminary examination of the longer penitential's relationship with Halitgar suggests that this approach may have potential). Two other sections of the manuscript are more fruitful where the question of culturally-embedded practices is concerned: the rubrics and a passage on commutation of penance for the wealthy on fols 42v–43v.

As noted earlier, the rubrics (both for the visitation of the sick and for the tending of the dying) are remarkable for their insistence that they are for the lay sufferer as well as for the ordained.[13] In the *uisitatio* the priest enters the house and asks the sick person why he has been summoned (*To hwi gecigdest þu, broðor, us hider to þe?*), to which he replies 'In order that you may anoint me' (*To þan þæt ge me smyrian*). The rubrics then envision three possible forms of response to the priest's invitation to confess, that of someone in orders (*gif se*

---

[13] They are paralleled in the less detailed CCCC 422: Fehr, 'Altenglische Ritualtexte', pp. 49–51.

mettruma gastlice drohtnunge sy) who is experienced at making his confession, that of a layman who refuses to confess and be reconciled (to whom unction must be refused), and finally that of a layman who agrees to confess and needs strengthening and encouragement by means of the scriptural anthology discussed above. The rubrics in the *ordo* for the dying show a similar discrimination. The most astute (*gesceadwisost*) of the available priests is to establish whether the dying person knows (*cunne*) his Creed and Pater Noster. If so, he is to sing them; if not

> þonne onwreo se sacerd him be þæs fyrstes mæðe, þe him þincð, þæt he wite hwæt sy riht geleaffulnes, þæt is, þæt he sceal gelyfan, þaet fæder 7 sunu 7 se halga gast is an god 7 þæt he sceal on domes dæge mid sawle and lichama arisan 7 æt godes dome standan 7 þær ealra þæra weorca edlean underfon, þe he her on worulde ær gefremode

> (then let the priest find out for himself during the period of that interval, as it seems to him, whether he knows what is true belief, that is, that he must believe that Father and Son and the Holy Ghost is one God, and that he must arise on Doomsday with body and soul and stand at God's judgment and there receive reward for all the deeds that he here in the world previously performed).

The rubrics to Laud Misc. 482 thus introduce a range of stock characters: the well-versed colleague who needs no guidance, the recalcitrant sinner who may have to be left to his fate, the compliant layman who does the priest's bidding, and the benighted soul who has no acquaintance even with the basic teachings of the Creed. These four characters schematise a complexity of response which every priest with an active ministry was likely to encounter. Finding them here built into the rubrics gives us a glimpse of how priests may have been trained to handle problematic parishioners with the appropriate measures of kindness and severity.

THE COMMUTATION OF PENANCE

Penitentials commonly repeat that penance is to be applied differently to different people, depending on their age, sex, health, status and so on, and this suggests that the tariffs listed with the relevant sins can only ever have been seen as a guideline, and that confessors were experienced in adapting the books' prescriptions to individual circumstances. As Barlow points out, the replacement of fasting with financial penalties was probably common.[14] Taking this one step further, Laud Misc. 482 and CCCC 201 (pp. 124–5) are the only manuscripts to preserve a text concerning the way in which penance could be performed partly by proxy for the very wealthy. A rich man (*mihtig man 7 freondspedig*) can in effect employ his followers to perform penance for him, and a seven-year penance can be expiated in only a few days if sufficient numbers of proxy-penitents are put to work. The clause suggests that there should be two phases to the penance, the first of three days when twelve men fast and the second for another three days when 840 men fast (*vii siþum cxx*), thus making up a total of 2,556, the number of days in seven

---

[14] Barlow, *The English Church 1000–1066*, p. 268 n.8.

years. The penance is to involve not only fasting on bread and water, but for the duration all worldly business must be put aside and the church resorted to, candles lit (*ælmesleohte*), and prayers performed with weeping and prostration in the form of the Cross.

Fowler calls these provisions 'lax', and remarks that this clause 'contradicts the principle on which commutation is based'.[15] However, it is meticulous in its calculations of how much penance this wealthy individual must perform, he is expected to spend a considerable amount of money, and although he does not have to carry out the full sentence himself, he is nonetheless a very high profile figure in the ritual, which is supervised by his confessor. After confession and reconciliation with those against whom he has transgressed, he is to be stripped of his weapons and *idele rænca*, symbols of worldly status. In their place, he is to take a staff and wear a hairshirt, and he is not to lie in a bed but on the floor. After the period of proxy-penance is over, he is to feed as many of God's poor as he can, bathe and entertain them and reward them, and he personally is to wash their feet (7 *silf se dædbeta beo ymbe heora forþweal*). After this as many masses as possible are to be sung for him, and only at the last of these is he to be given absolution and allowed to rejoin the eucharistic community. If this process was carried out to the letter, it would be an extremely high profile event, a local version of the national three-day penitential fast in response to the threat of Danish attack, enjoined by Æthelred, probably in 1009, and recorded only in CCCC 201.[16]

The kind of magnate that this clause discusses might have been an extremely problematic parishioner, very probably a patron or even the owner of the church to which his confessor was attached, and someone who could not easily be commanded. Such a ceremony would have obvious political as well as spiritual value. These 'lax' provisions may well represent a pragmatic, negotiated compromise, acceptable to the Church and to lay lords, who may themselves have been well aware (like Henry II after the murder of Thomas Becket) of the publicity value of such a penitential extravaganza.

CONCLUSION

Laud Misc. 482 gives every impression of being the product of empirical experience as well as the container of inherited wisdom. Its unusual qualities lie in its expanded, vernacular rubrics, and its juxtaposition of liturgical and penitential/confessional material, both of which suggest that this was a book for use in expounding the significance of these practices. The other texts it contains, such as the confessional prayer and the clause on commutation of penance, add to its complex construction of the often tense relationship between priest and parishioner. Laud Misc. 482 does not merely reflect this tension, however; it attempts to resolve it by enabling priests to perform the sacraments to the best of their ability, and to communicate with their parishioners with the utmost clarity. Penitentials

---

[15] Fowler, 'Old English Handbook', p. 14.
[16] D. Whitelock, *English Historical Documents*, i, *c. 500–1042* (London, 1955), pp. 409–11.

are often seen as unoriginal and therefore unfruitful texts for study; Fowler calls the ones preserved in Laud Misc. 482 'stereotyped' and 'conventional'.[17] However, to expect them and the allied material discussed here to be otherwise would be as misguided as to look for originality in the Highway Code. Nonetheless a close study of the Highway Code would give a reasonable idea of what it is like to drive the roads of contemporary Britain. Similarly, the texts preserved in Laud Misc. 482, through their use of quotation and metaphor, their moments of originality and their relationship with their sources, their unique combination and presentation, allow us a glimpse of the questions that troubled the minds of the mid eleventh-century Worcester clergy, at confession, by the sickbeds and death-beds of their flock, and in their imaginations, as they anticipated standing with their parishioners before Christ on Judgement Day.

---

[17] Fowler, 'Old English Handbook', p. 12.

7

Caring for the Dead in Late Anglo-Saxon England

Dawn M. Hadley and Jo Buckberry

Textual evidence concerning the treatment of the dead in later Anglo-Saxon England provides an incomplete picture, and this article examines the ways in which the study of the archaeology of funerary practices may cast new light on the issue. The burial practices of the earlier Anglo-Saxon period have been extensively studied, but those of the tenth and eleventh centuries have received comparatively little attention from archaeologists. While the results from a small number of well-excavated late Anglo-Saxon cemeteries have been published, either as full excavation reports or in summary form, the results of many other excavations remain unpublished and largely unknown.[1] However, recent research has identified large numbers of tenth- and eleventh-century cemeteries across England, and has begun to explore the potential of this evidence.[2] This article will highlight the diversity of both burial rite and burial location in the later Anglo-Saxon period and will examine the ways in which the archaeological evidence serves to complement the contemporary written evidence for the treatment of the dead. As we shall see, although burial was not as elaborate as it had been in earlier centuries, the funerary ritual was still used to convey important messages about the status of the dead and perhaps also about the likely fate of their souls in the afterlife. The variability of such signalling both in the grave and through the location of the burial suggests that they depended upon locally divergent initiatives and beliefs within individual communities, and that this continued even as the Church attempted to gain firmer control over burial during the tenth and eleventh centuries.

[1] The results of the excavations of the late Anglo-Saxon cemetery at York Minster have been extensively published: D. Philips and B. Heywood, ed., *Excavations at York Minster*, i (2 parts) (London, 1995), pp. 75–92. Other cemetery excavations have been partially published, for example, Winchester Old and New Minsters: B. Kjølbye-Biddle, 'A cathedral cemetery: problems in excavation and interpretation', *World Archaeology* 7 (1975), pp. 87–108.

[2] For example, D.M. Hadley, 'Burial practices in the northern Danelaw, c.650–1100', *Northern History* 36.2 (2000), pp. 199–216; *eadem*, 'Burial practices in Northern England in the later Anglo-Saxon period', in *Burial in Early Medieval England and Wales*, ed. S. Lucy and A. Reynolds (London, 2002), pp. 209–28; J.L. Buckberry, 'Later Anglo-Saxon Cemeteries in Lincolnshire and Yorkshire', University of Sheffield PhD thesis, 4 vols (2004); and on-going doctoral research at the University of Sheffield by Annia Cherryson.

TEXTUAL EVIDENCE

The textual evidence for attitudes to death and the regulations surrounding burial in the tenth and eleventh centuries includes law-codes, penitentials and homilies. There have been numerous studies of this evidence, including that by Tinti elsewhere in this volume, and therefore only a brief review is offered here. Law-codes reveal concern with where the dead should be buried and with ensuring that various payments, including those for mortuary provision, should be made to the appropriate church. The payment known as soul-scot, a burial tax which was paid to the minster church, is not codified until the early eleventh century, but is clearly of earlier origin given that it is mentioned in charters of the late ninth century.[3] In a law-code issued by King Æthelred in 1008 it is stated that 'if any body is buried elsewhere outside the proper parish (*rihtscriftscire*), the payment for the soul is nevertheless to be paid to the minster to which it belongs', which implies that the income to minster churches was under threat.[4] Indeed, the observations of Ælfric of Eynsham c.1006 imply that there was sometimes priestly competition to tend to the bodies of the deceased, and doubtless also to claim the funerary dues: 'Some priests are glad when men die and they flock to the corpse like greedy ravens when they see a carcass, in wood or in field; but it is fitting for [a priest] . . . to attend the men who belong to his parish (*hyrnysse*) at his church; and he must never go into another's district to any corpse, unless he is invited.'[5]

A distinction was also drawn in the tenth and eleventh centuries between churches with burial rights and churches without, and this suggests that such a distinction had become an important test of status for churches. For example, Edgar's second law-code (962 x 963, or possibly 970s) distinguished between a church with a graveyard and one without, a factor which determined the amount of tithe to be paid by the thegn on whose land the church was located. If a thegn had on his land a church with a graveyard he was 'to pay the third part of his own tithes into his church', whereas if there was no graveyard he was 'then to pay to his priest from the [remaining] nine parts what he chooses'.[6] It is apparent from the evidence of law-codes that burial was not limited to minster churchyards in the later Anglo-Saxon period, and it also implies that the minsters faced competition in the provision of pastoral care to local communities. As these thegnly foundations acquired burial rites it is likely that members of the local community

---

[3] H. Gittos, 'Creating the sacred: Anglo-Saxon rites for consecrating cemeteries', *Burial in Early Medieval England and Wales*, ed. Lucy and Reynolds, pp. 195–208, at p. 201; for charter evidence on soul-scot see S 1275 and S 1279. A number of reviews of the evidence for soul-scot cite the clause in Athelstan's law-code of the late 920s in which reeves are called upon to ensure that, among other payments, soul-scot went to its lawful recipients. However, this law-code survives only in later manuscripts, and Patrick Wormald has recently argued that this clause was an interporlation by Archbishop Wulfstan in the early eleventh century: P. Wormald, *The Making of English Law: King Alfred to the Twelfth Century*, i: *Legislation and its Limits* (Oxford, 1999), pp. 295, 314.

[4] V Æthelred, c. 12.1, in *Councils and Synods*, i, p. 352.

[5] 'Ælfric's First Old English Letter for Wulfstan', c. 182, in *Councils and Synods*, i, pp. 295–6.

[6] II Edgar, cc. 1.1–2.1, in *Councils and Synods*, i, pp. 97–8. On the development of the payment of church dues, see the article by Francesca Tinti in this volume.

would have been encouraged, if not forced, to bury their dead at the new church – a supposition borne out by excavations of extensive churchyards attached to such foundations (discussed below). These developments must have had major implications for the social rituals and commemorative practices of local communities, and if the new foundations were problematic for minster churches they must also sometimes have been contentious among the laity.

The distinction between consecrated and unconsecrated ground is first documented in the tenth century. This is when we first find legislation excluding certain individuals from burial in consecrated ground. For example, in Athelstan's law-code issued at Grately (Hants) (926 x c. 930) it is stated that 'he who swears a false oath' is not to be buried in a consecrated cemetery when he dies unless his bishop confirms that he has performed the prescribed penance.[7] Edmund's first law-code (939 x 946) stated that burial in consecrated ground was forbidden to murderers, adulterers and men who had intercourse with a nun, while Æthelred later extended this proscription to offences including lack of surety and violent burglary.[8] The earliest surviving evidence for the consecration of churchyards comes from the late tenth and eleventh centuries, although, as Helen Gittos has observed, the homogeneity of the earliest recorded consecration rites implies that the relevant manuscripts recorded well-established practices.[9] Moreover, the earliest recorded reference to the collection of soul-scot comes from late ninth-century charters and this source of revenue, which was to be collected at the grave side, may, as Gittos has observed, have given rise to 'a concomitant desire to define burial places liturgically'. This suggests that the origins of the interest of churches, if only major ones, in defining consecrated ground may lie rather earlier than the earliest surviving documentary records.[10] We should note, however, that consecrated ground did not invariably lie adjacent to a church. John Blair has drawn attention to the cemetery at Chimney Farm (Oxon), which was on land owned by the minster at Bampton located some three miles away.[11]

Despite this legislation concerning burial location, there was apparently no interest in prescribing the *form* that burial should take, either in law-codes or any other written source. Occasional descriptions of the burials of prominent individuals in the tenth and eleventh centuries provide information on the funeral procession, the forms of commemoration adopted and, in the case of would-be saints, the miracles that sometimes ensued at their tombs, but little information is provided on the form that their burials took. At the end of our period, Edward the Confessor is depicted on the Bayeux Tapestry in a shroud, and this may have been common for the laity by this time, although members of the clergy were probably

---

7   II Athelstan, c. 26, in *Councils and Synods*, i, p. 53.
8   I Edmund, c. 4, in *Councils and Synods*, i, p. 63; A.J. Robertson, ed., *The Laws of the Kings of England from Edmund to Henry I* (Cambridge, 1925), pp. 48, 72–3. We are grateful to Andrew Reynolds for bibliographical assistance on these matters.
9   See, for example, H.M.J. Banting, ed., *Two Anglo-Saxon Pontificals (the Egbert and Sidney Sussex Pontificals)*, Henry Bradshaw Society 104 (London, 1989), pp. 57–60; and H.A. Wilson, ed., *The Benedictional of Archbishop Robert*, Henry Bradshaw Society 24 (London, 1903), pp. 101–3. This evidence is discussed in detail in Gittos, 'Anglo-Saxon rites'.
10 Gittos, 'Anglo-Saxon rites', p. 201.
11 J. Blair, *Anglo-Saxon Oxfordshire* (Stroud, 1994), p. 73.

sometimes buried in their ecclesiastical robes, as famously was St Cuthbert in the late seventh century.[12]

In a recent paper Victoria Thompson has analysed later Anglo-Saxon ecclesiastical attitudes to the post-mortem fate of the body and the soul, observing that the Church did not offer precise guidelines about either matter, and that it did not offer coherent advice on how to ensure salvation either.[13] Thompson has argued that there emerges from the written record a fear of the grave as a dark and dirty place where the body would be subject to the horrors of decay.[14] For example, in *Soul's Need*, a homily probably dating to the early tenth century, it is stated that after death bodies 'shall lie in the earth and turn to dust, the flesh become foul and swarm with worms and pour down and ooze at all the joints'.[15] In a late tenth-century version of the poem *Soul and Body* both the Damned and the Saved bodies are subject to decay. As punishment for its animal lusts the Damned body is devoured by worms with teeth 'sharper than a needle', leading to the torment of the Damned soul. By contrast, as Thompson has observed, for the Saved body and soul decay is not an element of damnation; it is 'merely an unpleasant part of the common experience of burial', which contrasts with the exalted state of the soul.[16] Anglo-Saxon saints are often described as avoiding bodily corruption, especially virgin saints, and this is presented as evidence of, and deriving from, their holiness.[17] Their continuing bodily perfection also hinted at their fate in the afterlife. In his account of the death of Bishop Æthelwold (d. 984), Wulfstan Cantor observes that on his deathbed the body of the bishop became rosy and youthful, adding that 'in this observed change of the flesh appeared even on earth some hint of the glory of the resurrection'.[18] Victoria Thompson has concluded that the perfect corpse was perceived by later Anglo-Saxon ecclesiastical authors as one 'in which growth, change and decay are absent', and she suggests that these concerns were mirrored in the increasing tendency evident in the archaeological record to enclose the body in the grave, in the ninth to eleventh centuries, with various forms of coffin and grave lining.[19] Others have suggested that the later Anglo-Saxon practice of placing charcoal in the grave may symbolise humility and penance, and may have been informed by the contemporary revival of penitential traditions in England.[20] Yet, it is questionable how widely known

---

[12] C. Daniell and V. Thompson, 'Pagans and Christians: 400–1150', in *Death in England: an Illustrated History*, ed. P. Jupp and C. Gittings (Manchester, 1999), pp. 65–89, at pp. 84–5; J. Campbell, ed., *The Anglo-Saxons* (London, 1982), pp. 80–1.

[13] V. Thompson, 'Constructing salvation: a homiletic and penitential context for late Anglo-Saxon burial practice', in *Burial in Early Medieval England and Wales*, ed. Lucy and Reynolds, pp. 229–40.

[14] *Ibid.*, pp. 234–8.

[15] R. Morris, ed., *The Blickling Homilies of the Tenth Century*, EETS os 58, 63, 73 (London, 1880), pp. 100–1; discussed in Thompson, 'Constructing salvation', p. 234.

[16] G. Krapp, ed., *The Vercelli Book* (New York, 1932), pp. 54–8; Thompson, 'Constructing salvation', p. 235.

[17] W. Skeat, *Ælfric's Lives of Saints*, i, EETS os 76, 82 (London, 1881), p. 439; *idem*, *Ælfric's Lives of Saints*, ii, EETS os 94, 114 (London, 1881), p. 333.

[18] M. Lapidge and M. Winterbottom, ed., *Wulfstan of Winchester: Life of St Æthelwold*, Oxford Medieval Texts (Oxford, 1991), pp. 62–3.

[19] Thompson, 'Constructing salvation', p. 238.

[20] B. Kjølbye-Biddle, 'The disposal of the Winchester dead over 2000 years', in *Death in Towns. Urban*

these literary traditions would have been, and while a need to protect the body from corruption and to express penance may have been factors dictating burial form, the archaeological evidence reveals that conspicuous social display was also important to at least some members of society. Moreover, *where* a person was buried as much as *how* appears to have been important, both to the Church and to the laity, and may also have been used to convey messages about both social status and the anticipated fate of the soul, as we shall now discuss.

ARCHAEOLOGICAL EVIDENCE: BURIAL LOCATION

Archaeologists have long assumed that burial in churchyards was the norm by the eighth century. While some have suggested that there was a rapid transformation of burial practices attendant on the conversion of the various pagan kingdoms to Christianity, others have argued that there was a more gradual transition from the burial practices of the earlier Anglo-Saxon centuries to churchyard burial. The former were characterised by elaborate assemblages of grave goods in cemeteries typically thought to have been located away from settlements, whereas the latter were unadorned burials, adjacent to churches located within settlements, and it has often been suggested that the transition between the two was via an interme- diate phase of burial provision dating to the seventh century and characterised by small numbers of grave goods in cemeteries located nearer to settlements than had hitherto been the case.[21] The disappearance of grave goods from burials in the eighth century was believed to have been the result of ecclesiastical prohibition, and was taken as an indication of the direct influence of the Church on funerary practices, even though there was no documentary evidence to support this assumption. Nonetheless, it was a logical assumption for its time, not least because the disappearance of grave goods (or easily datable examples, at any rate) meant that the burial practices of the Anglo-Saxons ceased to be visible from the eighth century, and it was reasonable to have concluded that burials of the later Anglo-Saxon centuries were hidden beneath medieval and later churchyards.[22] Recent research has, however, cast doubt on this interpretation of the available evidence. In particular, the application of radiocarbon dating techniques has recently permitted the identification of many cemeteries of eighth-century and later date, and not all are to be found adjacent to churches or devoid of grave goods. The abandonment of many mid-later Anglo-Saxon cemeteries and their churches has also been identified, sometimes after only a short period of use,

---

Responses to the Dying and the Dead, 100–1600, ed. S.R. Bassett (London, 1992), pp. 210–47, at p. 231; C. Daniell, *Death and Burial in Medieval England* (London, 1997), pp. 158–60; Thompson, 'Con- structing salvation', pp. 239–40.

21 The relevant literature is reviewed in A. Boddington, 'Models of burial, settlement and worship: the final phase reviewed', in *Anglo-Saxon Cemeteries: a Reappraisal*, ed. E. Southworth (Stroud, 1990), pp. 177–99.

22 See, for example, A.L. Meaney and S.C. Hawkes, *Two Anglo-Saxon Cemeteries at Winnall, Winchester, Hampshire*, Society for Medieval Archaeology Monograph 4 (London, 1970); M. Faull, 'The location and relationship of the Sancton Anglo-Saxon cemeteries', *Antiquaries Journal* 56 (1976), pp. 227–33.

revealing that even once churchyard burial emerged in a particular place, this did not invariably set a pattern that would persist for centuries.[23]

This revised view of the archaeological evidence corresponds far better with the documentary evidence than did earlier interpretations. Documentary sources convey little ecclesiastical interest in burial prior to the tenth century.[24] There is little to suggest that burial in a cemetery at, or belonging to, a mother church, or indeed any church, was either expected or demanded much before the tenth century, which is when the earliest surviving legislative control over burial location is found, as we have seen. It may be that it was only in the tenth century that the majority of people were for the first time told where they must bury their dead. Thus, much of the legislation concerning burial location may represent a new departure in Anglo-Saxon religious and social life. The provisions in law-codes concerning burial were apparently a response to a newly-emerged situation, and it is probably not coincidental that the tenth century witnessed a proliferation of church foundations, many of which had an associated graveyard at their foundation, according to both excavation and the distribution of funerary sculpture.[25]

Given that the archaeological evidence for Anglo-Saxon burial during the later Anglo-Saxon centuries has been little studied, other than on a site-specific basis, it is necessary to begin our discussion of this material by outlining the available evidence. Although churchyard burial may not have been the norm until the tenth century, excavation suggests that between the seventh and ninth centuries both ecclesiastics and, on occasion, members of the laity, were buried adjacent to churches. At Monkwearmouth (County Durham) a cemetery accompanied the monastic buildings of the seventh or eighth century, and it appears to have catered for the laity, given the presence of females and infants. These burials were to the south of the church, and it is believed that there was another cemetery for the monastic community nearby, since Bede states that the monks were buried to the south of the church.[26] At least two, and possibly as many as four, cemeteries dating to the seventh to ninth centuries have been excavated near to the seventh-century monastic foundation at Ripon (Yorks). One of these cemeteries, at Ailcy Hill, seems to have included only adult male burials in one burial phase (phase 2) radiocarbon dated to the late seventh to ninth centuries, while other cemeteries at Ripon, and also an earlier phase of burial at Ailcy Hill, appear to have been for the laity.[27] At Crayke (Yorks), where a religious community was founded in the late seventh century, burials of adult males and females and infants

---

[23] For discussion of recent debates see Hadley, 'Burial practices in the Northern Danelaw', pp. 199–201.

[24] D. Bullough, 'Burial, community and belief in the early medieval West', in *Ideal and Reality in Frankish and Anglo-Saxon Society*, ed. P. Wormald (Oxford, 1983), pp. 177–201, at pp. 185–6.

[25] J. Barrow, 'Urban cemetery location in the high Middle Ages', in *Death in Towns*, ed. Bassett, pp. 78–100, at pp. 88–91; D.M. Hadley, *Death in Medieval England: an Archaeology* (Stroud, 2001), pp. 34–9.

[26] R. Cramp, 'Excavations at the Saxon monastic sites of Wearmouth and Jarrow, co. Durham: an interim report', *Medieval Archaeology* 13 (1969), pp. 21–66, at p. 33; Bede, *Historia Abbatum*, in C. Plummer, ed., *Venerabilis Baedae opera historica* (Oxford, 1896), ii, c. 20.

[27] R.A. Hall and M. Whyman, 'Settlement and monasticism at Ripon, North Yorkshire, from the 7th to 11th centuries A.D.', *Medieval Archaeology* 40 (1996), pp. 62–150.

have been excavated and radiocarbon dated to the eighth to eleventh centuries.[28] At Old Minster, Winchester (Hants) both monastic and lay burials have been excavated right through the Anglo-Saxon period of use of the cemetery from the seventh century.[29]

However, burial near to churches does not appear to have been universal even as late as the tenth century. Numerous burials of the seventh century are associated with barrows and other prehistoric features, but later examples of this phenomenon, while not numerous, have been identified.[30] For example, burials in or near barrows and seemingly unassociated with any church have been dated to the eighth century at Kemp Howe, Cowlam (Yorks), to the ninth and tenth centuries at Bevis Grave (Hants), to the eleventh century at Swinhope (Lincs) and to the mid-later Anglo-Saxon period at Winwick (Ches).[31] Excavations in urban centres, such as Newark (Notts), Staple Gardens in Winchester (Hants) and Barnstaple (Devon), and at rural sites such as Fillingham (Lincs), Riccall (Yorks), Caister-on-Sea (Norfolk) and Winwick (Ches) have located other later Anglo-Saxon cemeteries that appear not to have been adjacent to a church.[32] Such negative evidence is, of course, hardly conclusive and a church may have been positioned beyond the limits of the excavation, although in the cases of Bevis Grave and Winwick where burial was focused on a pre-existing barrow this might reflect the absence of any other focal point in the form of a church. Whichever way the archaeological evidence is interpreted, it should be noted that a cemetery did not necessarily have to be adjacent to a church to be under its direct control, as we have seen in the case of the outlying cemetery at Chimney Farm associated with the minster at Bampton.[33] It has also been argued by Steven Bassett that a cemetery at Saffron Walden (Essex), founded perhaps in the Romano-British

---

28 K.A. Adams, 'Monastery and village at Crayke, North Yorkshire', *Yorkshire Archaeological Journal* 62 (1990), pp. 29–50. It is not clear whether the monastery was located near to the medieval parish church where the later Anglo-Saxon burials were excavated, or further down the hill where fragments of a ninth-century cross-shaft were found.

29 Kjølbye-Biddle, 'Winchester dead', pp. 222–33.

30 On seventh-century burials associated with barrows and prehistoric features see, J. Shephard, 'The social identity of the individual in isolated barrows and barrow cemeteries in Anglo-Saxon England', in *Space, Hierarchy and Society: Interdisciplinary Studies in Social Area Analysis*, ed. B. Burnham and J. Kingsbury, BAR British Series 59 (Oxford, 1979); H. Williams, 'Ancient landscapes and the dead: the reuse of prehistoric and Roman monuments as early Anglo-Saxon burial sites', *Medieval Archaeology* 41 (1997), pp. 1–32.

31 H. Geake, *The Use of Grave-Goods in Conversion-Period England, c.600–c.850*, BAR British Series 261 (Oxford, 1997), pp. 154, 158; P. Phillips, *Archaeology and Landscape Studies*, 2 vols, BAR British Series 208 (Oxford, 1989), i, p. 5; D. Freke and A. Thacker, 'The inhumation cemetery at Southworth Hall Farm, Winwick', *Journal of the Chester Archaeological Society* 70 (1987–8), pp. 31–8.

32 J. Samuels, 'Newark Castle', *Current Archaeology* 156 (1998), pp. 458–61; R. Kipling and G. Scobie, 'Staple Gardens 1989', *Winchester Museums Service Newsletter* 6 (1990), pp. 8–9; T.J. Miles, 'The excavation of a Saxon cemetery and part of the Norman castle at North Walk, Barnstaple', *Proceedings of the Devon Archaeological Society* 44 (1986), pp. 59–84; J.L. Buckberry and D.M. Hadley, 'Fieldwork at Chapel Lane, Fillingham', *Lincolnshire History and Archaeology* 36 (2001), pp. 11–18; R. Hall, 'The blood of the Vikings – the riddle of Riccall', *Yorkshire Archaeology Today* 2 (2002), p. 5; M.J. Darling and D. Gurney, *Caister-on-Sea: Excavations by Charles Green 1951–55*, East Anglian Archaeology 60 (Gressenhall, 1993); Freke and Thacker, 'Winwick'.

33 Blair, *Anglo-Saxon Oxfordshire*, p. 73.

period, continued in use even after a church had been founded elsewhere, and may have served as an outlying cemetery for this church.[34]

It is evident from excavation that whatever interest the Church took in burial it did not prevent cemeteries and the churches with which they were often associated from going out of use. The loss of churches and abandonment of cemeteries is increasingly visible in the archaeological record for the later Anglo-Saxon period, and has been demonstrated at both rural sites – such as Fillingham, Thwing (Yorks), Flixborough (Lincs), North Elmham (Norfolk), Cherry Hinton (Cambs) and Brandon (Suffolk) – and urban sites – such as Pontefract (Yorks), Barnstaple, Black Gate in Newcastle-upon-Tyne, Newark and Norwich (Norfolk).[35]

Tenth-century law-codes indicate that felons and executed individuals would be excluded from burial in consecrated ground, as we have seen. Although excavation obviously cannot identify criminality, it can, in certain circumstances, reveal evidence of execution. Decapitation can be identified through the examination of the skull, jaw and vertebrae of skeletons, providing these bones are both present and well preserved. Evidence of decapitation is typically one or multiple blows to the back of the neck, mandible or head that succeeded in severing the neck, although such evidence may not distinguish between judicial execution and, say, decapitation during battle.[36] This having been said, an individual who died in battle might be expected to display much additional unhealed skeletal trauma across the body, unlike the victim of judicial execution.[37] Examples of Anglo-Saxon cemeteries in which the skeletal pathology is indicative of judicial execution include Walkington Wold (Yorks), where two individuals had blade injuries to the occipital bones at the back of the skull and two individuals had blade injures to the back of the mandible, consistent with decapitation from behind (Plate 1). In addition, one skeleton had a fine blade injury to the front of a cervical vertebra, which is more consistent with a knife injury rather than a blow with a sword or axe. Thus this individual may have had the throat slit rather than having been decapitated.[38] At the execution cemetery at Staines (now Surrey,

---

[34] S. Bassett, *Saffron Walden: Excavations and Research*, CBA Research Report 45 (London, 1982), pp. 13–14.

[35] Buckberry and Hadley, 'Fillingham'; Geake, *Conversion-Period England*, p. 159; C. Loveluck, 'Wealth, waste and conspicuous consumption: Flixborough and its importance for middle and late Saxon settlement studies', in *Image and Power in the Archaeology of Early Medieval Britain: Essays in Honour of Rosemary Cramp*, ed. H. Hamerow and A. MacGregor (Oxford, 2001), pp. 79–130, at pp. 85–6; P. Wade-Martins, *Excavations in North Elmham Park 1967–72*, 2 vols, East Anglian Archaeology 9 (Gressenhall, 1980); J. Bradley and M. Gaimster, 'Medieval Britain and Ireland', *Medieval Archaeology* 44 (2000), pp. 235–354, at p. 252; R.D. Carr, A. Tester, and P. Murphy, 'The middle Saxon settlement at Staunch Meadow, Brandon', *Antiquity* 62 (1988), pp. 371–7; T. Willmott, 'Pontefract', *Current Archaeology* 106 (1987), pp. 340–4; Miles, 'Barnstaple'; S. Lucy, 'Changing burial rites in Northumbria AD 500–750', in *Northumbria's Golden Age*, ed. J. Hawkes and S. Mills (Stroud, 1999), pp. 12–43, at pp. 42–3; Samuels, 'Newark'; B. Ayres, *Excavations within the North-East Bailey of Norwich Castle*, East Anglian Archaeology 28 (Gressenhall, 1985), pp. 123–9.

[36] C. Roberts and M. Cox, *Health and Disease in Britain from Prehistory to the Present Day* (Stroud, 2003), p. 153.

[37] See, for example, the medieval battle victims excavated at Towton (Yorks), in V. Fiorato, A. Boylston and C. Knüsel, *Blood Red Roses: the Archaeology of a Mass Grave from the Battle of Towton AD 1461* (Oxford, 2000), pp. 90–103.

[38] J.L. Buckberry and D.M. Hadley, 'An Anglo-Saxon execution cemetery at Walkington Wold, York-

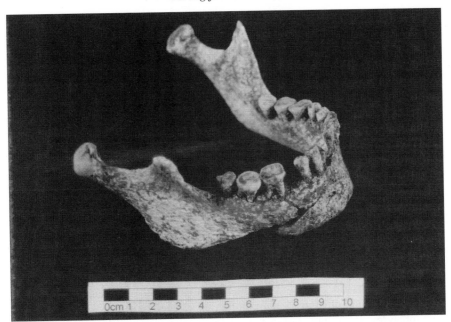

1. Mandible from the execution cemetery at Walkington Wold (Yorks). Note the smooth cut along the bottom of the mandible, which removed a section of the bone, and is consistent with decapitation from the rear. Photographed by Jo Buckberry.

formerly in Middlesex) six of the thirty-one individuals excavated had been decapitated, and six individuals had their hands tied.[39] In a late Anglo-Saxon cemetery excavated at Meon Hill (Hants) six individuals had been decapitated, and the skulls of four of them had been placed between the legs.[40] At Old Dairy Cottage, Littleton (Hants) seventeen individuals were excavated, many of whom were decapitated with the head being placed at the foot end of the grave.[41]

A number of tenth- and eleventh-century cemeteries have been excavated in which the pathology of some of the deceased suggests that they had experienced bodily mutilation, which tenth-century law-codes also reveal to have been the punishment meted out to felons. These include a skeleton with an amputated forearm from a cemetery at School Street, Ipswich, an individual with the legs cut off at the knees and another with the arms cut off at Guildown (Surrey), and an individual at Bokerley Dyke (Dorset) from which toes had been amputated, yet

shire', forthcoming. Since the skulls were found separately from the bodies at this site, the skulls with blade injuries may have belonged to the individuals with blade injuries to the mandible.

[39] A. Reynolds, 'Executions at Staines: regional and national perspectives', (forthcoming).

[40] D.M. Liddell, 'Excavations at Meon Hill', *Proceedings of Hampshire Field Club and Archaeological Society* 12 (1934), pp. 127–62, at pp. 132–9.

[41] P.M. McCullough, 'Littleton – Old Dairy Cottage', *Archaeology in Hampshire. Annual Report for 1990* (1990), pp. 38–9.

which displayed evidence for healing, demonstrating that this person lived for some time after the amputation.[42]

Execution cemeteries have commonly been dated to the tenth or eleventh centuries, when the earliest relevant documentary sources provide evidence for the exclusion of felons from consecrated ground. However, radiocarbon dates have recently been obtained for three skeletons from Walkington Wold of AD 640–775, 775–980 and 900–1030, while a series of radiocarbon dates indicate that the execution cemetery at Staines was in use from the eighth to the twelfth centuries.[43] The evidence from Walkington Wold and Staines suggests that not only were separate execution cemeteries established long before they are first documented in the tenth century, but that they were used periodically over a long period of time. Recently acquired radiocarbon dates for the execution cemetery at Old Dairy Cottage suggest that one of the burials was made in the late eighth or ninth century, while another dates to the tenth century.[44] While this evidence does not prove that the Church was influential in such burial arrangements as early as the eighth century, it raises the possibility that felons may have been buried separately from the majority of the population long before the tenth century, and this at the very least should lead us to consider whether burial arrangements not documented until the tenth century may, in fact, have been of greater antiquity.

A phenomenon noted during our research, and also commented upon elsewhere by John Blair and Helen Gittos, is the high incidence of burials of middle to later Anglo-Saxon date to be found immediately outside of churchyard boundaries.[45] This phenomenon has been observed at Crayke, Addingham and Kirkdale (Yorks), Whitton and Great Hale (Lincs), Repton (Derbys), Shipton-under-Wychwood and Charlbury (Oxon), Brixworth (Northants) and Aylesbury (Bucks).[46] Helen Gittos has recently suggested that this may have been due to the later Anglo-Saxon trend for enclosing cemeteries, a process which appears to have resulted in the area devoted to burial being reduced.[47] Another factor explaining the presence of burials of mid-later Anglo-Saxon date outside churchyards may relate to the status of the churches concerned. Many of the churches listed above were of early origins, housing important religious communities, and it may be that the reduction of their burial grounds was related to a change in function for the church from that of a sizable religious community, to that of,

---

[42] A. Reynolds, 'The definition and ideology of Anglo-Saxon execution sites and cemeteries', in *Death and Burial in Medieval Europe*, ed. G. de Boe and F. Verhaeghe (Zellik, 1997), pp. 33–41; and A. Reynolds, personal communication. It should, however, be noted that these amputations may have been undertaken for medical, rather than judicial, reasons.

[43] The dates from Walkington Wold were all calibrated to 2 sigma, and were at the 95% confidence range: Buckberry and Hadley, 'Walkington Wold'; Reynolds, 'Staines'.

[44] Annia Cherryson, personal communication

[45] Blair, *Anglo-Saxon Oxfordshire*, pp. 66, 72; Gittos, 'Anglo-Saxon rites', p. 204.

[46] Adams, 'Crayke', pp. 39–44; M. Adams, 'Excavation of a pre-Conquest cemetery at Addingham, West Yorkshire', *Medieval Archaeology* 40 (1996), pp. 151–91; P. Rahtz and L. Watts, 'Kirkdale Anglo-Saxon minster', *Current Archaeology* 155 (1998), pp. 419–22; D.M. Hadley, 'Whitton, Lincolnshire', *Current Archaeology* 186 (2003), pp. 234–7; J.L. Buckberry and D.M. Hadley, 'Great Hale', *Lincolnshire History and Archaeology* 36 (2001), p. 59; Blair, *Anglo-Saxon Oxfordshire*, pp. 66, 72.

[47] Gittos, 'Anglo-Saxon rites', pp. 203–4.

effectively, a parish church. For example, the medieval parishes of both Addingham and Crayke served no more than a single township, and while the size of the district for which they provided burial in the Anglo-Saxon period is unknown, that both were important religious communities – possessions of the archbishops of York and the community of St Cuthbert respectively – implies that they may previously have had pastoral responsibility for wide areas.[48] A second, and related, explanation for a reduction in the size of churchyards may be that the lay population for which a church provided burial declined in size, perhaps as a result of the foundation of other churches in the vicinity that were permitted burial grounds. For example, the medieval mother church of Repton served an enormous parish and had at least eight chapels, but several of these performed burial rites in the later Middle Ages.[49] It is possible that this evidence reflects not a shrinking single cemetery, but that the churches concerned had more than one cemetery, each, perhaps, associated with a different group within the religious community or local society. It is also, however, possible that mid-later Anglo-Saxon rural settlements sometimes had multiple places of burial, which came into and went out of use at various times. The eventual emergence of the churchyard as a place of burial may have derived from an increased sense of the settlement as constituting a church community.[50]

Both the documentary and archaeological record suggest that the interest of the Church in controlling the location of burial was growing during the later Anglo-Saxon centuries. However, this precludes neither the possibility that the Church was actively concerned with burial location for at least some members of society at an earlier date, nor the possibility that burial at a distance from churches continued into the tenth century. Moreover, whatever interest the Church had in burial location and in the desirability of protecting the deceased body, it did not prevent cemeteries, or parts of them, from being abandoned and superseded by either secular occupation or cultivation. For example, at Addingham the manorial complex had extended over the ninth- and tenth-century cemetery by the twelfth century, while domestic occupation and a Norman castle succeeded part of a late Anglo-Saxon cemetery at Pontefract.[51] In the late eleventh century castles were built over cemeteries at Norwich, Newark, Barnstaple, York and Black Gate, Newcastle, and although this normally resulted in the truncation or destruction of burials, at Barnstaple there is evidence for the exhumation of bodies prior to the building of the castle.[52] The cemetery at Swinegate, York was superseded by

---

48 D.M. Hadley, *The Northern Danelaw: its Social Structure, c.800–1100* (London, 2000), pp. 258–61; Adams, 'Addingham', p. 153.
49 Hadley, *The Northern Danelaw*, pp. 220–5.
50 E. Zadora-Rio, 'The making of churchyards and parish territories in the early medieval landscape of France and England in the 7th–12th centuries: a reconsideration', *Medieval Archaeology* 47 (2003), pp. 1–19 at p. 9.
51 Adams, 'Addingham', p. 188; Willmott, 'Pontefract', pp. 343–4.
52 Ayres, *Norwich Castle*, p. 129; Samuels, 'Newark', p. 460; Miles, 'Barnstaple', p. 68; D. Evans, 'The former female prison "skeletons in the cupboard"', *York Archaeological Trust Interim Report* 23.1 (2000), pp. 17–22; L. Webster and J. Cherry, 'Medieval Britain', *Medieval Archaeology* 23, (1979), pp. 234–78, at p. 246.

domestic buildings in the twelfth century.[53] At both Kirkdale and Crayke areas of Anglo-Saxon burial subsequently came under the plough.[54] At Aylesbury late eighth- to early tenth-century burials were discovered in an area that had ceased to be a burial ground by the late Anglo-Saxon period.[55] Churches also often occupied former burial grounds. At St Peter's, Barton-upon-Humber (Lincs) the building of a church in the tenth century led to the careful exhumation of bodies in the pre-existing cemetery to make way for the digging of foundations.[56] However, in other cases graves were truncated or completely destroyed by Anglo-Saxon church-building campaigns, such as at neighbouring Barrow-upon-Humber (Plate 2) and also at Holton-le-Clay (Lincs) and Pontefract (Plate 3).[57] Thus, even though those operating within learned ecclesiastical circles may have written of the desirability of the body remaining incorrupt, in practice churches were as likely as anyone, if not more so, to disturb bodies in their graves.[58]

ARCHAEOLOGICAL EVIDENCE: BURIAL FORM

The form of burial in the tenth and eleventh centuries was highly varied, suggesting that local communities exercised considerable initiative in the provision of what they deemed appropriate burial for their members. Burial in various types of coffin was common. Evidence for wooden coffins normally survives only in the form of iron nails and various iron coffin fittings, such as those recovered during excavation at York Minster, Pontefract, Old Minster in Winchester and Barnstaple.[59] However, in waterlogged conditions the coffins themselves sometimes survive, as at St Peter's, Barton-upon-Humber, Swinegate in York (Plate 4) and the Guildhall site in London.[60] Given that in these cases most of the coffins were held together with wooden dowels, not nails, apparent lack of evidence for any type of coffin from non-waterlogged sites should not be taken as

---

[53] N. Pearson, 'Swinegate excavation', *York Archaeological Trust Interim Report* 14.4 (1989), pp. 2–9, at p. 7.

[54] Rahtz and Watts, 'Kirkdale', p. 421; Adams, 'Crayke', p. 36.

[55] D. Allen and C.H. Dalwood, 'Iron Age occupation, a Middle Saxon cemetery and 12th to 19th-century urban occupation: excavations in George Street, Aylesbury, 1981', *Records of Buckinghamshire* 25 (1983), pp. 1–60, at pp. 6–8.

[56] W. Rodwell and K. Rodwell, 'St Peter's church, Barton-upon-Humber: excavation and structural study, 1978–81', *Antiquaries Journal* 62 (1982), pp. 283–315, at p. 294.

[57] J.M. Boden and J.B. Whitwell, 'Barrow-upon-Humber', *Lincolnshire History and Archaeology* 14 (1979), pp. 66–7; J. Sills, 'St Peter's church, Holton-le-Clay', *Lincolnshire History and Archaeology* 17 (182), pp. 29–42, at pp. 30, 32; Willmott, 'Pontefract', p. 342.

[58] Thompson, 'Constructing salvation'; also see A.K. Cherryson, 'Disturbing the dead: urbanisation, the Church and the post-burial treatment of human remains in early medieval Wessex, c.600–1100 AD', forthcoming.

[59] B. Kjølbye-Biddle, 'Iron-bound coffins and coffin-fittings from the pre-Norman cemetery', in *Excavations at York Minster*, ed. Philips and Heywood, pp. 489–521; Willmott, 'Pontefract', p. 342; Kjølbye-Biddle, 'Winchester dead', pp. 226–8; Miles, 'Barnstaple', p. 63.

[60] Rodwell and Rodwell, 'Barton-upon-Humber', pp. 291–2; Pearson, 'Swinegate', p. 7; T. Bagwell and I. Tyres, *Dendrochronological Analysis of a Coffin Assemblage from Swinegate, York, North Yorkshire*, ARCUS Project Report no. 575 (2001), p. 5; N. Bateman, 'The early 11th to mid 12th-century graveyard at Guildhall, City of London', in *Death and Burial in Medieval Europe*, ed. de Boe and Verhaeghe, pp. 115–20.

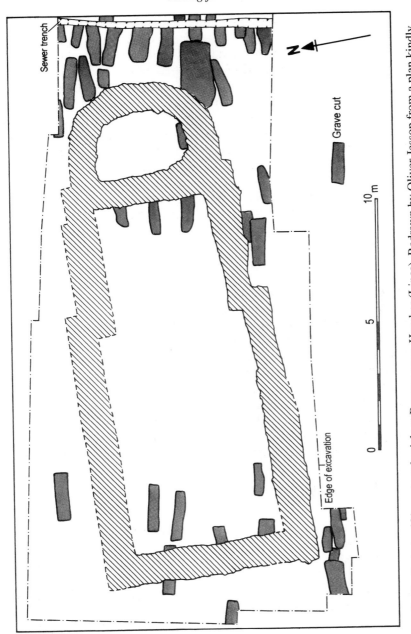

2. Tenth- to twelfth-century burials at Barrow-upon-Humber (Lincs). Redrawn by Oliver Jessop from a plan kindly provided by Humber Archaeology Partnership.

3. Tenth-century burial from Pontefract (Yorks). The wall of the church clearly cut through the earlier burial. Reproduced with permission from West Yorkshire Archaeology Service.

proof of the absence of coffins. Where coffins survive, there is evidence for innovation in coffin production. For example, dug-out logs were used at St Peter's, Barton-upon-Humber and Swinegate, the re-use of domestic chests with hinges and locks has been identified at York Minster (Plate 5), Ripon and Winchester Old Minster, and clinker built coffins, possibly utilising parts of old boats, have been detected at both St Peter's, Barton-upon-Humber and York Minster.[61] At Caister-on-Sea it has been suggested that boat parts were used as grave covers or coffin lids.[62] Lead coffins are occasionally found, such as that from Staple

[61] Rodwell and Rodwell, 'Barton-upon-Humber', p. 291; Bagwell and Tyres, *Swinegate*, p. 3; Kjølbye-Biddle, 'Coffins and coffin-fittings', p. 517; Whyman and Hall, 'Ripon', pp. 99–110.
[62] Darling and Gurney, *Caister-on-Sea*, pp. 253–4. The dating of this cemetery is not certain. It is often stated to be middle Saxon, but a range of artefacts of later Anglo-Saxon date has been recovered from the cemetery, in some cases from within graves (*ibid.*, p. 252).

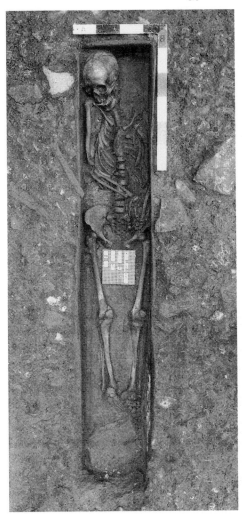

4. A coffined burial of tenth- or eleventh-century date from Swinegate, York. Reproduced with permission from York Archaeological Trust.

Gardens, Winchester, and a possible example from Kilham (Yorks).[63] Examples of stone sarcophagi have been found at York Minster, Kirkdale and at Winchester Old Minster.[64]

A cheaper alternative to a sarcophagus may have been the provision of a stone lining in graves. This phenomenon has been encountered during excavation at many later Anglo-Saxon cemeteries including Fillingham (Plate 6), York Minster, Barrow-upon-Humber, Newark and Raunds (Northants).[65] Many tenth- and eleventh-century graves demonstrate more limited use of stone to enclose the

---

63 Kipling and Scobie, 'Staple Gardens'; Hull Sites and Monuments Record, no. 7437.
64 Philips and Heywood, *York Minster*, p. 82; L. Watts *et al.*, 'Kirkdale – the inscriptions', *Medieval Archaeology* 41 (1997), pp. 51–99, at p. 89; Kjølbye-Biddle, 'Winchester dead', p. 227.
65 Buckberry and Hadley, 'Fillingham', pp. 13–15; Philips and Heywood, *York Minster*, pp. 84–5; Buckberry, 'Later Anglo-Saxon Cemeteries', ch. 6; Samuels, 'Newark'; A. Boddington, *Raunds Furnells: the Anglo-Saxon Church and Churchyard* (London, 1996), p. 40.

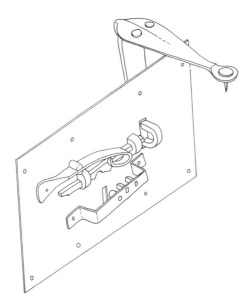

5. Reconstruction of a coffin lock from a tenth-century burial at York Minster. Redrawn by Melissa Peet after B. Kjølbye-Biddle, 'Iron-bound coffins and coffin-fittings from the pre-Norman cemetery', *Excavations at York Minster, Volume 1* (2 parts), ed. D. Philips and B. Heywood (London, 1995), pp. 489–521.

body. In particular stones are often placed around or underneath the head, and are commonly, if misleadingly in many cases, called pillow stones by excavators. Examples have been found in cemeteries excavated at Fillingham, St Andrew's, Fishergate in York, St Peter's, Barton-upon-Humber, Barnstaple, Staple Gardens in Winchester, Raunds, and both the Guildhall site and St Nicholas Shambles in London.[66] These have been found in apparently plain earth graves, in burials with wooden coffins and in stone-lined graves. Scatters of charcoal in burials have been identified at York Minster, Barrow-upon-Humber, Hereford, Exeter and at both Old Minster and Staple Gardens in Winchester.[67] This charcoal is sometimes found above the burial, although it is more common beneath. The amount of charcoal provided varies from a small scatter to a layer up to 15 cm in depth.[68]

What does this variation in burial form reveal? The first observation to be made is that it seems to confirm the impression to be gleaned from the silence of the documentary record, that the Church did not concern itself with the form that burial took. The archaeological evidence seems to suggest highly localised

[66] Buckberry and Hadley, 'Fillingham', p. 13; G. Stroud and R. Kemp, *Cemeteries of the Church and Priory of St Andrew, Fishergate*, The Archaeology of York 12.2 (London, 1993), p. 153; Rodwell and Rodwell, 'Barton-upon-Humber', p. 301; Miles, 'Barnstaple', p. 66; Kipling and Scobie, 'Staple Gardens'; Boddington, *Raunds*, pp. 38–40; Bateman, 'Guildhall', p. 117; W. White, ed., *Skeletal Remains from the Cemetery of St Nicholas Shambles, City of London* (London, 1988), pp. 18, 20–2. It would be helpful if excavators used the term 'pillow stones' to refer only to stones placed under the head.

[67] Philips and Heywood, *York Minster*, pp. 87–8; Boden and Whitwell, 'Barrow-upon-Humber', p. 67; R. Shoesmith, *Hereford City Excavations*, i: *Excavations at Castle Green*, CBA 36 (London, 1980), pp. 28–9; C. Henderson and P. Bidwell, 'The Saxon minster at Exeter', in *The Early Church in Western Britain and Ireland*, ed. S.M. Pearce, BAR British Series 102 (Oxford, 1982), pp. 145–75, at pp. 154–5; Kjølbye-Biddle, 'Winchester dead', pp. 228–33.

[68] Kjølbye-Biddle, 'Winchester dead', pp. 228–9; A. Cherryson, 'In the Shadow of the Church', University of Sheffield PhD thesis (forthcoming), ch. 5.

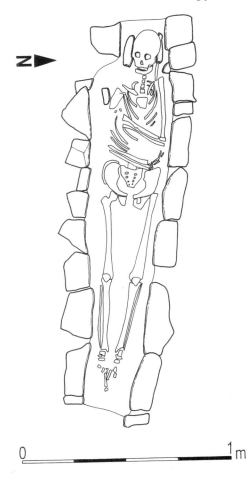

6. Late Anglo-Saxon burial at Fillingham (Lincs). This burial was in a stone-lined grave and additional stones had been placed on either side of the head. Drawn by Oliver Jessop.

patterns of burial provision that may vary between neighbouring settlements or even within the same settlement. For example, at St Peter's, Barton-upon-Humber, just over half of the late Anglo-Saxon burials were placed in wooden coffins of various types or buried in graves lined or covered with planks, one individual was buried in a partially stone-lined grave and the remainder were apparently in plain earth graves. By contrast, in the neighbouring village of Barrow-upon-Humber, although there is similarly some evidence for wooden coffins (in the form of iron nails), many more individuals were buried in stone-lined graves than at Barton.[69] At the same time, just 15 miles away at Fillingham all of the tenth- and eleventh-century burials excavated were in stone-lined graves.[70]

Within later Anglo-Saxon towns it can be shown that the burial practices employed commonly varied between cemeteries. For example, in York there is a

[69] Buckberry, 'Later Anglo-Saxon Cemeteries', ch. 6.
[70] Buckberry and Hadley, 'Fillingham', p. 13.

great degree of variety of burial form in the Minster cemetery (including stone-lined graves, a grave with a mortar bed, a tile-lined grave, a sarcophagus, coffined burials, chest burials, a burial under a plank, and one individual placed on part of a boat), which presumably was the burial place of high-status members of the urban community, while at Swinegate the burials were either in plain earth graves or in simple wooden coffins (i.e. without elaborate metal fittings) (Plate 4) or covered by planks, and at St Andrew's, Fishergate burials were either in plain earth graves or simple coffins.[71] At Winchester Old Minster there was great diversity of burial practice in the tenth century (simple earth graves, wooden coffins, graves with pillow-stones, charcoal graves, graves with yellow sand, graves with a stone coffin, and burial in a monolithic coffin), and similar diversity was encountered at New Minster, but in the Staple Gardens cemetery the burials were mostly either plain earth graves or in simple wooden coffins, although one wooden coffin contained a lead lining (a unique feature in Winchester cemeteries) and charcoal was found in five graves.[72]

Although grave goods had long ceased to be common, artefacts are occasionally found in tenth- and eleventh-century graves, although they constitute a miscellaneous corpus. They include jewellery and dress-fittings, coins, combs, and small knives. For example, later Anglo-Saxon burials in York have produced a pair of bronze tweezers, as well as a belt mount and finger rings at St Helen-on-the-Walls, while a burial at Swinegate has produced a knife blade, and at the Minster cemetery earrings and finger rings were found in various graves.[73] Combs were found in burials at Ripon and Heysham (Lancs), and a hairpin 'of late Saxon type' was found in a grave at Caister-on-Sea.[74] A burial from Thwing radiocarbon dated to the ninth or tenth century contained an amber and glass bead and a knife, while a late Anglo-Saxon burial at Exeter included a gold finger ring.[75] Six tenth-century burials from Staple Gardens, Winchester contained Roman coins, either held in the hand or placed on the chest, and although these had presumably been disturbed from Roman contexts during grave digging, it was clearly a deliberate decision to place them in the graves.[76] Excavations of a cemetery at Scarborough (Yorks) revealed a coin of Cnut (1016–35) in one grave and a ninth-century jet cross on the breast of another skeleton. A ninth- or tenth-century bronze cross, possibly from a book cover, a ninth-century strap-end and a spear-head were also found during the excavations, and may have been associated with graves.[77] Indeed, although they were not definitely disturbed from graves, it is notable that artefacts of tenth- and eleventh-century date have frequently been

[71] Discussed in Buckberry, 'Later Anglo-Saxon Cemeteries', ch. 6.

[72] Kjølbye-Biddle, 'Winchester dead', pp. 227–8; Kipling and Scobie, 'Staple Gardens'.

[73] J. Magilton, *The Church of St Helen-on-the-Walls, Aldwark*, The Archaeology of York 10.1 (London, 1980), pp. 15; Buckberry, 'Later Anglo-Saxon Cemeteries', ch. 6; Philips and Heywood, *York Minster*, pp. 88–92.

[74] Whyman and Hall, 'Ripon', pp. 127–8; T. Potter and R. Andrews, 'Excavation and survey at St Patrick's Chapel and St Peter's Church, Heysham, Lancs, 1977–78', *Antiquaries Journal* 74 (1994), pp. 55–134, at p. 124; Darling and Gurney, *Caister-on-Sea*, p. 252.

[75] Geake, *Conversion-Period England*, p. 159; Henderson and Bidwell, 'Exeter', p. 154.

[76] Kipling and Scobie, 'Staple Gardens', p. 8.

[77] A. Rowntree, ed., *The History of Scarborough* (London, 1931), pp. 146–8.

recovered during excavation of cemeteries of this date, including tenth-century copper alloy pins, a buckle, needle and strap-end discovered during excavations of burials at Holton-le-Clay.[78] Finally, there are significant numbers of Anglo-Saxon burials that contained only iron knives, and although these are not usually closely datable, some may date to the later Anglo-Saxon period. Indeed, a knife burial has been found in the cemetery at Chimney, near Bampton (Oxon), which has yielded radiocarbon date-ranges between the mid tenth and mid eleventh centuries, and at Lewknor (Oxon) two graves contained knives in a cemetery dated to the mid tenth to mid eleventh century.[79]

Our understanding of the significance of the presence of such small objects as coins and rings in graves is sometimes hampered by the difficulty of determining whether they originally belonged to the grave or whether they were residual from earlier contexts or have been disturbed from later contexts during excavation. Nonetheless, the variety of items found in graves of the tenth and eleventh centuries is greater than is often supposed, and is found in a wide range of cemeteries. Many burials containing artefacts of tenth-century date have been labelled as examples of 'viking' burial. In some cases, such a conclusion is warranted, including the extremely elaborate assemblages of grave goods in burials at Repton (grave 511) (Derbys), Claughton Hall (Lancs), Hesket-in-the-Forest, Eaglesfield and Aspatria (Cumbria), and the female burial from Adwick-le-Street (Yorks) containing a pair of oval brooches, a bronze bowl and an iron knife and key, which has produced an isotopic signature indicating that the origins of the woman lay in Norway.[80] However, not all burials labelled as those of Scandinavians are so elaborate, and they may be further examples of what appears to be a widespread pattern of burial with occasional artefacts, which continued through the later Anglo-Saxon period.[81]

A trait of later Anglo-Saxon burials that may sometimes be missed during excavations concerns the placing of stones in the grave other than those outlining the grave or surrounding the head. At Kellington (Yorks) white quartz pebbles were placed in later Anglo-Saxon graves, in a practice mirrored in contemporary cemeteries at Llandough (Glam) and Whithorn (Dumf).[82] At Barnstaple quartz pebbles were placed not only around the head but also on the chest and in one case across the neck, and such pebbles were sometimes scattered on top of coffins. Flat stones were also set on edge between the knees of two skeletons, and one burial had stones placed around the feet, although not the head.[83] Recent excavations at

---

78 Sills, 'Holton-le-Clay', pp. 31, 40–1.

79 Blair, *Anglo-Saxon Oxfordshire*, p. 73.

80 J.D. Richards, *Viking Age England*, second edn (Stroud, 2001), pp. 144–9; G. Speed and P. Walton Rogers, 'A burial of a Viking woman at Adwick-le-Street, South Yorkshire', *Medieval Archaeology* 48 (2004), pp. 51–90.

81 See also G. Halsall, 'The viking presence in England? The burial evidence reconsidered', in *Cultures in Contact: Scandinavian Settlement in England in the Ninth and Tenth Centuries*, ed. D.M. Hadley and J.D. Richards (Turnhout, 2000), pp. 259–76, at pp. 264–8.

82 H. Mytum, 'Kellington church', *Current Archaeology* 133 (1993), pp. 15–17; A. Selkirk, 'Llandough', *Current Archaeology* 146 (1996), pp. 73–7; P. Hill, *Whithorn and St Ninian: The Excavation of a Monastic Town, 1984–91* (Stroud, 1997), pp. 472–3.

83 Miles, 'Barnstaple', p. 66.

Fillingham revealed that oval-shaped stones had been placed on the eye-sockets of one individual, and stones had been placed in the mouth of both this and another skeleton.[84] Pebbles were placed in the mouths of four skeletons at St Nicholas Shambles, London and in the mouth of one burial at Raunds (see also below).[85] Organic materials rarely survive in graves, but where the burial environment is conducive to organic preservation, a miscellaneous array of items has been recovered. Examples include the hazel rods found in ten burials at Barton-upon-Humber, and the hazel rods from at least five of the eleventh-century burials at the Guildhall site in London.[86] Pillows made of organic materials were placed under the head of one burial at Barton, while at Raunds charcoal stains under the heads of two individuals have been tentatively interpreted as decayed organic pillows.[87]

Given the rarity of the artefacts found in graves and the absence of a consistent pattern it is difficult to ascribe meaning to this evidence. Most of the artefacts found within graves can be interpreted as the result of clothed burial. Indeed, there is additional evidence for clothed burial in the form of fragments of gold thread from costumes at both York Minster and Repton, although clothed burial was not universal as evidence for shrouded burial has also been recovered, in the form of shroud pins at St Helen-on-the-Walls, York and preserved linen at St Nicholas Shambles.[88] Some items found in graves – such as coins, bone combs, hazel rods, stones of distinctive type and stones placed on and around the body – must have been deliberately placed there. The significance of such items doubtless relates to individual or community beliefs that are now almost certainly beyond our ability to reconstruct. It has, however, been suggested that the deposition of hazel rods may have been linked to ideas about the Resurrection, as hazel 'if coppiced regularly, becomes effectively eternal'.[89] Although what are termed 'grave goods' are rare in burials of the tenth and eleventh centuries, it is increasingly apparent that what was placed in the grave and on and around the body continued to be important. Moreover the variation within and between cemeteries suggests that even though funerary arrangements may have come increasingly under the direct control of the Church, there was still opportunity for localised and individual traditions and beliefs to be expressed through the medium of burial.

Above-ground markers, both stone and wooden, have been detected in many excavations, particularly in northern England, where the tradition of monumental stone carving seems to have been more common than in southern England in the tenth and eleventh centuries. For example, carved stone grave covers and head

---

[84] Buckberry and Hadley, 'Fillingham', pp. 15–16.

[85] White, *St Nicholas Shambles*, p. 24; Boddington, *Raunds*, p. 42.

[86] Rodwell and Rodwell, 'Barton-upon-Humber', p. 312; Bateman, 'Guildhall', p. 117.

[87] W. Rodwell and C. Atkins, personal communication; Boddington, *Raunds*, p. 37.

[88] Philips and Heywood, *York Minster*, p. 91; M. Biddle and B. Kjølbye-Biddle, 'Repton and the "great heathen army", 873–4', in *Viking and the Danelaw: Select Papers from the Proceedings of the Thirteenth Viking Congress*, ed. J. Graham-Campbell, R. Hall, J. Jesch and D. Parsons (Oxford, 2002), pp. 45–96, at pp. 85–6; Magilton, *St Helen-on-the-Walls*, p. 14; White, *St Nicholas Shambles*, p. 20.

[89] Bateman, 'Guildhall', p. 120; Daniell, *Death and Burial*, p. 163.

7. Sculpture from Weston (Yorks). The sculpture depicts a warrior with his sword in one hand, who is grabbing, or protecting, a woman with his other hand. The scene was added to an earlier sculpture in the tenth century. Drawn by Oliver Jessop.

and foot stones have been excavated *in situ* at York Minster, and stone grave markers and covers, both carved (at St Mark's Lincoln and Old Minster, Winchester) and plain (at Newark and Raunds), have also occasionally been excavated *in situ* elsewhere.[90] Evidence for wooden markers, in the form of post-holes associated with individual graves, has also been identified at St Mark's, Lincoln, and Thwing.[91] At the Guildhall site in London one burial appears to have been marked with a wooden board that projected above the grave cut.[92] Most of the stone sculpture of the tenth and eleventh centuries was not found *in situ* above a grave, but much of it is clearly funerary, in particular the grave slabs and covers, while the crosses may have served either to mark a grave or to commemorate an individual or family. Indeed, a cross-shaft from Crowle (Lincs) incorporates an inscription, which – though fragmentary – reveals that the cross was commemorative as it included the element *līcbæcun*, 'corpse monument, memorial stone' – it may have commemorated one or more of the men depicted on the cross, one on horseback and another grasping a sword.[93] Other crosses lacking inscriptions but depicting secular figures, almost always men, may also have been commemorative monuments (Plates 7 and 8).[94]

From an analysis of these grave variations – the form of the grave, additional artefacts placed in the grave and above-ground markers – it emerges that they do not appear to be constrained by either the age or the sex of the deceased. That is to

[90] Philips and Heywood, *York Minster*, p. 84; B. Gilmour and D. Stocker, *St Mark's Church and Cemetery*, The Archaeology of Lincoln 13.1 (London, 1986), pp. 20–1; B. Kjølbe-Biddle and R. Page, 'A Scandinavian rune-stone from Winchester', *Antiquaries Journal* 55 (1975), pp. 389–94; Samuels, 'Newark', p. 40; Boddington, *Raunds*, p. 40.

[91] Gilmour and Stocker, *St Mark's*, pp. 20–21; Geake, *Conversion-Period England*, p. 159.

[92] Bateman, 'Guildhall', p. 117.

[93] P. Everson and D. Stocker, *Corpus of Anglo-Saxon Stone Sculpture*, v: *Lincolnshire* (Oxford, 1999), pp. 147–52.

[94] Discussed in D.M. Hadley, 'Negotiating gender, family and status in Anglo-Saxon burial practices', in *Gender in the Early Medieval World. East and West, 300–900*, ed. L. Brubaker and J. Smith (Cambridge, 2004), pp. 301–23, at pp. 315–19, and note 55.

8. Tenth-century sculptures from northern England. (a) Sockburn
(Durham) (b) Leeds (Yorks) (c) Sockburn (d) Middleton (Yorks). Three
of these sculptures depict armed warriors; of these, two are cross-shafts
and the third, from Sockburn, is a so-called hogback monument. The
cross-shaft from Leeds depicts the flying scene from the legend of
Wayland the smith. Drawn by Oliver Jessop.

say, adult males and females, as well as infants, could be accorded any given grave
type, although there seems to be a tendency for more elaborate burial to become
more frequent with increasing age.[95] It is also apparent that rural cemeteries, and
some urban cemeteries, tend to be limited to two or three basic grave forms, while
greater variation in grave form is generally to be found in high-status urban cemeteries, in particular those associated with major churches, such as York Minster
and Winchester Old Minster. In a recent paper David Stocker has noted that
tenth-century stone funerary monuments in northern England appear to have been
more common in cemeteries located in urban and trading centres, rather than in
the cemeteries of rural churches, even including the mother churches of the
region. He suggests that the graveyards with exceptional numbers of monuments
may belong to unusual settlements with distinctive elite populations, with a

---

[95] Buckberry, 'Later Anglo-Saxon Cemeteries', ch. 6.

sizable number of new-comers (in the form of merchants) whose social competitiveness was played out, amongst other ways, through funerary display.[96] Although what went into the grave may no longer have been a primary focus of social display, the fact that some urban cemeteries have greater variations in grave form suggests that this social environment gave rise to greater investment in funerary provision, below ground as well as above. Wealth may have been a factor, but the higher numbers of incomers, bringing new traditions and, perhaps, greater access to learned ideas about the fate of the body in the grave, may have combined to produce the variation evident in the archaeological record. Victoria Thompson has recently observed that the increasingly enclosed nature of later Anglo-Saxon burials may have been a response to the above-mentioned literary notions of the perfect body, giving rise to an attempt to protect the body and separate it from the soil in various forms of container and lining – if so, the influence of literary ideals is more likely to have been manifest in these high-status contexts.[97]

ARCHAEOLOGICAL EVIDENCE: CEMETERY TOPOGRAPHY

Where a person was buried was important in the tenth and eleventh centuries. For example, it is clear from the documentary record that burial in consecrated ground was not permitted to felons and excommunicates, and the reality of this prohibition, as we have seen, is supported by archaeological evidence. The archaeological record also implies that where a person was buried within a consecrated cemetery, as much as how, seems to have been significant in conveying messages about the status of that person. The control of cemetery topography by the Church may have hinted at the post-mortem fate believed to await individuals.[98]

The study of tenth- and eleventh-century cemetery topography is compromised by the disturbance of burials during the digging of later graves, and by the limited scale of most excavations. Nonetheless, a few cemeteries of this date have been extensively excavated, and distinct patterns in the distribution of certain types of burial have been identified. Our recent spatial analysis of five later Anglo-Saxon cemeteries from Lincolnshire and Yorkshire reveals significant clusters of particular types of burial, which may have been related to the status of the deceased.[99] While most grave types were shown to be evenly distributed across the cemeteries, more unusual grave types were shown to occur in clusters. At York Minster these more unusual burial types included burials in re-used chests, graves lined with stones or tiles, burials under stone grave slabs and a sarcophagus. These burials were notably located near to each other, as were

---

[96] D. Stocker, 'Monuments and merchants: irregularities in the distribution of stone sculpture in Lincolnshire and Yorkshire in the tenth century', in *Cultures in Contact*, ed. Hadley and Richards, pp. 179–212, at pp. 183–91, 200–6.

[97] Thompson, 'Constructing salvation', pp. 232, 240.

[98] For discussion of this idea in an earlier context see B. Effros, 'Beyond cemetery walls: early medieval funerary topography and Christian salvation', *EME* 6.1 (1997), pp. 1–23.

[99] This analysis was undertaken by Jo Buckberry, and the results are presented in detail in her thesis, 'Later Anglo-Saxon Cemeteries', ch. 6.

unusual burials at Swinegate in York (under a wooden plank), St Peter's Barton-upon-Humber (clinker-built coffins and burials containing hazel rods or 'wands'), and St Mark's Lincoln (stone-lined graves and graves with above-ground markers). Similar patterns in the distribution of more unusual burial types have been noted elsewhere. For example, the burials in coffins with elaborate iron fittings, and those with charcoal packing, in monolithic coffins or with stone covers at Old Minster, Winchester are found in the most prominent positions, either around the east end of the church or arranged axially with the west end.[100] These findings suggest that the use of these relatively unusual grave types at each cemetery may have been restricted to a small social group which was usually buried close together. Most of these grave forms imply a greater level of invest-ment in burial than was the case for the majority of the population, who were more commonly buried in plain earth graves or simple coffins, and whose burials were evenly distributed across the cemeteries studied. It seems a reasonable conclusion that these burials with evidence for greater investment belonged to the elite members of society, although it is difficult to say whether this elevated status derived from family connections, wealth, profession or the personal attributes of the deceased.

The cemeteries studied in our recent survey were found to have clusters of burials of individuals of different ages. This was particularly true of the burials of infants and children. For example, the burials of children under twelve years of age were largely encountered in the north-western part of the excavations at York Minster (referred to in publications as area ST), while in the Swinegate cemetery all of the infants and most of the young children (under the age of six years) were found during the excavation of the southern-most trenches. There was a cluster of sub-adult burials in the south-west of the excavated area at St Andrew's, Fishergate, and there was also a notable cluster of infant burials in the mid tenth- to mid eleventh-century cemetery at St Mark's, Lincoln. Unfortunately, in none of these cases is the location of the associated church known with certainty, so it is unknown whether these burials were close to the church walls, as they were in the late Anglo-Saxon cemetery at St Peter's, Barton-upon-Humber.[101] Clusters of infant graves around the walls of churches have been identified at several other tenth- to eleventh-century cemeteries, including Raunds, Cherry Hinton, Compton Bassett (Wilts) and both Old Minster and Nunnaminster in Winchester.[102] The location of infant burials close to church walls has led to the interpretation that the mourners believed that these infants would be blessed every time rainwater dripped off the church roof onto the graves. However, it is possible that the symbolism of 'eaves-drip' burials might have varied from cemetery to cemetery. Moreover, it does not seem to have been a universal phenomenon, and no clusters

---

[100] Kjølbye-Biddle, 'Winchester dead', p. 228.

[101] Buckberry, 'Later Anglo-Saxon Cemeteries', ch. 6.

[102] Boddington, *Raunds*, p. 55; Bradley and Gaimster, 'Medieval Britain', p. 252; S. Lucy and A. Reynolds, 'Burial in early medieval England and Wales: past, present and future', in *Burial in Early Medieval England and Wales*, ed. Lucy and Reynolds, pp. 1–23, at pp. 17–18; Kjølbye-Biddle, 'A cathedral cemetery', pp. 99–100; S. Crawford, *Childhood in Anglo-Saxon England* (Stroud, 1993), p. 88; Annia Cherryson, personal communication on the unpublished cemetery at Nunnaminster.

of infant graves adjacent to church walls have been observed at extensively excavated cemeteries at Barrow-upon-Humber or St Nicholas Shambles, London.[103] Nonetheless, whatever the intended symbolism of burials clustered near to the church walls, they do indicate that certain types of burial may have been seen to be more appropriate for different age groups at some, if not all, cemeteries.

There is little evidence from the study of excavated late Anglo-Saxon cemeteries that they were organised according to sex. This evidence suggests that there had been significant transformations in the ways in which gender was signalled in burial rite through the Anglo-Saxon period. In the earlier Anglo-Saxon centuries, there were clear gendered differences between the burials of some, but not all, adults. Masculine burial assemblages typically included weapons, while feminine assemblages were commonly comprised of jewellery, and such burials often account for around a half to a third of burials in a cemetery, with the remainder of adult burials containing a common range of artefacts or none at all (these are often dubbed 'gender neutral' burials).[104] Our survey suggests, by contrast, that by the later Anglo-Saxon period such distinctions between male and female burials do not occur. What can be said, however, is that in some extensively excavated cemeteries males were sometimes slightly more likely to be buried in certain locations than females, and vice versa. That was the case, for example, at St Mark's, Lincoln, which had a higher number of male burials to the north of the earliest (phase VIII) church, and a higher number of female burials to the south of the later (phase IX) church, and at Raunds, where a higher number of male burials was encountered immediately south of the church.[105] This uneven distribution may have been prompted by a desire to bury some of the dead of a community in prominent locations in the cemetery. Funerary sculpture was excavated *in situ* on the south side of the church at Raunds, where there was also a higher number of coffined burials, while at St Mark's in Lincoln the most accessible part of the cemetery of the earliest church was to the north of the building.[106]

Excavation reveals that occasionally burials located on the outskirts of Anglo-Saxon churchyards display unusual characteristics, implying that some individuals were segregated from the rest of society in death. In some of these instances the individual concerned was physically distinct. Examples include an adult male with a severely deformed leg buried just beyond the boundary wall at North Elmham. This was the only burial with the head placed to the east rather than the west. An adult male buried beneath the boundary wall of the same cemetery had apparently met a violent death. He had blade injuries to the skull and right arm, and a cut mark to the front of the vertebra suggests that his throat had

103 Daniell, *Death and Burial*, p. 128; White, *St Nicholas Shambles*, pp. 14–17.

104 For recent surveys, see S. Lucy, *The Early Anglo-Saxon Cemeteries of East Yorkshire: an Analysis and Reinterpretation*, BAR British Series 282 (Oxford, 1998); N. Stoodley, *The Spindle and the Spear: a Critical Enquiry into the Construction and Meaning of Gender in the Early Anglo-Saxon Burial Rite*, BAR British Series 288 (Oxford, 1999).

105 Buckberry, 'Later Anglo-Saxon Cemeteries', ch. 6; Boddington, *Raunds*, pp. 55–6.

106 The location of the earliest church is conjectural, although it probably lies between the southern part of the cemetery and High Street. The mid eleventh-century church appears to have been approached by a pathway from St Mark's Street to the north: Gilmour and Stocker, *St Mark's*, p. 19.

been cut – he may have been an execution victim, given the location of his burial and the similarities of his injuries to those of individuals in execution cemeteries.[107] At Ripon the probable monastic cemetery at Ailcy Hill was later used for a series of distinctive burials. One of these burials was of a juvenile who suffered from spinal tuberculosis, and whose lower back was hunched and twisted to the right side. This burial produced a radiocarbon date of AD 780–990, and it was excavated in the same phase as a multiple burial containing three individuals, which may have been an execution burial. At any rate, the form of the burial implies that less care had been taken over it than was normally the case, and it has been suggested that by this time the cemetery was being used to bury the socially excluded, including felons and the physically different.[108] The treatment in the grave of some individuals may have been related to some aspect of their health or social status. For example, one individual at Raunds with a large stone in its mouth had suffered from poliomyelitis and tuberculosis.[109]

Burial strategies may have been intended to convey strong messages about the fate of the soul of the deceased, and while some unfortunate individuals may not have been excluded from burial in consecrated ground, their life experiences, and perhaps also the fate that might await them, was signified through their treatment in death. Having said this, some individuals suffering severe health problems were buried alongside everybody else in an apparently indistinctive fashion. Examples include the adult with ankylosing spondylitis (resulting in an entirely fused spine) at Swinegate in York, three lepers at Raunds and one at York Minster.[110] This suggests that the treatment of individuals in the funerary rituals was a localised affair. Moreover, not all individuals given a distinctive treatment in the grave were necessarily suffering from health-related problems, unlike the Raunds burial with the stone in its mouth (see above). For example, at Fillingham the two adults with stones placed in their mouths were not suffering from any condition that left a mark on their skeletons, although, of course, this does not remove the possibility that they were suffering from some health condition that did not affect the skeleton, or else were treated in this way because of their behaviour in society.

CONCLUSIONS

The archaeological record has much to contribute to our understanding of the treatment of the dead in the tenth and eleventh centuries. While the Church had long been concerned with the burials of some members of the laity, it was probably not until the tenth century that churchyard burial became the norm. Many mid-later Anglo-Saxon rural settlements have more than one location for burial,

---

[107] Wade-Martins, *North Elmham*, pp. 185–91.
[108] The radiocarbon date was calibrated at the 95% confidence range; Hall and Whyman, 'Ripon', pp. 123–4.
[109] Boddington, *Raunds*, pp. 41–2.
[110] Buckberry, 'Later Anglo-Saxon Cemeteries', ch. 7; Cox and Roberts, *Disease*, p. 218.

and while these may have been satellite burial grounds of the associated church it remains possible that burial was brought into the midst of the places of the living by factors independent of the Church.[111] It is clear that even when churchyard burial had commenced at a particular site, this was no guarantee that it would be a long-lived location for burial, and the nascent parish communities may often have seen the burial places of their ancestors abandoned and obliterated by agriculture or buildings, and have been encouraged, if not forced, to bury their dead in newly founded churchyards at the behest of their lords. Whatever the views of learned ecclesiastics, local rituals and superstitions appear to have continued and are occasionally manifested through the presence of, for example, stones and wooden rods on or near the corpse. Together the textual and archaeological evidence suggests that caring for the dead in later Anglo-Saxon England was a matter not only for the Church but also for families, local communities, and lords. Local communities seem to have been permitted a fair degree of latitude in determining the form of burial and commemoration deemed appropriate for their family and friends. It is striking that during the course of the tenth and eleventh centuries burial rites, grave furniture and above-ground markers became increasingly diverse and elaborate, and it may be that as regulations for burial practices became more established and ecclesiastical expectations of the fate of the soul became more widely known, families and communities sought out ever more innovative ways to respond to these requirements and expectations while continuing to use funerary practice for social display.[112]

---

111 Zadora-Rio, 'The making of churchyards', p. 7.

112 We are grateful to Annia Cherryson for discussion of sites in southern England, to Francesca Tinti for valuable feedback on an earlier version of the paper, and to Andrew Reynolds for permission to cite his unpublished paper on the execution cemetery at Staines and for information about mutilated individuals in Anglo-Saxon cemeteries. Unfortunately, Victoria Thompson's *Dying and Death in Later Anglo-Saxon England* (Woodbridge, 2004) appeared too late to be addressed in this article; in this book she develops many of the points summarised above, p. 124. We would like to thank Warwick Rodwell, Caroline Atkins, English Heritage, York Archaeological Trust and Humber Archaeology Partnership for granting us access to the site archives for St Peter's Barton-upon-Humber, Swinegate and Barrow-upon-Humber in advance of publication. We are also grateful to York Archaeological Trust and West Yorkshire Archaeology Service for permission to reproduce photographs, and to Oliver Jessop and Melissa Peet for the illustrations.

Index

Index